Where Wrath and Mercy Meet
Proclaiming the Atonement Today

The Oak Hill School of Theology Series

Where Wrath and Mercy Meet
Proclaiming the Atonement Today

*Papers from the Fourth Oak Hill College
Annual School of Theology*

Edited by
David Peterson

MILTON KEYNES • COLORADO SPRINGS • HYDERABAD

First published 2001 by Paternoster

Reprinted 2002, 2005, 2008, 2009

15 14 13 12 11 10 09   11 10 9 8 7 6 5

Paternoster is an imprint of Authentic Media
9 Holdom Avenue, Bletchley, Milton Keynes, Bucks., MK1 1QR
1820 Jet Stream Drive, Colorado Springs, CO 80921, USA
OM Authentic Media, Medchal Road, Jeedimetla Village,
Secunderabad 500 055, A.P., India
www.authenticmedia.co.uk
Authentic Media is a division of IBS-STL U.K., limited by guarantee, with
its Registered Office at Kingstown Broadway, Carlisle, Cumbria CA3 0HA.
Registered in England & Wales No. 1216232. Registered charity 27016

British Library Cataloguing in Publication Data
A catalogue record for this book is available from the British Library

ISBN 978-1-84227-079-0

Cover Design by Campsie, Glasgow
Typeset by WestKey Ltd, Falmouth, Cornwall
Printed in Great Britain by Bell & Bain Ltd, Glasgow

Contents

    Predicament**   **100**
    MICHAEL OVEY

    Introduction: the Question of Sin   100
    Redemption as Re-creating Creation   105
    Sin and 'De-creation'   106
    The Implications of Sin as 'De-creation'   117
    Creation and 'Recapitulation'   123
    Conclusion   132

5. **Proclaiming Christ Crucified Today:
    Some Reflections on John's Gospel**   136
    PAUL WESTON

    Introduction   137
    John's Crucifixion Narrative   139
    Concluding Observations   159

    **Appendix – Justification by Faith:
    The Reinstatement of the Doctrine Today**   **164**
    ALAN M. STIBBS

Abbreviations

AB	Anchor Bible
AnB	Analecta Biblica
BNTC	Black's New Testament Commentaries
CBQ	*Catholic Biblical Quarterly*
ExpT	*Expository Times*
HUCA	*Hebrew Union College Annual*
ICC	The International Critical Commentary
IDB	G.A. Buttrick (ed.), *The Interpreter's Dictionary of the Bible*, 5 vols. (Nashville: Abingdon, 1976)
JBL	*Journal of Biblical Literature*
JSOT	*Journal for the Study of the Old Testament*
JSOTS	Journal for the Study of the Old Testament Supplement Series
NCB	New Century Bible
NEB	New English Bible
NICNT	The New International Commentary on the New Testament
NICOT	The New International Commentary on the Old Testament
NIDNTT	C. Brown (ed.), *The New International Dictionary of New Testament Theology*, 3 vols. (Exeter: Paternoster, 1975–8)
NIDOTTE	W.A. VanGemeren (ed.), *The New International Dictionary of Old Testament Theology and Exegesis*, 5 vols. (Carlisle: Paternoster, 1997)
NIV	New International Version
NRSV	New Revised Standard Version

NTS	*New Testament Studies*
RB	*Revue Biblique*
SJLA	Studies in Judaism in Late Antiquity
SJT	*Scottish Journal of Theology*
SNTSMS	Society for New Testament Studies Monograph Series
TDNT	G. Kittel and G. Friedrich (eds.), *Theological Dictionary of the New Testament*, 10 vols. (Grand Rapids: Eerdmans, 1964–74)
TynBul	*Tyndale Bulletin*
VT	*Vetus Testamentum*
VTS	Vetus Testamentum Supplements
WBC	Word Biblical Commentary
WMANT	Wissenschaftliche Monographien zum Alten und Neuen Testament
WTJ	*Westminster Theological Journal*
WUNT	Wissenschaftliche Untersuchungen zum Neuen Testament

Foreword

There can hardly be a more important topic for the ongoing cause of God and truth today than the theme of this book. If Christianity is essentially Christ himself, and if he came (as he claimed) to seek and save the lost, then the question of how he saves them is, in the strictest sense, the crux of the faith.

This book examines, expounds, defends and applies the central truth of the atonement – and all four verbs are important. It looks at the belief that Christ's death on the cross had the character of penal substitution, and that it is that fact that makes it saving.

The authors draw attention to both 'wrath and mercy' in relation to the atonement that is, both to 'the personal involvement of God in punishing sin' and to his mercy in 'the one who will be the acting subject in the Last Judgment becoming its object in the place of sinners'. This emphasis is vital for at least two reasons.

First, at the popular level, because the gospel is often reduced to a vague, undefined and ultimately unsatisfying message that somehow 'God loves us'. The authors show the depth and seriousness of the issues the gospel addresses and the predicament from which it delivers.

Second, at the academic level, because within the evangelical orbit some are rejecting the penal view of Christ's work. The authors here address and answer those criticisms in detail, by scholarly analysis and with biblical rigour.

The genius of this symposium is that it weds clear, profound and well-reasoned biblical theology to practical Christian concern for evangelism and pastoral care. The result is a volume that is rewarding intellectually in its thoroughness, satisfying spiritually in its exposition and stimulating both evangelistically and pastorally.

It has all this, plus a typical *multum in parvo* contribution from a former Vice-Principal of Oak Hill Theological College, Alan Stibbs. His short essay on 'Justification of the sinner by God and in God's sight by faith in Christ, crucified and exalted' is a masterpiece, showing how justification and atonement hang together.

Overall, this book demonstrates what riches await those who pay close attention to the text of the Bible – particularly on such a theme as 'proclaiming the atonement today'.

Happy the students who have these authors as their teachers. Happy the readers who have this addition to Oak Hill's 'School of Theology' series.

Bob Horn
(Former General Secretary, the Universities
and Colleges Christian Fellowship).

Introduction

The cross of Christ is absolutely central to the teaching of the New Testament. Much is made of it in connection with the promise of salvation through Jesus, but it is also the focus of teaching about discipleship, ministry and ethics. The focus in this book is on its saving or atoning significance. A variety of images or models – such as redemption, justification, reconciliation and victory over the powers of evil – are used in Scripture to proclaim this. Throughout church history, the cross has been at the heart of various expressions of orthodox Christianity and numerous attempts have been made to explain how it is effective for us, including the satisfaction, moral influence, dramatic, governmental, ransom and penal substitution models.

Satisfaction for our sins was a major medieval category for defining Jesus' atoning work. This was developed in a number of ways, so that some spoke of satisfying the devil, while others spoke of satisfying God's honour or God's justice.[1] Returning to the insight of earlier theologians such as Augustine and Gregory the Great, the Reformers of the sixteenth century, including Luther, Calvin, Zwingli and Melanchthon, redefined the notion of satisfaction in the light of their own rigorous examination of Scripture. Anselm (*Cur Deus Homo* 1.12, 13, 15) had written of satisfaction being made so that there is no need for sin to be punished. But the Reformers saw Christ's death precisely as 'the undergoing of

---

[1] Note the helpful survey of these views in J.R.W. Stott, *The Cross of Christ* (Leicester: IVP, 1986), pp. 111–32.

vicarious punishment (*poena*) to meet the claims on us of God's holy law and wrath (i.e. his punitive justice)'.[2]

In this tradition, the Prayer of Consecration in the *Book of Common Prayer* speaks of Christ's death as 'a full, perfect, and sufficient sacrifice, oblation, and satisfaction, for the sins of the whole world', and Article 31 of the Articles of Religion states that

> The offering of Christ once made is that perfect redemption, propitiation and satisfaction, for all the sins of the whole world, both original and actual; and there is none other satisfaction for sin, but that alone.

A classic critique of this position was offered by the Unitarian Faustus Socinus in 1578.[3] His polemic held the attention of exponents of the Reformation view for more than a century, 'and created a tradition of rationalistic prejudice against that view which has effectively shaped debate about it right down to our own day'.[4] Nevertheless, the penal view of the atonement remained a central element of Protestant orthodoxy in the seventeenth century and became a particular focus of Evangelicalism from the eighteenth century onwards. It has been powerfully reargued and defended in more recent times by writers such as James Denny, Leon Morris, James Packer and John Stott.

The penal view has had a succession of formidable critics throughout the centuries, questioning whether it is biblical, moral, and appropriate as a way of explaining and proclaiming the saving work of Christ. But what is unusual about the last decade is the fact that several writers from the evangelical movement have stepped forward to join them.

---

[2] J.I. Packer, *Celebrating the Saving Work of God*, The Collected Shorter Writings of J.I. Packer (Carlisle: Paternoster, 1998), vol. 1, p. 86.

[3] Socinus, F., 'De Iesu Christo servatore', in *Opera omnia*, vols. 1–2 of Bibliotheca fratrum Polonorum quos unitarios vocant, 8 vols. (Irenopoli: post 1656), vol. 2, pp. 115–246.

[4] Packer, *Celebrating*, p. 86. He goes on to show how Reformed theologians in trying to beat Socinian rationalism at its own game became defensive rather than declaratory, analytic and apologetic rather than doxological and kerygmatic. Packer's own reworking of the penal substitutionary view of the atonement seeks to avoid the pitfalls he identifies in previous formulations.

For example, in 1995 John Goldingay edited a volume of essays entitled *Atonement Today*. Goldingay himself denies that there is any link between atonement and punishment in the Old Testament and argues that the improper linking of punishment with sacrifice in much Christian thought is particularly due to a misunderstanding of Isaiah 53.[5] Stephen Travis surveys some of the key texts in Paul's letters that have traditionally been taken to mean that Christ suffered the punishment due for our sin and concludes, for example, that Galatians 3:13 is not a statement about atonement in general or about the salvation of individuals. Paul's concern is to show how the death of Christ 'makes possible the coming of God's blessing to the Gentiles (Gal. 3:14)'.[6] In 2 Corinthians 5:21, Christ is said to identify with sin as our representative and to break its power, thereby freeing those who are in him to share his righteousness. But Travis does not believe that either here or in Romans 3:24–6 Paul taught that Christ experienced retributive punishment on behalf of humanity. Rather, 'standing where we stand, he bore the consequences of our alienation from God. In so doing he absorbed and exhausted them, so that they should not fall on us.'[7]

In America, Joel Green combined with John Carroll and others to produce a volume entitled *The Death of Jesus in Early Christianity*. Almost the first half of the book is devoted to the Gospels and a consideration of the death of Jesus within the framework presented by each evangelist. However, the sacrificial dimension of Jesus' suffering is not well explored. Examining the Pauline letters in only twenty-nine pages, Carroll and Green seem determined to exclude any sense of vicarious punishment from the apostle's thought. The concluding chapter specifically argues that 'Paul uses an almost inexhaustible series of metaphors to represent the significance of Jesus' death, and penal substitution (at least as popularly defined) is not one of them'.[8] These writers are particularly sensitive to the concerns of feminist theologians, who argue that the penal view of the cross

---

[5] J. Goldingay (ed.), *Atonement Today* (London: SPCK, 1995).

[6] S. Travis, 'Christ as Bearer of Divine Judgement in Paul's Thought about the Atonement', in Goldingay, *Atonement Today*, pp. 21–38 (24).

[7] Ibid., p. 37.

[8] J.T. Carroll and J.B. Green with others, *The Death of Jesus in Early Christianity* (Peabody: Hendrickson, 1995), p. 263.

makes God the patriarch who punishes his son in order to satisfy his own parental honour and sense of justice. Although there have always been moral objections to this view of the atonement, the notion that our salvation can only be accomplished at the expense of 'the abuse of one perfect child' is particularly abhorrent in an age when issues of parental punishment and child abuse are so prominent.[9]

Responding to such challenges and believing that the penal view of the cross is a valid and necessary aspect of the biblical gospel, the contributors to this volume decided to focus on this issue at the Annual Oak Hill School of Theology on 3 May 2000. We happily agree that there is more to the cross than penal substitution and want the biblical teaching to be presented in all its fullness. But we are convinced that the true significance of the cross has not been grasped until this particular dimension has been acknowledged. Papers were read and discussed at several faculty meetings in preparation for the day on which about 150 clergy and other Christian workers gathered in the Chapel to participate in the debate. As in previous years, this time of theological reflection was set within the context of corporate prayer and praise. We now continue the practice of offering the fruit of our work to a wider public through the publication of this volume of essays.[10]

The title of this book echoes the chorus of a song by Graham Kendrick, entitled 'Come and see' (© 1988, Make Way Music). With the words, 'we worship at your feet, where wrath and mercy meet', Kendrick expresses the biblical truth that wrath and mercy are simultaneously expressed by God at the cross. The Son whom we worship actually experienced that wrath in our place.

My own contribution to the School of Theology was a paper entitled 'The Atonement in Scripture', now much expanded and divided into a chapter on the Old Testament and a chapter on the

---

[9] Ibid., pp. 259–60; M.G. Houts, 'Classical Atonement Imagery: Feminist and Evangelical Challenges', *Catalyst* 19.3 (1993), pp. 1, 5–6; R.N. Brock, 'And a Little Child Will Lead Us: Christology and Child Abuse', in J.C. Brown and C.R. Bohn (eds.), *Christianity, Patriarchy, and Abuse: A Feminist Critique* (New York: Pilgrim, 1989), pp. 42–61.

[10] Publications from previous schools of theology are Peter M. Head (ed.), *Proclaiming the Resurrection* (Carlisle: Paternoster, 1998), and David Peterson (ed.), *Witness to the World* (Carlisle: Paternoster, 1999).

New Testament. The aim was to focus on key areas of debate in the interpretation of Scripture. Chapter one treats the provisions in the Pentateuch for atonement and then considers the surprising lack of teaching in the Psalms and prophetic literature on the theme, as a prelude to examining Isaiah 53. Chapter two offers a study of some of the teaching of Jesus in the Gospels and an analysis of critical passages on atonement in the rest of the New Testament. The subject is vast and the treatment of some texts is too brief. But after this re-examination of the evidence, I find myself wondering whether those who downplay or deny the theme of penal substitution are driven by personal or cultural agendas, rather than by biblical theology.

The significance of a topic or theme is not revealed by the number of times it is mentioned but by the place and prominence it is given in the unfolding of the divine plan. Teaching about atonement in the Pentateuch must therefore be understood as part of the wider question of what it meant for Israel to be the holy people of God, called to live within the framework of the Mosaic covenant, with its blessings and curses. Prophetic denunciation of Israel's failure is also to be viewed within this context. The ultimate judgement of exile is not, in fact, the last word. The prophets indicate that there will be a restoration of the covenant people and of God's plan to bless the whole world through them. The pattern once established is not abandoned by God. At the heart of this restoration, there must be atonement, redemption from the consequences of sin and the renewal of the covenant, re-establishing a God-honouring worship. The singular importance of Isaiah 53 can be seen within this theological context.

Jesus' focus on the fulfilment of certain Old Testament texts in his life and death seems to have been the stimulus for much theological reflection on the part of his disciples, particularly those who wrote the New Testament. Isaiah 53 is critical in this connection, because it leads back to the wider issues outlined above: how is God's covenant purpose fulfilled and the problems created by human sin dealt with once and for all? Although there are various ways of explaining the achievement of Christ's cross, the idea that he suffered the divine penalty for sin in our place appears to be foundational to various strands of New Testament teaching.

Garry Williams picks up the wider issues of divine law and punishment, which are intimately connected with the penal view of the cross. Garry recently completed a doctorate at Oxford, under the supervision of Professor Oliver O'Donovan, on the subject of Hugo Grotius's view of the atonement. He joined the faculty at Oak Hill in 1999 as a lecturer in Church History and Doctrine. Garry's chapter first examines a particular strand of biblical evidence, to show that the expression 'he bore our sins' means that Jesus bore the divine punishment for sin in our place. Moreover, Jesus' punishment was atoning since it brings wholeness, healing and righteousness to those who believe.

Garry then turns to the widespread theological criticism that the penal view of the cross represents atonement in too *mechanical* a fashion. It appears to some scholars to exclude God's intimate involvement in the process. But law in Scripture is a means by which God expresses his most intimate nature and concerns. It is not an alien code to which he is somehow subject. Furthermore, God is so personally involved in the punishment of sin in biblical teaching that we cannot speak of that punishment as a mechanical process. Ironically, it is often the critics of penal substitution themselves who introduce a mechanistic view of punishment.

Michael Ovey is now the Kingham Hill Fellow, engaged in research for a doctorate at Kings College London under the supervision of Professor Colin Gunton. His subject is the eternal relations between the persons of the Trinity. Michael has also been teaching Doctrine at Oak Hill since 1998. His contribution to this book addresses two further objections to penal substitution. The first is that it is *immoral* to argue that someone can be either condemned for another person's sins or acquitted for another person's righteousness. The second is that the penal view is *redundant* in God's plan to renew or restore his fallen creation: what it demands is met, and more, by the logic of re-creation in Christ. Some who adopt this view even argue that the re-creative position takes sin more seriously and does more justice to the wrath of God than penal substitution.

Michael expresses his approval of any attempt to encompass the whole sweep of salvation history by associating redemption with re-creation. But he establishes from Scripture that sin is that which profoundly 'de-creates' or is 'anti-creational'. It inverts creational relationships and frustrates God's purposes for the whole created order. There must be a profound solution to the problem of sin if creation's purpose is to be fulfilled. The captivating nature of sin is particularly apparent in the delusion of false faith and idolatry. It thus impinges on our theology and the way we do it! Sin enslaves us and holds us in death. Most importantly, it has eternal consequences in terms of our alienation from God.

God's glory requires that his creation purposes be fulfilled by an act of redemption that involves re-creation. Only *the creator* God can achieve this end, and he does it through Christ as the new or second Adam. The cosmos, and humans in particular, must become righteous, in a right relationship with God. Our condition as sinners, unable to save ourselves, means that we need the alien righteousness that is found in Christ alone. This righteousness becomes ours through faith-union with him. Such a personal union means that it is not immoral for us to be acquitted on the basis of an alien righteousness: what is his is ours.

The creation order to be restored is a creation stipulating punishment for sin (Gen. 2:17). A restoration soteriology must therefore face the question of what happens to the penalty for sin, whether that penalty is ignored or applied. If it is ignored, then God's word is broken and the original creation order not restored. Happily, faith-union provides the answer for this too. Christ's righteousness becomes ours because he assumes our guilt and punishment. Faith-union enables a double transfer (2 Cor. 5:21). Thus, a restoration exclusive of penal substitution is not a full restoration, 'for it involves a God whose word has been and remains broken'. 'Restoration may well involve more than penal substitution, but it cannot be less and still be restoration.'

Paul Weston's chapter is entitled 'Proclaiming Christ Crucified Today: Some Reflections on John's Gospel'. At the time of writing, Paul was Vice-Principal and lecturer in Homiletics and Mission Studies. Sadly for Oak Hill, he has now become the General Secretary of the Universities and Colleges Christian Fellowship. Paul's passion for evangelism and for expository preaching motivates his concern to proclaim the cross from John 19. He observes that what is really happening in John's narrative cannot be ascertained simply by means of a surface reading. John's crucifixion narrative keeps on informing the reader that an Old Testament text or prediction is being fulfilled in what happened. Connections between the crucifixion of Jesus and the Passover are particularly compelling.

Paul observes three paradoxes in John's narrative. First there is the implication that, despite appearances, the death of Jesus is the fulfilment of God's plan. God was in Christ reconciling the world to himself. The biblical gospel of the cross will always transcend our frames of understanding and so we must be cautious about calls to revise our models of the atonement to make them more comprehensible today. Scripture must be allowed to speak for itself and proclaim the divine logic of the atonement.

John's second paradox is that, despite appearances, the death of Jesus is entirely voluntary. This is the mirror image of the first. The Father's sending of the Son must not be presented in a way that excludes the Son's own active and willing co-operation in all that the cross involves. Jesus is not simply an unwitting pawn in a divinely executed plan. John's third paradox is that, despite appearances, the death of Jesus is a revelation of divine glory. The cross itself is the revelation of his majesty and kingly victory over all the forces of evil.

Paul Weston's conclusion is that there is evidence in John's Gospel for the so-called 'objective' view of the cross (that God the Father is reconciled by Jesus' action on the cross), for the 'subjective' view (that sinners are transformed and inspired by his sacrificial love shown there), and for the 'classic' view (that Satan is defeated and the powers of evil are overcome on the cross). Each perspective should have its proper place in our preaching and teaching.

The appendix to this volume is a brief essay by Alan Stibbs, formerly Vice-Principal of Oak Hill College. Originally delivered as 'The Latimer Day Lecture of the Fellowship of Evangelical Churchmen' in 1958, this was subsequently published in the *Evangelical Quarterly* and in the *Evangelical Churchman*. Against a background of neglect and challenge, Stibbs urged reinstatement of the doctrine of justification by faith to its proper place in the preaching and theological argumentation of Christians. Recent decades have brought forth new challenges, requiring extensive and detailed responses. There is, however, a continuing vitality, relevance and power in this contribution to the debate. In particular, Stibbs shows how the doctrine of justification by faith and a penal substitutionary doctrine of the atoning work of Christ are interdependent and complementary. Together, these doctrines offer the 'solid and unshakeable ground of full and abiding assurance' that many professing Christians seem to lack.

Since the penal, substitutionary dimension of the cross continues to be rejected or neglected by many today, this volume aims to reaffirm that it is *theologically foundational* to New Testament teaching about the atoning work of Jesus. What is theologically foundational must also be *evangelistically* important, as a key element of the message that God wants people to hear, to experience salvation by his grace. What is theologically foundational must also be *pastorally* important, for the strengthening of God's people in their devotion to him.

It is appropriate to conclude this introduction with some words written by R.T. France in 1971, in connection with the related topic of Jesus' use of the Old Testament (and Isaiah 53 in particular):[11]

> Perhaps the most revolutionary suggestion that can be made in contemporary theological debate is that the traditional viewpoint is not axiomatically wrong, that even among the heady outpourings of today's avant-garde exegetes, it may still sometimes be true that the old is better, not because it is old, but because it is rooted in the sheer exegetical common sense which is one of the first casualties of the scholar's quest for originality.

David Peterson
Principal of Oak Hill College

---

[11] R.T. France, *Jesus and the Old Testament* (London: Tyndale, 1971), p. x.

1

Atonement in the Old Testament
David Peterson

Introduction

In this chapter and the next, my aim is to take a biblical-theological approach to the subject of atonement, to set questions of detail within the widest possible context and thereby open up some different perspectives on the issues. Biblical Theology as a discipline can be pursued in different ways, but its general aim is to bring the contents of the Bible to a greater degree of systematization than is found immediately in the Bible itself, while remaining 'as close as possible to the method God himself has used in giving us his revelation.'[1] It is primarily concerned with the final form of the canonical text, rather than with sources or patterns of interpretation based on theories of composition. Interpretation of Old Testament books in their canonical form is particularly important as a basis for understanding the way New Testament writers used Scripture, since this was the form in which the material was available in the time of Jesus and the apostles.

Scholars sometimes trace the meaning of the term 'atonement' to its roots in Middle English – 'at-one-ment' – and so understand it as essentially a synonym for *reconciliation*. But the inadequacy of this equation soon becomes obvious when the relevant Hebrew terminology is examined in its context. There are several dimensions to 'atonement' in the Old Testament and 'reconciliation' is not an

---

[1] F.I. Andersen, 'Biblical Theology', in G.G. Cohen (ed.), *The Encyclopedia of Christianity* (Marshalltown, DE: National Foundation for Christian Education, 1968), vol. 2, pp. 65–6.

adequate term to cover this semantic field. Furthermore, although 'reconciliation' is an important New Testament word, it has no exact Hebrew equivalent.

This chapter begins with a brief review of the significance attributed to sacrifice in the Pentateuch, with special reference to rituals involving the use of blood. The Day of Atonement provisions in Leviticus are then examined in some detail and the meaning of atonement terminology in the Pentateuch is explored. Given the centrality of atonement rituals to the Mosaic Law, the second half of this chapter is concerned to discover what the psalmists and the prophets have to say about this subject. When the judgement of the Babylonian exile calls into question the future of Israel's relationship with God, it is especially interesting to note what is said about God's provision for Israel's sin. Within this context, the prophecy of Isaiah 53 makes a unique and distinctive contribution to the unfolding revelation of God's purpose and plan.

Sacrifice and Atonement in the Pentateuch

The broadest biblical context for considering the subject of sacrifice is the earliest chapters of Genesis, with their picture of humanity's rebellion against the Creator and subsequent alienation from God. Even in their fallen state, both Cain and Abel are moved to bring their respective offerings to God and to express some sense of gratitude or debt for the blessings of creation (Gen. 4:1–7). But at this early stage in the biblical story it is implied that the only sacrifice pleasing to God is one offered from a pure heart or with right intentions (cf. Heb. 11:4).[2]

Sacrifice was common in the ancient world and it is regularly mentioned in the book of Genesis in connection with key individuals and significant moments in the outworking of God's purposes for his world (e.g. 8:20–2; 12:7–8; 22:1–19). Such incidents are often spontaneous expressions of devotion and gratitude to God. However, it is in Exodus that sacrifice is first established as an essential part of God's plan for Israel as a nation. From that point in the

---

[2] Five different ways of interpreting this passage are assessed by G.J. Wenham, *Genesis 1–15*, WBC 1 (Waco: Word, 1987), p. 104.

biblical narrative, various rituals are prescribed as God's gift to his people, to express and maintain the relationship he established with them by grace.[3] They are shown to be an essential part of the covenant code, with its blessings and curses.

In the book of Exodus, the celebration of the Passover is intimately linked with Israel's redemption from Egypt (12:1 – 13:10). Sacrifice is then associated with the giving and receiving of the covenant (24:4–8), and a whole system of sacrifice is prescribed in connection with the building of the tabernacle, so that God can continue to 'dwell among them' and 'be their God' (29:38–46). The details of the sacrificial system are set out more fully in the book of Leviticus, where it is made clear that the annual Day of Atonement is at the heart of God's gracious provision for the continuance of Israel as his holy people. In the next chapter, I will examine the extent to which New Testament writers interpret the death of Jesus in the light of these rituals and the theology associated with them.

Salvation and covenant

When the Passover is first described in Scripture, the meaning of the Hebrew word *pesaḥ* is explained in terms of the Lord's 'passing over' the houses of the Israelites when he brought judgement against the Egyptians (Exod. 12:11–13, 23–7). Two separate but related feasts, the Passover and the Feast of Unleavened Bread, were to be celebrated one after the other as 'a perpetual ordinance', to remember the mighty deliverance of Israel from bondage in Egypt (Exod. 12:14–20; 13:3–10). Originally a purely domestic occasion, the Passover involved the sprinkling of the two sideposts and lintel of the door with the blood of the sacrificed lamb. When the sacrificial aspect of the festival was transferred to the central sanctuary, this blood sprinkling was apparently applied to the altar (cf. 2 Chron. 35:11).[4]

---

[3] For an assessment of various theories about the origin and meaning of the Israelite sacrificial system, see R.E. Averbeck, 'Offerings and Sacrifices', *NIDOTTE*, vol. 4, pp. 996–1022.

[4] For an assessment of relevant biblical texts and theories about the origin and development of the Passover, see T.D. Alexander, 'The Passover Sacrifice', in R.T. Beckwith and M.J. Selman (eds.), *Sacrifice in the Bible* (Carlisle: Paternoster; Grand Rapids: Baker, 1995), pp. 1–24.

The first Passover involved God's deliverance of his people from the judgement of the final plague, in which the first-born son of every Egyptian household died (Exod. 11:4–8). Thus, from this early stage of the biblical story, *deliverance from divine judgement* is associated with the offering of animal blood as a substitute for human life. In this respect there is a resemblance to the sin offering prescribed later in the Pentateuch. However, unlike the sin offering, the Passover was a communal celebration, not individual, 'and this, together with the fact that it was eaten, makes it closer to the fellowship offerings in character'.[5] Like the fellowship offerings, it was thus also a sign of covenant fellowship with God. But what is most important for our purpose is the observation that a substitutionary blood sacrifice is linked with the deliverance that constituted Israel as God's distinct and holy people.

The wrath of God is consistently directed against the Egyptians in Exodus 7–14. Israel is delivered from each of the plagues by a merciful divine provision. With the last and most terrible plague, however, Israel is only delivered by obedience to the Lord's command and by the fulfilment of this sacrificial ritual. The Passover is more than a demonstration of God's love. The blood averts the judgement of God (12:12–13) and this deliverance initiates the whole process by which God brings the Israelites out of Egypt and enables them to function as his chosen people (12:50 – 13:16).

The covenant ratification ceremony in Exodus 24:3–8 involved burnt offerings and peace offerings, such as became a regular part of the Israelite sacrificial system. Uniquely on this occasion, however, the blood of the sacrifices was splashed on both altar and people, presumably to represent their consecration to God as a holy nation (Exod. 19:6). In between these applications of blood, the people swore an oath of covenant loyalty to the Lord (24:7). A striking similarity between the ritual on this occasion and the ritual for the consecration of priests in Exodus 29 has also suggested to some scholars that Israel was more specifically being consecrated at Sinai to fulfil its role as 'a priestly kingdom'. Richard Averbeck suggests

---

[5] A.M. Harman, 'Passover', *NIDOTTE*, vol. 4, p. 1043–6 (1045). Alexander, 'Passover Sacrifice', p. 17, argues that atonement, redemption, and the sanctification of Israel as God's holy people are all implied by the narrative in Exodus.

that 'in the offering and manipulation of blood something that already by nature belonged to the Lord, and the Lord alone, was used to make a connection between the Lord and the person or thing that was to be consecrated to him'.[6] However, accepting the possibility that the application of blood in such contexts has a consecratory significance, it is important to consider whether blood is also used here to convey the notion of 'atonement'.

The Pentateuch introduces a whole system of sacrifice in connection with the building of the tabernacle. Most important for my purpose here are the sin offering, the guilt offering and the burnt offering. The sin offering or purification offering was provided to deal with unintentional sin (e.g. Lev. 4:1–35). Hands were to be laid on the animal before it was slaughtered and then the blood was to be manipulated 'before the Lord', to 'make atonement' (Heb. *kipper*), so that the participants might be forgiven (Lev. 4:20, 26, 31, 35). The guilt offering or reparation offering involved some financial payment as well as the sacrifice of an animal to 'make atonement' (e.g. Lev. 5:14 – 6:7). The burnt offering, which was the most common of all the sacrifices, was meant to be an expression of consecration to the Lord but also to be a means of making atonement for sins (Lev. 1:3–17; 14:20; 16:24; cf. Gen. 8:21). 'Whereas the purification offering is concerned with cleansing the different parts of the tabernacle from the uncleanness caused by sin, the burnt offering makes atonement for sin in a more general sense.'[7] An important part of the ritual of the burnt offering was the preliminary laying of the hand on the head of the animal and the splashing of its blood 'against all sides of the altar' (Lev. 1:4–5; 8:18–19).

---

[6] Averbeck, 'Offerings and Sacrifices', p. 1003. Blood is also smeared on a *person* in the guilt offering ritual prescribed for the cleansing of a leper (Lev. 14), reconsecrating the leper into the people of God. Blood is smeared on certain *objects* in the ritual of the Day of Atonement (Lev. 16), reconsecrating them to the Lord after their defilement by the sin and uncleanness of Israel.

[7] G.J. Wenham, *The Book of Leviticus*, NICOT (Grand Rapids, 1979), p. 57. He observes that the idea of the burnt offering appeasing God's anger is expressed in many other passages (e.g. Num. 15:24; 2 Sam. 24:25; Job 1:5; 42:8; 2 Chron. 29:7–8). Cf. P.P. Jenson, 'The Levitical Sacrificial System', in Beckwith and Selman, *Sacrifice in the Bible*, pp. 25–40 (28–9), for different ways of viewing the burnt offering.

Descriptive texts suggest that the general sequence within the system was atonement, consecration, fellowship, though there is some overlap of meaning between the various sacrifices.[8] The whole ritual might begin with a sin or guilt offering or both. This could be followed by a burnt offering with its accompanying grain and drink offerings (e.g. Lev. 9:7–17). It appears that the making of full atonement normally required sin and/or guilt offerings and a burnt offering.[9] Peace offerings finally symbolized the fellowship thus restored or maintained between God and his people (e.g. Lev. 9:18–21). But what is meant by atonement in such contexts and why is it so important?

Atonement in Leviticus

The terminology of atonement is extensively used in Leviticus,[10] and structurally the chapter about the Day of Atonement is pivotal in the way the book is formed. Leviticus 1–16 contains regulations designed to maintain the purity of the tabernacle, so that the Lord may dwell in the midst of his people, to fulfil his covenant promises and bless them (cf. Lev. 26). Although the second half of the book is still concerned with the holiness and purity of the tabernacle, Leviticus 17–27 broadens the focus to encompass the holiness of the people in a range of everyday situations. 'One might say that the shift is from *tabernacle* holiness and purity to *national* holiness and purity.'[11]

Canonically, the book picks up the notion that Israel is 'a priestly kingdom and a holy nation' (Exod. 19:6; cf. Lev. 20:7–8; 22:32–3), consecrated to the Lord's service (cf. Exod. 24:3–8) and called to live in holiness and purity before him. They are saved by God's grace and set apart for his service from among the nations by the

---

[8] See A.F. Rainey, 'The Order of the Sacrifices in OT Ritual Texts', *Biblica* 51 (1970), pp. 485–98 (498).

[9] Ibid. Cf. Lev. 5:7; 9:7; 14:18–20.

[10] The verbal root *kpr* is used with reference to atonement 52 times in Leviticus, 14 of which are in ch. 16; the abstract term *kippurîm*, 'atonement', is found in Lev. 23:27, 28; 25:9; *kappôret*, 'place of atonement, mercy seat, or cover (over the ark)' is found in Lev. 16:2 (twice), 13, 14 (twice), 15.

[11] R.E. Averbeck, 'Leviticus: Theology of', *NIDOTTE*, vol. 4, pp. 907–23 (909).

redemptive activity which brings them to himself at Sinai (Exod. 19:4). But that holy status is to be expressed by obeying his voice and keeping his covenant (Exod. 19:5–6; Lev. 11:44–5; 20:23–6).[12] In practical terms, this meant maintaining certain moral standards and engaging in various cultic rituals that set them apart from the nations.

Within this framework of thought, Leviticus 1–16 deals with the special priestly responsibility of the family of Aaron, to maintain the holiness and purity of the tabernacle and thereby to sustain the nation in its holy calling. Leviticus teaches that pollution and sin affect not only the individual and the nation, but also the tabernacle, the seat of God's presence among his people. When this happens, 'Israel's holy redeemer can no longer dwell among them and their *raison d'être* is destroyed.'[13] Thus, although Leviticus 16 is the conclusion of the first major part of the book, it is also the theological centre and binds the two halves together. The Day of Atonement ritual is designed to make atonement for the sanctuary, the tent of meeting, the altar, the priests and 'all the people of the assembly' (16:33). Without atonement, Israel cannot function as God's holy people in a sinful and fallen world. But we still need to explore what is precisely meant by this language of atonement.

Atonement and judgement

In Leviticus 16:1–2 the Lord is said to have given the instructions about the Day of Atonement ritual 'after the death of the two sons of Aaron, when they drew near before the Lord and died'. The reference is to the incident in chapter 10, where Nadab and Abihu offered 'unholy fire before the Lord, such as he had not commanded them', and 'fire came out from the presence of the Lord and consumed them, and they died before the Lord'. This incident shows how priests who approached the Lord improperly might

---

[12] See D. Peterson, *Possessed by God: A New Testament Theology of Sanctification and Holiness* (Leicester: Apollos; Grand Rapids: Eerdmans, 1995), pp. 19–23.

[13] Wenham, *Leviticus*, p. 5. There is an important link between the inauguration of the tabernacle in Lev. 9 and the annual renewal of the tabernacle system in Lev. 16. In both cases the focus is clearly on the tabernacle itself, and there are separate sin offerings and burnt offerings for both priests and people (cf. 9:7–17 with 16:5–19, 24).

experience his judgement. Consequently, Aaron is warned 'not to come just at any time into the sanctuary inside the curtain before the mercy-seat that is upon the ark or he will die' (16:2; cf. 22:9).[14] Only by strict adherence to the Lord's commands could he safely enter the Lord's presence and do what was necessary for the preservation of God's people.

Again, the wider context here is the awesome revelation of the holiness of God in salvation and judgement, as experienced by Israel in the exodus (Exod. 15:1–12), at Mount Sinai (19:9–25), and in connection with the making of the golden calf (32:1 – 34:9). Those who rebelled against the Holy One experienced his fierce wrath. In the Pentateuch generally there is a close connection between sin and punishment. In certain cases it is possible to escape that punishment by means of the sacrifices provided by God (e.g. Lev. 4–5).

When God was about to consume the people in his anger and fulfil his covenant purposes through Moses, Moses sought to 'make atonement' for their sin by interceding for them and asking for his own name to be blotted out of God's 'book' (32:30–2). This incident shows that atonement is more generally concerned with *the removal of God's wrath against sin*. It involves an appeal to God for forgiveness but also the need for a penalty to be paid. Moses offers himself as a substitute for rebellious Israel, even though the Lord does not allow him to function as such at this time (32:33–5).

The ultimate threat of the Pentateuch is that the Lord will uproot Israel from the land 'in anger, fury, and great wrath', casting them into another land, because of their unfaithfulness and rebellion against him (Deut. 29:19–28; cf. Lev. 26:21–39). 'The Bible writers have nothing to do with pagan conceptions of a capricious and vindictive deity, inflicting arbitrary punishments on offending worshippers, who must bribe him back to a good mood by the appropriate offerings.'[15] Neither do they suggest that God 'needs'

---

[14] The Hebrew in Lev. 16:2 could imply a total prohibition against entry, but the context indicates that the high priest may enter the inner sanctum once every year, if the proper preparation is made.

[15] L. Morris, *The Apostolic Preaching of the Cross* (Leicester: IVP, 1965[3]), p. 148. Morris (pp. 147–54) has a very helpful section on the wrath of God in the Old Testament, as part of an argument for understanding atonement as propitiation.

sacrifice for his own satisfaction and welfare (e.g. Ps. 50:7–15). But they portray the wrath of God as his fixed and determined response to all that is unholy and evil. At the same time, they proclaim him as the God of mercy (e.g. Exod. 34:6–7), who provides ways in which the consequences of sin may be averted.

In a positive sense, the ritual provisions of the law are designed to maintain Israel's covenant status as a holy people living in the presence of a holy God. Negatively, they are designed to protect priests and people from experiencing the judgement of God. It is therefore quite misleading for John Goldingay to say that 'the idea of punishment belongs in the framework of law rather than the framework of worship, and we get into difficulties when we mix ideas from the different frameworks such as these'.[16]

For one thing, the provisions for worship in the Pentateuch are an integral part of God's law for Israel and cannot be separated from his moral and social demands. Worship involves obedience to God's commands and the terminology of worship fundamentally expresses submission and service to God as Israel's great king.[17] Furthermore, as we have noted, the avoidance of divine judgement is linked with ritual provisions in several important contexts and must be understood within the wider framework of Israel's covenant relationship with the Holy One and the threat of ultimate exclusion from the land and God's presence.

Goldingay's image of sacrifice being like the giving of flowers in a loving relationship is inadequate with respect to atonement offerings. These are God's merciful provision to deliver his people from the consequences of their rebellion against him. They have a saving function within the divinely established and maintained covenant between God and Israel that has no simple parallel in human relationships.

The meaning of the terminology

The Hebrew verb *kpr* is used 102 times in the Old Testament, almost always in intensive forms (such as the piel *kipper*) and mostly

---

[16] Goldingay, 'Old Testament Sacrifice and the Death of Christ', in idem (ed.), *Atonement Today* (London: SPCK, 1995), pp. 3–20 (10).

[17] See D. Peterson, *Engaging with God: A Biblical Theology of Worship* (Leicester: Apollos; Grand Rapids: Eerdmans, 1992), pp. 55–79.

in the priestly or ritual sections of Exodus, Leviticus, Numbers.[18] In non-priestly contexts it is said that God himself will 'make atonement for his land and people' (Deut. 32:43) or 'cleanse the land for his people' (NRSV; cf. Ezek. 16:33). Even where some ritual is prescribed, God is still asked to (lit.) 'atone for' or 'absolve' his people (Deut. 21:8; 2 Chron. 30:18–19). In other words, there is a recognition that *God is the true or ultimate source of atonement*, even if he provides certain rituals as the means by which his people obtain this benefit.

Some English versions quite rightly translate *kpr* 'forgive' or 'pardon' where God is the subject (e.g. Pss. 65:3[4]; 78:38; 79:9; Jer. 18:23). There is a close link between atonement and forgiveness in Scripture. But it is important to note that when *kpr* is used in parallel with the normal verb to forgive (*slḥ*), something else which we may broadly categorize as 'atonement' is clearly necessary before one can expect to be forgiven for the transgression (e.g. Lev. 4:20, 26, 31; 19:22; Num. 15:25).[19] In the Israelite cult, divine grace was sought by worshippers making the offerings prescribed by God himself.

Debate continues about the foundational meaning of the terminology of atonement, especially when it is used to describe an action that humans perform with respect to God. Some scholars have related the Hebrew root to the cognate Arabic verb 'cover, conceal', but there are serious problems with this proposal.[20] Others have argued that the root meaning is 'wipe clean, purge', noting the cognate Akkadian verb and the parallel in Jeremiah 18:23 with Hebrew *mḥh* ('wipe, blot out') or with *hsr* ('remove') in Isaiah 27:9.[21] Many of the cultic uses of *kpr* certainly suggest that blood was used to purge the sanctuary from contamination.

---

[18] The abstract noun *kippurîm* 'atonement' (cf. Exod. 30:16; Lev. 23:27) and *kappōret* 'place of atonement' or 'atonement seat' (cf. Lev. 16:2, NRSV 'mercy seat') are clearly derived from this root.

[19] The passive in such texts could be rendered 'that (he) may be forgiven' and suggest that God's forgiveness is not the automatic consequence of the priestly rite. See J. Milgrom, 'Atonement in the OT', *IDB*, Supplementary Volume (Nashville: Abingdon, 1976), pp. 78–82 (79).

[20] See R.E. Averbeck, '*kpr*', *NIDOTTE*, vol. 2, pp. 689–710 (692–3); B.A Levine, *In the Presence of the Lord*, SJLA 5 (Leiden: Brill, 1974), pp. 56–63.

[21] See J. Milgrom, *Leviticus 1–16*, AB 3A (Garden City, New York: Doubleday, 1991), pp. 1079–80; Levine, *Presence*, pp. 57–77.

But there is another possibility that the verb is a denominative from *kōper* ('bribe, ransom').[22] In Exodus 30:11–16 and Numbers 35:29–34, these terms occur together, suggesting that atonement is associated with the payment of a ransom. A range of other passages similarly indicate that atonement in non-cultic contexts involves the payment of a price, either of money or of life (e.g. Exod. 32:30; Num. 25:10–13; 31:50; Deut. 21:1–9; 2 Sam. 21:1–14). It is then important to note that the expression 'to make atonement for your lives', which is found twice in Exodus 30:15–16, is also found in Leviticus 17:11, which is a key text for explaining the significance of sacrificial blood within the Israelite cult: 'For the life of the flesh is in the blood; and I have given it to you *for making atonement for your lives* on the altar; for, as life [lit. 'in the life'], it is the blood that makes atonement' (NRSV, my emphasis).

The means of atonement for a human life in Exodus 30:11–16 is a monetary payment, whereas the means of atonement in Leviticus 17:11 is the blood or 'life' of a slaughtered animal. Atonement here is not simply a matter of removing guilt or defilement by purging, but of averting the wrath of God by offering the life of a substitute.

Are we then to conclude that *kpr* reflects two distinct verbal forms and derivations ('purge' and 'ransom')? Richard Averbeck argues that the base meaning of *kpr* is 'to wipe away, wipe clean, purge',[23] but that the verb sometimes takes on the meaning of 'ransom' when it refers to the overall effect of the action. The 'wiping away' is done by means of a substitute, 'specifically, the soul of the animal that is represented by its blood'.[24] Here the 'wiping' is

---

[22] See Averbeck, '*kpr*', *NIDOTTE*, vol. 2, pp. 689–710 (693–5); Levine, *Presence*, pp. 67–77; Morris, *Apostolic Preaching*, pp. 160–74. Positively, *kōper* is a legally legitimate payment, which delivers a guilty party from the punishment that is the right of the offended party to execute. It is usually a *mitigated penalty*, that rescues the life of the guilty and appeases the offended party.

[23] Averbeck, '*kpr*', *NIDOTTE*, vol. 2, p. 696. '*kpr* has a direct effect on sancta – it "wipes" sancta "clean".'

[24] Averbeck, '*kpr*', *NIDOTTE*, vol. 2, p. 698. N. Kiuchi, *The Purification Offering in the Priestly Literature*, JSOTS 36 (Sheffield: JSOT, 1987), pp. 87–109, concludes that 'make atonement' is a broad idea, involving several subsidiary ones, such as sanctify, cleanse, forgive and bear guilt.

achieved by more than the application of blood to an object as an act of cleansing. Jacob Milgrom somewhat similarly argues that *kpr* as 'purge' is restricted to the sanctuary and its objects: it is never used of a person directly. The sanctuary must be regularly purged of its impurities or else God will abandon both sanctuary and people to their doom. However, *kpr* as 'ransom/substitute' for the sins of the people is associated with the notion of the scapegoat and the heifer whose neck is broken. 'The common denominator of all these cases is their avowed goal: to siphon off the wrath of God from the entire community.'[25]

In a thorough review of the evidence, Jay Sklar argues that, in contexts addressing sin, *kipper* refers to the effecting of a *kōper* on behalf of the guilty party.[26] Where the sins addressed also result in impurity, it is possible that *kipper* also refers to some element of purgation. In contexts addressing impurity, *kipper* refers to the effecting of purgation on behalf of the person or item needing to be cleansed. However, particularly in contexts involving a major impurity, the person in need of cleansing defiles the holy things associated with the tabernacle, which is an inadvertent sin requiring a *kōper*. In short, Sklar argues that, whether the context is one of sin or impurity, it is possible that *kipper* refers to the effecting of a ransom or 'composition' payment as well as to the effecting of a purgation.[27]

The Day of Atonement

When the ritual of the Day of Atonement is outlined in Leviticus 16, the high priest is warned to approach the 'mercy-seat' on God's terms

---

[25] Milgrom, 'Atonement in the OT', p. 80.

[26] Sklar's doctoral research, which is being supervised by Gordon Wenham, is not yet published. It was kindly made available for me to read at a critical stage in the writing of this chapter. Sklar follows H.C. Brichto, 'On Slaughter and Sacrifice, Blood and Atonement', *HUCA* 47 (1976), pp. 19–55 (27–8), in arguing that the legal term 'composition', which is used for 'the settling of differences', best covers the meaning of *kōper*. This includes elements of 'ransom' and 'appeasement', but notably implies a *mitigated payment*. See n. 22 above.

[27] To satisfy both aspects of the biblical usage, he suggests that *kipper* comprehensively means 'to effect *kōper* – purgation'.

(vv. 1–2),[28] lest he experience the wrath of God by acting inappropriately as the two sons of Aaron did (10:1–3). He must first make atonement 'for himself and for his house', by sacrificing a bull and sprinkling some of its blood 'on the front of the mercy-seat and before the mercy-seat' (v. 14). As a preliminary to this last action, he must put incense 'on the fire before the Lord, so that the cloud of the incense may cover the mercy-seat, that is upon the covenant, or he will die' (v. 13).[29] He must then cast lots over the two goats, to determine which one is to be presented to the Lord as a sin offering for the people (cf. vv. 7–9).

The blood of one goat is sprinkled 'upon the mercy-seat and before the mercy-seat', to 'make atonement for the sanctuary, because of the uncleannesses of the people of Israel and because of their transgressions, all their sins' (vv. 15–16). These verses speak comprehensively of the need of the people for forgiveness and cleansing. They also indicate the need for the outer 'tent of meeting', as well as the inner sanctuary, to be atoned for. When this is done, the high priest sprinkles the blood of goat and bull on the horns of the altar, to 'make atonement on its behalf' (v. 18) and to 'cleanse it and hallow it from the uncleannesses of the people of Israel' (v. 19). Israel's failure to be a holy nation contaminates these vehicles by which their relationship with God is expressed and maintained, putting that relationship at risk.

When the high priest has finished atoning for the holy place and the tent of meeting and the altar, he presents the live goat (v. 20), chosen by lot 'for Azazel' (vv. 8–10). Although there has been considerable debate over the interpretation of this last expression, the meaning of the ritual seems clear enough:

> Whether Azazel means, the mountain where the goat is destroyed, the sin which is given to destruction, or the evil angel who is given the

---

[28] The Hebrew *kappōret*, which is probably derived from *kipper*, is best translated 'place of atonement', rather than 'cover, lid' (see Wenham, *Leviticus*, p. 229, n. 2). NRSV 'mercy-seat' reflects the notion of Ps. 99:1 that the Lord 'sits enthroned upon the cherubim'. These cherubim made the top of the ark appear like a throne (cf. Exod. 25:17–22).

[29] Incense may be used to prevent the high priest from gazing upon the holy presence represented by the mercy-seat. But it may also be used to avert God's wrath, as in Ps. 141:2; Num. 16:46–8. Cf. Wenham, *Leviticus*, p. 231.

bribe so that he does not become an accuser, it all comes back to the same basic idea: that sin is exterminated from Israel.[30]

Laying both his hands on the head of the live goat, the high priest confesses over it 'all the iniquities of the people of Israel, and all their transgressions, all their sins, putting them on the head of the goat, and sending it away into the wilderness by means of someone designated for the task' (v.21).[31]

It is interesting to reflect on the spatial significance of the ritual of the two goats:

> The blood of one goat reaches to the heart of holy space, whereas the other is driven out to where major impurities have their proper place (cf. Nu. 5:1–3). At no other time of the year are these spaces employed in priestly rituals.[32]

Both parts of this movement together restore harmony between God and Israel. The Day of Atonement appears to have been the occasion when all the serious impurities accumulated throughout the year were dealt with. 'The ordered world of the cult could be compromised by an unchecked multiplication of impure people and places, but on the Day of Atonement the appropriate boundaries were re-established and the sanctuary purified from every possible defilement.'[33] However, from a biblical-theological point of view it must be stressed again that the wider context of this activity is the maintenance of Israel as a holy nation before a holy God.

The goat that is set free is explicitly said to 'bear on itself all their iniquities to a barren region' (Lev. 16:22). When a person is the subject of the expression 'bear sin/iniquity' (Heb. *nāśā' 'āwōn/ḥēṭ*), the meaning is 'bear responsibility, punishment' for his or her sins (e.g. Lev. 5:1, 17; 7:18; 17:16; 19:8; Num. 5:31) or 'remove iniquity,

---

[30] Wenham, *Leviticus*, p. 235, citing D. Hoffmann, *Das Buch Leviticus* (Berlin: Poppelauer, 1905), vol. 1, p. 444.

[31] The laying-on of hands has been variously interpreted. E.R. Leach, *Culture and Communication* (Cambridge: CUP, 1976), p. 89, concludes that the most probable explanation is that the victim is thus identified as 'a vicarious substitution for the donor himself'.

[32] Jensen, 'Levitical Sacrificial System', p. 34.

[33] Ibid., p. 35.

forgive sin' (e.g. Gen. 50:17; Exod. 10:17; 1 Sam. 15:25). In the sacrificial system, the priest is authorized to 'remove the guilt of the congregation', by making atonement on their behalf 'before the Lord' (Lev. 10:17). Leviticus 16:22 is the only text where an animal is explicitly said to 'bear on itself' the iniquities of God's people. Although the sense of 'carry away' is implied by the movement 'to a barren region', there must also be a sense of vicarious punishment involved in putting all the transgressions 'on the head of the goat' (16:21) and sending it off to die.[34] As we shall shortly observe, the Servant of the Lord in Isaiah 53:12 is the only *person* in the Old Testament who is said to 'bear' the sins of others.

Sacrifice and Forgiveness in the Prophets and the Psalms

Sacrifice in the Psalms

Although the theme of sacrifice emerges at a number of points in the psalms, there is very little reference to atonement. Nigel Courtman identifies three distinct motives that are commonly associated with the offering of sacrifice by the psalmists. Thanksgiving and petition are the first two, 'corresponding to the situations of distress and deliverance regularly depicted in the psalms of thanksgiving and lament'.[35] Worship in the sense of homage, praise and devotion is the third motive, corresponding loosely to 'the purpose of the hymnic psalms, that is, to offer praise to God'. A positive view of sacrifice is thus presented in many contexts.

---

[34] The other goat is slaughtered and it seems logical to presume that the goat in the wilderness would soon die. The phrase at the end of Lev. 16:22 is lit. 'a land of cutting off', which quite likely means 'a place where the goat is cut off', i.e. dies/is killed. Combined with the possible rendering of Azazel as either 'total destruction' or 'precipice', this strongly suggests the destruction of the goat. See Wenham, *Leviticus*, pp. 233–5. Thus the punishment-bearing of the goat seems obvious from the context.

[35] N.B. Courtman, 'Sacrifice in the Psalms', in Beckwith and Selman, *Sacrifice in the Bible*, pp. 41–58 (41). Thanksgiving is the keynote in Pss. 27:6; 54:6; 56:12; 116:12, 17, and petition most obviously in Ps. 20:2–4. Worship is the general theme in contexts such as Pss. 4:5; 76:11; 96:8–9.

This positive perspective is particularly reflected in Psalm 50:14–15, 23, where it is indicated that God is honoured when people express their dependence on him through sacrifice. However, the same psalm warns about the danger of offering anything to put God in one's debt (Ps. 50:9–13) or to cover up one's disobedience (vv. 16–22). This psalm is one of a number that critique the *abuse*, rather than the institution of sacrifice (e.g. Pss. 40:6–8; 51:16–17). Here we find no 'axiomatic repudiation of the whole sacrificial cult',[36] but an expression of the true meaning implicit in this whole way of approaching God. In the next chapter we shall note how Hebrews 10:5–10 uses Psalm 40:6–8 to proclaim the fulfilment and replacement of the sacrificial system in the obedience of Jesus Christ. When the ideal of submission to the will of God is perfectly fulfilled in Jesus' death, a definitive cleansing and sanctification is made possible. This inaugurates the New Covenant of Jeremiah 31:31–4, with its promise of a once-for-all forgiveness of sins (Heb. 10:11–18).

Psalm 65:3 acknowledges God as the one who answers prayer and atones for sin: 'when deeds of iniquity overwhelm us, you forgive our transgressions' (lit. 'it is you who atone for our transgressions'). But the text does not explicitly mention the need for rituals of atonement. Elsewhere, even where sin is acknowledged as the cause of Israel's difficulties (e.g. Ps. 107:10–20), sacrifice is not identified as a means of securing God's forgiveness. In Psalm 51, which is clearly penitential, sacrifice is only mentioned in a positive light at the end, as an expression of thanksgiving and homage (v. 19). Prayer for pardon, confession, and contrition are regularly called for when sin looms large in the experience of the psalmists (e.g. Pss. 25:7, 11; 32:5; 51:1–18; 130).[37]

It would be wrong to conclude, however, that the psalms recognized no atoning role for sacrifice. Psalm 76:10–12 speaks of votive offerings in a context where God is wrathful and needs to be appeased. Psalm 40:6, with its apparently negative view of sacrifice, nevertheless lists 'burnt offering and sin offering' with the

[36] A. Weiser, *The Psalms* (London: SCM, 1962), p. 338. Contrast Courtman, 'Sacrifice in the Psalms', pp. 50–2.
[37] Cf. H. McKeating, 'Divine forgiveness in the Psalms', *SJT* 18 (1965), pp. 78–81.

other rituals provided by God to facilitate the true dedication of his servants to his will. Given the sequence of atonement, consecration and fellowship that was noted in connection with the pattern of sacrifice in Leviticus, perhaps it was assumed by the psalmists that atonement rituals would have preceded offerings to express praise and dedication to God. Generally, however, the hope of forgiveness in the psalms is centred on 'the nature and action of God, rather than on what might appear to be the human aspect of sacrifice'.[38]

Redemption and forgiveness in the Prophets

As in the psalms, so in the writings of the prophets, there are passages that condemn God's people for their corruption of the sacrificial system (e.g. Amos 4:4–13; Hos. 8:11–13; Jer. 7:21–6; Ezek. 16:15–21; 20:25–31). These deal with the introduction of pagan ideas and practices into Israelite worship, or the attempt to worship other gods while still claiming to serve the Lord, or the hypocrisy of engaging in sacrificial ritual without genuine repentance and a desire to live in obedience to God's moral law. Sometimes, in order to clarify the sort of response the cult was meant to inculcate, prophecies are worded in a way that appears to be a categorical rejection of the cult (e.g. Amos 5:21–7; Hos. 6:6; Isa. 1:10–17; 66:1–4; Mic. 6:6–8). However, such passages are condemnations of Israel's abuse of the cult rather than of the cult itself.[39]

The prophets also speak with approval of future sacrificial activity, portraying a time when God would renew his people and their worship (e.g. Isa. 19:19–21; 56:6–7; 60:7; Jer. 17:24–7; 33:10–11, 17–18; Ezek. 20:40–1). Some speak of the restoration of the temple after the judgement of the exile, envisaging it as the spiritual centre for Israel and the nations (e.g. Isa. 2:2–3; Mic. 4:1–3; Ezek. 40–8). In this connection, the closing chapters of Ezekiel reflect something of the original exodus structure and its theology: 'just as the meaning of the exodus was proclaimed in the "cultic" response of Israel to divine kingship, so here the new temple will function as

---

[38] Courtman, 'Sacrifice in the Psalms', p. 56.
[39] Cf. E.C. Lucas, 'Sacrifice in the Prophets', in Beckwith and Selman, *Sacrifice in the Bible*, pp. 59–74, and Peterson, *Engaging with God*, pp. 45–8.

Yahweh's kingly setting in the new holy city'.[40] But Ezekiel also indicates that God is going to do something quite new in the outworking of his purposes. His temple-plan, with all its marvellous symbolism, combines a number of biblical ideals and points to their ultimate fulfilment, not by some human building programme, but by the sovereign and gracious act of God (see 20:40–4).

The Babylonian exile is regarded by many of the prophets as such a devastating judgement of God that it calls into question Israel's covenant status and future as God's people. It is the final curse that the Law prescribes for a covenant-breaking nation (Deut. 29:19–28; Lev. 26:21–39). For this reason, we read of the need for a new act of divine redemption, paralleling the exodus from Egypt (e.g. Isa. 40:1–11; 42:14–17; 43:1–21). Associated with this are promises that the Lord himself will blot out Israel's transgressions (e.g. Isa. 43:25), 'forgive their iniquity and remember their sin no more' (Jer. 31:34), and cleanse them from all their idols and from all their uncleannesses (Ezek. 36:25; 37:23). Transformed cultic imagery is used to underline the fact that God himself must provide the way of atonement and reconciliation that is needed to renew the covenant and save his people (cf. Jer. 31:31–4; Ezek. 36:24–31). Only in this way can he dwell in their midst again, to bless them and enable them to function as his holy people among the nations.

These prophets teach that the removal of God's wrath against sin and the restoration of his relationship with Israel comes from the Lord himself. Although the terminology of atonement is not much used outside the Pentateuch, some of the same categories of thought are found in prophetic proclamations of salvation. Where the Hebrew verb *kpr* is used, God rather than a priest is normally the subject, and sin rather than contaminated objects is the direct object (e.g. Jer. 18:23; Ezek. 16:63; Ps. 78:38). Other terminology is also employed to convey the need for divine forgiveness and the removal of sin (e.g. Hos. 14:2; Mic. 7:18–19). Ezekiel in particular stretches cultic language creatively to speak of 'a forgiveness that knows the depths of sin, that wants to separate God's people from the habit of defection. It knows that sin stains, and that sin estranges people from God.'[41]

---

[40] W.J. Dumbrell, *The End of the Beginning: Revelation 21–22 and the Old Testament* (Homebush West: Lancer; Grand Rapids: Baker, 1985), p. 57.

[41] T.M. Raitt, *A Theology of Exile Judgment/Deliverance in Jeremiah and Ezekiel* (Philadelphia: Fortress, 1977), p. 191.

But how is God's wrath to be satisfied and how will his just condemnation of human sin be maintained through gracious acts of forgiveness and renewal? What ransom or substitute will God provide if animal sacrifice cannot fulfil his purpose?

The Suffering Servant

From a New Testament point of view, Isaiah 53 is the most important passage in the prophetic literature for illuminating and explaining the death of Jesus. Scholars continue to debate whether Jesus was the first to interpret his own ministry as a fulfilment of this passage, even though there appears to be sufficient evidence in the Gospels that he was.[42] More fundamentally, there are those who question the legitimacy of any reading of the text, which sees in Isaiah 53 a pattern of penal substitution.[43]

Some argue that the so-called 'Servant Songs' had a separate existence and meaning before being incorporated into the canonical form of Isaiah, but we are surely bound to explain their significance in the context in which we now find them. The wider setting indicates that God will deliver his people in exile from the punishment due to their sin, restoring them to himself by his own 'hand' or 'arm' (40:10; 48:14; 50:2; 51:5, 9; 52:10). The Servant of the Lord, who is first mentioned in 42:1–4, is mysteriously identified with Israel in 49:1–6, but is paradoxically also the means by which Israel is restored to God and God's salvation is brought to the nations. Suffering first appears to be the Servant's lot in 50:4–9, resulting from his prophetic activity. However, the Servant's sufferings appear to be *redemptive* in Isaiah 53. The chapter begins with the claim that 'the arm of Lord', by which Israel's relationship with God is restored and her destiny is fulfilled, is revealed in what happens to the Lord's Servant.

The language of the fourth song (52:13 – 53:12) portrays an individual who not only acts for 'the many' in a representative way but

---

[42] Against the sceptical position of Morna Hooker on this issue, note the discussion in W.H. Bellinger Jr. and W.R. Farmer (eds.), *Jesus and the Suffering Servant: Isaiah 53 and Christian Origins* (Harrisburg: Trinity Press International, 1998), pp. 70–151.

[43] E.g. R.N. Whybray, *Thanksgiving for a Liberated Prophet: An Interpretation of Isaiah 53*, JSOTS 4 (Sheffield: JSOT, 1978).

also as their substitute. In him, the true Israel has been reduced to one.[44] The framework of the song (52:13–15; 53:10–12) proclaims that the Servant will ultimately be exalted and prosper, but the intervening verses speak of rejection, terrible anguish and an unjust death (53:1–9). All forms of suffering – physical, mental and spiritual – are encompassed by the language of verses 1–3. It is because the Servant suffers so comprehensively that he first appears to be of no significance to the onlookers. Such a person could hardly be the one through whom the Lord's saving arm is revealed! However, verses 4–6 report how the onlookers came to perceive that the Servant was actually 'wounded for our transgressions, crushed for our iniquities'. With this confession, the prophet offers a profound solution to the problem of Israel's unfaithfulness and rebellion. P.D. Hanson puts it like this:

> What happens when a people is stumbling toward extinction under the burden of its sin-induced infirmities and diseases, and the traditional institutions of sacrifice and atonement have proven ineffectual to relieve them of their sin and guilt? What can be done about these infirmities and diseases? The surprising answer given in 53:4 is that they have already been lifted from the afflicted community *by the Servant*.[45]

Even those who deny any substitutionary element in Isaiah 53 admit that the Servant suffers undeservedly because of human sin. However, writers such as Orlinsky and Whybray argue that the people of Israel had already suffered the full measure for their sins in the destruction of their land and their captivity (cf. 40:2).[46] The Servant only suffers because they do – as a *result* of their sin – but not in their place, as a *substitute*. Oswalt offers two significant responses

---

[44] See C.R. North, *The Suffering Servant in Deutero-Isaiah* (London: Oxford University, 1956), p. 216.

[45] P.D. Hanson, 'The World of the Servant of the Lord in Isaiah 40–55', in Bellinger and Farmer, *Jesus and the Suffering Servant*, pp. 9–22 (18).

[46] See H.M. Orlinsky, 'The so-called "Servant of the Lord" and "Suffering Servant" in Second Isaiah', in H.M. Orlinsky and N. Snaith, *Studies in the Second Part of the Book of Isaiah*, VTS 14 (Leiden: Brill, 1967), pp. 1–133; R.N. Whybray, *Isaiah 40–66*, NCB (London: Oliphants, 1975), pp. 171–2, expanded in Whybray, *Thanksgiving for a Liberated Prophet*, pp. 134–40.

to this approach. He first observes how the passage in its context points to the Servant as the means of salvation anticipated in chapters 49–52. The people are then invited to participate in the salvation that the Servant achieves in chapters 53–5.[47] Oswalt further points out that the exile was a temporal punishment for sin but that this did not automatically restore the people to fellowship with God. Something more was needed because of the seriousness of their situation under the curse of God. Only the affliction of the Servant could make them 'whole' and only 'by his bruises' could they be healed (53:5).

We should also note that the Servant's treatment is portrayed as unjust from start to finish (53:7–9), whereas the prophets insist that Israel's punishment in the exile was completely just (e.g. Neh. 9; Dan. 9). The Servant cannot simply be identified with Israel or with one of the prophets who were caught up in the consequences of Israel's rebellion against God. Moreover, the injustice that the Servant suffers is not simply the result of a corrupt legal system, since 'he is stricken for the transgression of my people' (53:8). He suffers in the place of those who ought to have suffered, 'although he had done no violence and there was no deceit in his mouth' (53:9).[48]

As Israel's substitute, the Servant is punished in a manner that exceeds the just punishment of the Babylonian exile. The salvation or 'healing' that is achieved in this way is profound and comprehensive. A decisive reconciliation with God is implied, together with a restoration of God's people that involves more than a return from exile (e.g. the Servant shall 'make many righteous', 53:11). Those who deny the theme of penal substitution in this chapter appear to be guilty of special pleading.

Isaiah 53 speaks about the need for an entirely novel means of atonement, which is nevertheless explained in terms that would have been familiar to the Jews from the sacrificial system. The metaphor of the lamb being led to the slaughter is certainly reminiscent of the sacrificial system. Jeremiah uses the same image to stress his own trusting *naïveté* (Jer. 11:19), but the emphasis in Isaiah 53:7 is much more on willing submission without protest (cf. 42:2–4;

---

[47] Oswalt, *Isaiah 40–66* (Grand Rapids: Eerdmans, 1998), pp. 377, 385.

[48] See ibid., pp. 393–4 (esp. nn. 25, 26) for a criticism of Whybray in this connection.

50:5–7). Further sacrificial language is found in the promise that God will heal and restore his people by making his servant 'an offering for sin' (53:10, Heb. *āśām*, Gk. *peri hamartias*). Whybray thinks it is unwise to press the significance of this statement because nowhere else in the Old Testament is it stated that a person's life can be a guilt offering, 'whether in a literal or metaphorical sense'.[49] However, this is a natural development of the view expressed in the psalms and the prophets that the sacrifice which really pleases God is the life of the offerer. The novelty of Isaiah 53 is the claim that one person's obedient service may be accepted by God as an atoning sacrifice for others.

Again, it should be noted that the language of 'carrying' and 'bearing' in verses 4, 11, 12, points to the Servant's death as substitutionary, just as the death of animals in the sacrificial system appears to have been substitutionary. This terminology in the context suggests that the Servant bears the sin of others by enduring its consequences for them. He is 'stricken, struck down by God, and afflicted' (53:4), because 'the Lord has laid on him the iniquity of us all' (53:6). 'The effect in the Servant is the measure of how seriously God takes our rebellion and crookedness.'[50]

The final stanza of the poem in Isaiah 53:10–12 makes it clear why 'it was the will of the Lord to crush him with pain'. Since the Lord was prepared to regard him as 'an offering for sin', extraordinary benefits flow for his 'offspring' and for the Servant himself. His 'offspring' shall be 'made righteous', because the Righteous One, God's Servant, 'shall bear their iniquities'. The benefit for the Servant is that 'he shall see his offspring and shall prolong his days'. He will also be allotted 'a portion with the great' and shall 'divide the spoil with the strong' (53:12; cf. 52:13). Although it is disputed, the most obvious reading of this section is that the Servant will be resurrected from death to see the fruit of his suffering. He was 'numbered with the transgressors', but it was not because he was a rebel himself. Indeed, by 'bearing the sin of many' he was actually 'interceding' for them, that is, intervening on their behalf to rescue and redeem them (cf. 59:16).

---

[49] R.N. Whybray, *Isaiah 40–66*, NCB (London: Oliphants, 1975), p. 179. Contrast R.E. Averbeck, '*šm*', *NIDOTTE*, vol. 1, pp. 553–66 (564).
[50] Oswalt, *Isaiah 40–66*, p. 387.

Many questions remain about the detail of Isaiah 53 and scholars will continue to debate how the prophet expected this chapter to be understood by his contemporaries. But Christians throughout the ages have recognized the person and work of Christ in every verse, so that 'what had formerly been opaque becomes patently clear',[51] in the light of its fulfilment. In the next chapter, I will confront certain contemporary challenges to this reading of the text.

Conclusion

Atonement in the Pentateuch is not simply to be identified with ritual cleansing. It involves the notion of ransom from the divine penalty for sin, which is sometimes represented as physical death and sometimes as alienation from God, as in the prediction of exile from the Promised Land. Animal substitution is a key to this notion of ransom or redemption, especially in the Day of Atonement ritual, where the notion of bearing human sin is highlighted.

The theological importance of atonement within the framework of Israel's covenant relationship with God is highlighted in the Pentateuch by the Passover narrative in Exodus, the focus in Leviticus on the Day of Atonement provisions, and the general prominence given to atonement in the sacrificial system. Christian interpreters ought to keep their eyes open to this broad picture and not get lost in debates about the meaning of particular terms and sacrificial rites. This portion of Scripture teaches that sinful men and women can only draw near to the Holy One and continue in his presence by the means which he himself provides.

The psalmists and prophets point to the maintenance of a right relationship with God as the Lord's ultimate purpose in establishing the sacrificial system. At the same time, they identify God as the true and only source of atonement and redemption, especially in the context of the Babylonian exile, where a definitive restoration of Israel's relationship with God is seen to be necessary. Within the framework of Biblical Theology, this prepares for the extraordinary message of Isaiah 53, where the perfect obedience of the Servant in his suffering and death is presented as the Lord's provision for Israel

---

[51] Ibid., p. 408.

and ultimately the nations. Attempts to remove the penal substitutionary dimension to the Servant's self-offering appear to be an exercise in special pleading. Indeed, there is a train of thought about sin-bearing in the Old Testament that comes to an awesome climax in this unique prophecy.

Questions for Further Study

1. What was the significance of the daily burnt offerings, according to Exodus 29:38–46?
2. Why then was the Day of Atonement ritual in Leviticus 16 necessary?
3. Why are there so many restrictions about the use of blood in the Old Testament (see Lev. 17:10–16)?
4. Read through the so-called 'Servant Songs' in Isaiah 42:1–4; 49:1–6; 50:4–9; 52:13 – 53:12 and consider how the different aspects of the Servant's role fit together.
5. Given the teaching of the Pentateuch about atonement, why is the teaching of Isaiah 53 so important in the revelation of God's plan of salvation?

Select Bibliography

Beckwith, R.T., and M.J. Selman (eds.), *Sacrifice in the Bible* (Carlisle: Paternoster; Grand Rapids: Baker, 1995)

Bellinger Jr., W.H., and W.R. Farmer (eds.), *Jesus and the Suffering Servant: Isaiah 53 and Christian Origins* (Harrisburg: Trinity Press International, 1998)

Milgrom, J., 'Atonement in the OT', *IDB*, Supplementary Volume (Nashville: Abingdon, 1976)

Morris, L., *The Apostolic Preaching of the Cross* (Leicester: IVP, 1965[3]), ch. 5

Peterson, D., *Engaging with God: A Biblical Theology of Worship* (Leicester: Apollos; Grand Rapids: Eerdmans, 1992), ch. 1

2

Atonement in the New Testament
David Peterson

Introduction

In *The New International Dictionary of New Testament Theology*, there is no separate entry for 'atonement'. The subject is specifically addressed in an article where 'reconciliation, restoration, propitiation, atonement' are considered together. The rationale for this is stated in these terms:

> Reconciliation means the restoration of a good relationship between enemies. In order to achieve this good relationship in the confrontation of God and man, it is necessary that the factors which produce the enmity be removed. This is achieved by atonement.[1]

Reconciliation is a comprehensive notion in the New Testament, involving the restoration of relationships between God and humanity, and the consequent restoration of relationships at a human level (e.g. Eph. 2:11–18). The restoration of creation from all the effects of sin also flows from the work of Christ (e.g. Acts 3:19–21). Indeed, there is a cosmic dimension to the reconciliation which takes place 'through the blood of his [Christ's] cross' (Col. 1:20; cf. 2:15). Atonement is specifically identified in this dictionary with the group of words linked to the Greek verb *hilaskomai*, which is translated 'propitiate, expiate, conciliate, make gracious, be gracious'.

---

[1] H.-G. Link, C. Brown, 'Reconciliation, Restoration, Propitiation, Atonement', *NIDNTT*, vol. 3, pp. 145–76 (145).

It will certainly be my concern in this chapter to focus on the use of such terminology and to relate this to wider perspectives on the reconciling work of God in Christ. However, the subject of atonement cannot simply be explored in connection with the *hilaskomai* word group. There are other terms and concepts that must be drawn into the discussion. Investigation of atonement categories from the Old Testament suggests further clues for exposing the atoning dimension to Christ's cross. Furthermore, contemporary scholars continue to raise important questions that must be answered in connection with the meaning of atonement in the New Testament.

For example, did Jesus interpret God's will for himself in terms of Isaiah 53 or was the influence of that passage upon Christian faith subsequent to his ministry? In a recent set of essays, Morna Hooker maintains that the apostle Paul may have been the first to use that passage to interpret Jesus' death, but only in Romans 4:25.[2] Other contributors to the same volume differ strongly with her on this point. Moreover, the extent to which Isaiah 53 has determined New Testament thinking about Jesus' death is still much debated. To the exploration of such issues we now turn.

Jesus and his Sacrifice

The redemptive significance of Jesus' ministry

Each of the Gospels presents a broad framework of teaching about the saving significance of Jesus' life and ministry. Thus, for example, the opening chapter of Matthew interprets Jesus' name to mean that 'he shall save his people from their sins' (Mt. 1:21), Luke soon makes it plain that the promised messianic salvation involves the forgiveness of sins (Lk. 1:77), and John identifies Jesus from the beginning as 'the Lamb of God, who takes away the sin of the world'

---

[2] M.D. Hooker, 'Did the Use of Isaiah 53 to Interpret His Mission Begin with Jesus?', in W.H. Bellinger Jr. and W.R. Farmer (eds.), *Jesus and the Suffering Servant: Isaiah 53 and Christian Origins* (Harrisburg: Trinity Press International, 1998), pp. 88–103. She had previously argued that 1 Peter might be the earliest example of that prophecy being used to interpret Jesus' death.

(Jn. 1:29). However, in the Synoptic Gospels it is not until the narrative of the Last Supper that Jesus' *death* is explicitly identified as the means of effecting that salvation from sins. Matthew alone includes the words 'for the forgiveness of sins' in Jesus' saying about the cup (Mt. 26:28). But Luke makes it clear that 'the new covenant' is inaugurated by Jesus' death, thereby implying the definitive forgiveness of sins predicted by the prophet Jeremiah (Jer. 31:34; cf. Lk. 22:20; 1 Cor. 11:25). The evidence of the Fourth Gospel will not be examined here.[3]

Prior to Jesus' teaching at the Last Supper, his most pointed saying in the Synoptic Gospels about the redemptive significance of his death occurs in Matthew 20:28 (= Mk. 10:45). There he claims that the Son of Man 'came not to be served but to serve, and to give his life as a ransom for many'. James and John had sought precedence and rank in the kingdom which they believed Jesus would soon establish. Jesus responded by telling them that they did not know what they were asking. There was a cup which he must drink and a baptism with which he must be baptized before he could enter into his glorious reign as the Christ (Mt. 20:22–3; Mk. 10:38–40). The implication of this challenge was that they could not share in the suffering which he alone must endure.

In the Old Testament, the cup of wine is a common metaphor for suffering experienced as a divine judgement for sin (e.g. Ps. 75:8; Isa. 51:17–23; Jer. 25:15–28). Jesus' application of that image to himself here and in his prayer to the Father in Gethsemane (Mt. 26:39, 42; Mk. 10:35) suggests that he viewed his death in such a way. This is indeed a paradox, since the Gospels present him as one who was consistently faithful and obedient to the Father, not as one deserving his wrath. The image of Jesus' death as a baptism (cf. Lk. 12:50) indicates that it was to be an overwhelming disaster for him and should be taken as a parallel to the image of the cup.[4] When he

---

[3] For an assessment of what the Gospels say about the sacrificial nature of Jesus' death, see P.M. Head, 'The Self-Offering and Death of Christ as a Sacrifice in the Gospels and the Acts of the Apostles', in R.T. Beckwith and M.J. Selman (eds.), *Sacrifice in the Bible* (Carlisle: Paternoster; Grand Rapids: Baker, 1995), pp. 111–29.

[4] See W.L. Lane, *The Gospel of Mark*, NICNT (Grand Rapids: Eerdmans, 1974), pp. 380–1, and A. Feuillet, 'La coupe et le baptême de la passion (Mc, x, 35–40; cf. Mt, xx, 20–3; Lc, xii, 50)', *RB* 74 (1967), pp. 377–82.

applies the same imagery to James and John, he is prophesying that they too will endure great tribulation and suffering for the sake of the kingdom. However, the idea that there is something unique and unrepeatable about his suffering becomes clear as the narrative draws to a close.

Jesus contrasts the conduct of pagan rulers with the submission to service and sacrifice which is appropriate to his disciples, presenting himself as a model to be followed. There is clearly an exemplary dimension to Jesus' suffering and death in the New Testament (cf. Jn. 13:1–17; 1 Pet. 2:18–25), but this is not the heart of the matter. Jesus concludes:

> whoever wishes to be great among you must be your servant, and whoever wishes to be first among you must be your slave; just as the Son of Man came not to be served but to serve, and to give his life a ransom for many. (Mt. 20:26–8, NRSV)

The reference to his life being given 'as a ransom for many' (Gk. *lytron anti pollōn*) suggests that he viewed his death as a substitutionary payment for the benefit of others.

R.T. France rightly proposes that the redemptive role of the Servant in Isaiah 53 had so penetrated Jesus' thinking that it emerges here 'even in an incidental illustration'.[5] He argues that with one formal quotation of Isaiah 53 by Jesus in the Synoptic Gospels (Lk. 22:37), two indisputable allusions (Mk. 10:45; 14:24 and parallels), three possible allusions (Mk. 9:12; Mt. 3:15; Lk. 11:22) and the numerous passion predictions, 'Jesus saw the events of Good Friday as the destined fulfilment of the suffering of the Servant depicted in Isaiah 53, and that his thoughts turned especially to the impending imputation of guilt to one who did not deserve it'.[6]

The terminology in Matthew 20:28 / Mk. 10:45 implies that the 'many' are held in a captivity from which only the death of Christ can release them. The wider context of Jesus' teaching indicates that this captivity is caused by sin and that human beings need deliverance from the divine hostility to sin that culminates in the final judgement

---

[5] R.T. France, *Jesus and the Old Testament* (London: Tyndale, 1971), p. 121.
[6] Ibid., p. 116.

(e.g. Mt. 5:22; 18:8–9; 25:41, 46; Mk. 9:42–8; Lk. 12:5; 13:27–8; Jn. 5:28–9).[7] The focus seems to be on where we are before God. For that reason, Jesus' proclamation of the kingdom of God is linked with a call to repent (Mt. 4:17 / Mk. 1:15). The expression 'to give his life' signifies the voluntary nature of his death and recalls Isaiah 53:10–12, which speaks of the Servant of the Lord offering his life as a compensation or payment for the sins of his people. Another link with that prophecy is provided by the word 'many', a term used to describe the beneficiaries of the Servant's sacrifice (LXX, *pollois, pollōn*).

The word *lytron*, meaning 'payment for loosing' or 'ransom price', does not occur in the Greek translation of Isaiah 53:10, but is a possible rendering of the Hebrew word *āšām* in that text.[8] In the LXX more generally, *lytron* (singular or plural) can translate Hebrew *kōper*, where the reference is to 'the gift in exchange for a life, which according to the sacred law is forfeit or has come under the punishment of God'.[9] Jesus could have had in mind Isaiah 43:3–4, where ransom terminology is used to explain how God will rescue Israel from exile (Heb. *kpr*). God promises to let other nations pay the price, so that Israel may live, rather than die for her sins. If both texts are drawn together by Jesus' saying, we may conclude that he viewed himself as the ultimate 'guilt offering' for the sins of his people and the ransom to redeem Israel and the nations from judgement and death (cf. 1 Tim. 2:6).[10] Jesus' whole life was a ministry to others, designed to

---

[7]   See S.H. Travis, 'Judgment', in J.B. Green, S. McKnight, I.H. Marshall (eds.), *Dictionary of Jesus and the Gospels* (Leicester: IVP, 1992), pp. 408–11. Here, as elsewhere in his writings, Travis seeks to play down the retributive aspect of divine judgement.

[8]   *āšām* can mean 'guilt offering', with or without sacrifice (cf. 1 Sam. 6:3–4, 8, 17), or simply 'payment' (cf. 2 Kgs. 12:16 [MT 17]). *Lytron* never translates *āšām* in the LXX but is not far from equivalent to the latter meaning. See France, *Jesus and the Old Testament*, pp. 119–20, R.E. Watts, 'Jesus' Death, Isaiah 53, and Mark 10:45: A Crux Revisited', in Bellinger and Farmer, *Jesus and the Suffering Servant*, pp. 125–51.

[9]   C. Brown, 'Redemption', p. 190. See Exod. 21:30; 30:12; Num. 35:31, 32; Prov. 6:35; 13:8. Brown goes on to discuss the use of the *lytron* word group in the LXX to translate other Hebrew terms for ransom.

[10]   The link between Isa. 43:3–4 and 53:10–12 is helpfully argued by S. Kim, *'The "Son of Man"' as the Son of God*, WUNT 30 (Tübingen: Mohr, 1983), pp. 52–8.

serve their needs. But ultimately his service to them meant offering himself in death, in perfect obedience to the will of his Father, as a payment for their sins.

There is no parallel to Matthew 20:28 and Mark 10:45 in the third Gospel. Nevertheless, on the eve of Jesus' death, Luke has him making an explicit identification of himself with the Suffering Servant, providing the only formal quotation from Isaiah 53 by Jesus in any of the Gospels: 'For I tell you, this scripture must be fulfilled in me, "And he was counted among the lawless"; and indeed what is written about me is being fulfilled' (Lk. 22:37; cf. Isa. 53:12).

The wording of this verse makes the strongest possible assertion that the prophecy in question must be fulfilled in him. Indeed, there is no reason to doubt that the whole of Isaiah 53, with its presentation of the redemptive suffering of the Servant, is in view, not simply the particular verse quoted. Jesus' focus on the phrase 'he was counted among the lawless' shows that 'he was preoccupied with the fact that he, who least deserved it, was to be punished as a wrongdoer'.[11]

The Last Supper

The so-called 'eucharistic words' of Jesus occupy 'the central place in Jesus' self-disclosure, and therefore they offer a crucial key to understanding his person and work'.[12] There are differences of emphasis in the various Gospel accounts but each one points to the fact that it was in the context of a traditional Passover meal that Jesus enjoyed his last supper with his disciples.[13] According to Jewish tradition, the

---

[11] France, *Jesus and the Old Testament*, p. 115. France rightly opposes those who question whether Jesus used this text to point to his death as vicarious and redemptive. Cf. P.M. Head, 'The Self-Offering and Death of Christ', p. 119.

[12] S. Kim, *'The "Son of Man" ' as the Son of God*, p. 38. I am not convinced by Kim's argument (pp. 43–50) that the saying recorded in Mk. 10:45 was originally spoken in the context of the Last Supper. However, it is reasonable to conclude that Mk. 10:45 is an anticipation and alternative expression of the eucharistic words of Jesus.

[13] I.H. Marshall (*Last Supper and Lord's Supper* [Exeter: Paternoster, 1980], pp. 57–75) reviews the arguments for and against the conclusion that the meal was a Passover celebration, particularly noting the problem of the

blood of the lambs sacrificed at the time of the exodus had redemptive power and made God's covenant with Abraham operative.[14] When families or groups of friends gathered in Jerusalem to eat the Passover meal, they were reminded in a very personal way of the whole basis of their relationship with God and their existence as a people. Additionally, the Passover had become an occasion for Israelites to express their confidence in a future redemption by God, associated with the coming of the Messiah.[15]

Jesus' longing to celebrate this last Passover with his disciples is especially emphasized in Luke's account: 'He said to them, "I have eagerly desired to eat this Passover with you before I suffer; for I tell you, I will not eat it until it is fulfilled in the kingdom of God"' (Lk. 22:15–16; cf. 22:18, NRSV).

Yet his hope of celebrating it anew, when it would be fulfilled 'in the kingdom of God', is expressed in each of the Gospels (cf. Mt. 26:29; Mk. 14:25). The notion of fulfilment indicates that for Jesus the Passover had a typological significance. In other words, he was endorsing the Jewish tradition that this rite pointed forward to an eschatological deliverance of God's people and the subsequent possibility of enjoying the messianic banquet together in the End time (e.g. Isa. 25:6–7; Lk. 14:15; 22:30). The context makes it clear that his approaching death would be the event to accomplish that deliverance.

We do not know whether Jesus identified himself explicitly with the Passover lamb, but that link was soon made by early Christian writers (1 Cor. 5:7–8; cf. 1 Pet. 1:18–19). Jesus himself took the unusual step of accompanying the distribution of the bread and at least one of the Passover cups with his own words of interpretation. In this way, the food was presented to the disciples as a symbol of his approaching death and of the salvation he would accomplish. Their eating and drinking appears to be an anticipation and symbolic

---

[13] (*continued*) chronology of John's Gospel. He concludes that 'Jesus held a Passover meal earlier than the official Jewish date, and that he was able to do so as the result of calendar differences among the Jews.' (p. 75) For another assessment of the differences between John and the Synoptics at this point cf. Lane, *Mark*, p. 498 (esp. n. 33).

[14] See J. Jeremias, *The Eucharistic Words* (London: SCM, 1966), pp. 225–6.

[15] Ibid., pp. 252, 256–62.

reception of the benefits to be obtained by his death: 'Jesus uses the grace before and after eating to give his disciples one after another the additional personal assurance that they share in the kingdom because they belong to the many for whom he is about to die.'[16]

Some commentators interpret the bread-word and the cup-word differently, since they were separated by the main course of the meal and each saying was meant to be complete in itself. Thus 'this is my body' is taken to refer to Jesus' *person* – the bread broken and distributed is to be a pledge of his continuing presence with them[17] – and 'this is my blood' is taken to refer to his sacrificial death. However, even though the two sayings were originally separate,

> we must surely grant that Jesus intended the two sayings to be in some way complementary to each other. If, then, the second saying speaks of Jesus' sacrificial death, we should expect something similar to be present in the former saying.[18]

With mention of the fact that his blood is to be 'poured out' as a sacrificial offering 'for many' (Mt. 26:28 = Mk. 14:24; Lk. 22:20 has 'for you'), there are allusions again to the role of the suffering Servant of Isaiah 53, who 'poured out his life unto death and . . . bore the sin of many' (Isa. 53:12; cf. Mt. 20:28 = Mk. 10:45; Lk. 22:37).

The cup-word speaks of the inauguration of a new covenant by Jesus' blood. In the version of the saying in Matthew 26:28 and Mark 14:24, the strange expression 'my blood of the covenant' occurs. This recalls Exodus 24:8, where the covenant established by God at Mount Sinai is said to have been sealed by means of animal sacrifice. Only the version of the saying in Luke 22:20 and 1 Corinthians 11:25 mentions explicitly that Jesus had in view the New Covenant promised in Jeremiah 31:31–4. Jeremiah said nothing

---

[16] J. Jeremias, 'This is My Body. . .', *ExpT* 83 (1972), pp. 196–203 (203).

[17] The argument that the Aramaic behind *to sōma mou* is *gûpî*, meaning 'my person' or 'myself', is proposed by J. Behm, '*klaō*', *TDNT*, vol. 3, pp. 726–43 (736), Lane, *Mark*, p. 506, and others. Jeremias, *Eucharistic Words*, pp. 198–201, 221–2, strongly contests this.

[18] Marshall, *Last Supper and Lord's Supper*, p. 87. Marshall (pp. 86–8) assesses the arguments of Jeremias in the light of significant challenges to his position.

about sacrifice or blood but pointed to a definitive and permanent solution to the problem of Israel's sin as a basis for the renewal of God's relationship with his people. Yet, it is obvious even from the words '*my* blood of the covenant' that Jesus envisaged some renewal of the covenant with Israel, effected by his death. Since Matthew 26:28 indicates that Jesus' death was specifically 'for the forgiveness of sins', the link with Jeremiah 31:34 is clear. Thus the various forms of the cup-word in each of the Gospel narratives express materially the same meaning.

Jesus implies that his death would re-establish the underlying covenant with Israel on a new basis. A new or renewed covenant was effected by his shed blood, fulfilling the typology of Exodus 24:8 and the prediction of Jeremiah 31:31–4. Jesus' allusion to Isaiah 53:12 implies also that his blood shed as the Servant of the Lord was the means of atonement 'for many'. Indeed, the idea of a covenant established through the death of a human being, rather than through the shedding of animal blood, probably stems from the Servant passages in Isaiah. The Servant is made by God 'a covenant to the people, a light to the nations' (Isa. 42:6; 49:8). These passages indicate that the restoration of a right relationship between Israel and the Lord will also mean the ultimate fulfilment of that ancient promise to Abraham to bring blessing to all peoples on earth (cf. Gen. 12:2–3). Through the death of Jesus, Jews and Gentiles together will experience atonement and consecration to God as his people.

Conclusion

N.T. Wright concludes a volume of essays on Jesus and the Suffering Servant with this assessment:

> I believe, therefore, that Jesus did not consider his own death in terms of an abstract or ahistorical atonement theology. He did not think of himself going to his death in order to set in motion a piece of celestial mechanics whereby a timeless system of purely spiritual salvation would be set up. He saw himself as possessed of the awesome vocation to bring Israel's history to its climax; to be the means of ending the exile at last, of defeating paganism as a good Messiah should do, and of overturning the renegade and faithless Judaism that was still occupying

center stage. He saw himself as being called upon not merely to announce, but more importantly to enact, the end of exile, the return of Yahweh to Zion, *in other words*, the forgiveness of sins.[19]

Wright helpfully places Isaiah 53 in its context and views Jesus' fulfilment of the Servant's role in holistic terms. However, he fails to grasp the particular contribution that Isaiah 53 makes to the progressive unveiling of God's purposes for Israel and the nations within that context. In the last chapter I argued that it is inadequate to identify the end of exile with the forgiveness of sins. It is the *unjust* punishment of the Servant and not the punishment of guilty Israel by exile that makes possible the forgiveness and restoration of God's people. The Gospels lay such stress on the way Jesus is innocent and his suffering unjust that any account which downplays this seems seriously defective. And debates about the meaning of Jesus' atoning work are not advanced by parody and the use of emotive expressions such as 'a piece of celestial mechanics'!

Pauline Perspectives on the Atoning Work of Christ

'For Paul the cross of Christ was critical for Christian reflection and life, especially as the means by which God has provided for salvation and as the instrument and measure of new life in Christ.'[20] The apostle seems to have drawn to some extent on primitive Christian tradition in 'handing on' to his converts what he himself had 'received', specifically 'that Christ died for our sins according to the scriptures' (1 Cor. 15:3). Variations of the confession 'Christ died for us' are found throughout his letters (e.g. Rom. 5:6, 8; 14:9; 1 Cor. 8:11; 2 Cor. 5:14, 15; Gal. 2:21; 1 Thes. 5:10). Another stereotypical expression for the atoning significance of the cross

---

[19] N.T. Wright, 'The Servant and Jesus: The Relevance of the Colloquy for the Current Quest for Jesus', in Bellinger and Farmer, *Jesus and the Suffering Servant*, pp. 281–97 (292–3).

[20] J.B. Green, 'Death of Christ', in G.F. Hawthorne, R.P. Martin, D.G. Reid (eds.), *Dictionary of Paul and his Letters* (Leicester: IVP, 1993), pp. 201–9 (201). Cf. M. Hengel, *The Atonement: The Origins of the Doctrine in the New Testament* (Philadelphia: Fortress, 1981), pp. 34–9.

presents the 'giving up' of Jesus for our salvation as a divine act (e.g. Rom. 4:25; 8:32) or as Jesus' self-giving (e.g. Gal. 1:4; 2:20). But how did he develop and express this shared tradition?

The cross is at the heart of Paul's teaching in many contexts and he employs many biblical images to explain its significance. Joel Green insists that, like the apostle, we need to contextualize our presentation of Jesus' death, seeking out metaphors that speak to various contemporary cultures and circumstances.[21] Others speak of Paul's teaching as being like a diamond, with many facets, each of which we must allow to shine into different situations today. However, the problem with this approach is that important biblical themes can be downplayed or ignored because of their seeming incompatibility to the culture and/or circumstances. The doctrine of penal substitution is a case in point. Some would deny that Paul teaches it, while others would say that it is only one among many representations, but not foundational or essential to Paul's gospel.

Reconciliation and atonement

Reconciliation with God through the death of Jesus is the central theme of 2 Corinthians 5:14 – 6:2 and Romans 5:1–11 (cf. Rom. 11:15; Eph. 2:16; Col. 1:20, 22). A number of important dimensions to the cross are highlighted in both contexts: the cross is an expression of divine love; it is the motivation for godly living, especially the endurance of suffering and perseverance in gospel work; it brings about justification, access to God and 'a new creation'. But the notion of Jesus' bearing the punishment for our sin is foundational to both passages.

Paul asserts in 2 Corinthians 5:14–21 that 'the God of the cosmos and of history has reconciled rebellious humankind to himself through the "one" (v. 14) whom he "made sin", on account of whom trespasses are no longer reckoned (vv. 19, 21)'.[22] Paul is talking in this context about a *universal* ('all' – vv. 14, 15; 'the world' – v. 19), *cosmological* ('new creation' – v. 17), and *eschatological* ('no

---

[21] Green, 'Death of Christ', p. 204. Green, however, is quick to point out that contemporary interpreters need to be guided by the apostle in this task.

[22] P. Barnett, *The Second Epistle to the Corinthians*, NICNT (Grand Rapids: Eerdmans, 1997), p. 300.

longer . . . now' – vv. 15–17) act of God in Christ. The natural starting point for such thinking is the early chapters of Genesis, with
their account of the rebellion of humanity against God and its dire
consequences (cf. Rom. 5:12–21). But there are surely also echoes
of Isaiah 53 here. God's plan of salvation, which focuses canonically
for a time on Israel, comes to its climax in Christ as sin-bearer and is
potentially for the benefit of 'the many'.[23]

A relational blessing ('reconciliation with God') rests on forensic
forgiveness (v. 19 'not counting their trespasses against them'; v. 21
'righteousness'). In the parallel passage in Romans, 'being reconciled to God' (5:10) similarly depends on 'being justified by faith'
(5:1, 9). The logic of the argument in both contexts is the same and
we do Paul a great disservice if we ignore it! Reconciliation with
God is only possible because of Christ's sin-bearing. Forensic forgiveness or justification is based on the fact that God made his Son
'to be sin who knew no sin, so that in him we might become the
righteousness of God' (2 Cor. 5:21; cf. Rom. 3:24–5). *Structurally
and theologically, 2 Corinthians 5:21 is the key to everything that precedes
it.*

The efficacy of Christ's death arises from the sinlessness of his
life. Paradoxically, in his death, God made this sinless one 'sin for us'
(Gk. *hyper hēmōn hamartian*). Paul means that Christ 'came to stand
in that relation with God which normally is the result of sin, estranged from God and the object of his wrath'.[24] It is therefore
special pleading for Stephen Travis to write, 'But God's wrath is not
mentioned in the context, and the focus is in fact on Christ's death
absorbing or neutralizing the effects of sin. And that does not
involve notions of retribution.'[25]

---

[23] G.K. Beale, 'The OT Background of Reconciliation in 2 Corinthians
5–7 and its Bearing on the Literary Problem of 2 Corinthians 6:14 – 7:1',
NTS 35 (1989), pp. 550–81, sees the theme of Israel's restoration to the
land in terms of *creation* in Isa. 40–55 as the primary source of Paul's words
in 2 Cor. 5:17–21. But the precise vocabulary of reconciliation is not
found in Isaiah and it is relatively undeveloped within Judaism by Paul's
time. Cf. F. Büchsel, *'allassō'*, *TDNT*, vol. 1, pp. 251–9.
[24] C.K. Barrett, *The Second Epistle to the Corinthians*, BNTC (London:
Black, 1973), p. 180.
[25] Travis, 'Christ as Bearer of Divine Judgement', p. 27.

This is an extraordinary conclusion to reach after Paul has just indicated that all must appear before the judgement seat of Christ to receive recompense for what has been done in the body (2 Cor. 5:10). God's wrath certainly features in the parallel passage about reconciliation in Romans 5:1–11. Furthermore, God's wrath in Romans is more than the intrinsic consequence of our refusal to live in a relationship with him, as Travis proposes. What human beings experience in the present, as a result of God's abandoning them to the consequences of their sin (1:24, 26, 28), is an anticipation of 'God's righteous judgement' on 'the day of wrath', when he will personally 'repay according to each one's deeds' (2:3–10). A properly formulated view of penal substitution will speak of retribution being experienced by Christ because that is our due. Moreover, the penalty inflicted by God's justice and holiness is also a penalty inflicted by God's love and mercy, for salvation and new life. God's loving provision through the sacrifice of Christ enables us to be *'saved through him* from the wrath of God' (Rom. 5:8–10).

The purpose of the divine act of substitution was 'so that in him we might become the righteousness of God' (2 Cor. 5:21, Gk. *dikaiosynē theou*). 'Righteousness' or 'justification' is the opposite of 'condemnation' in Paul's teaching (cf. 2 Cor. 3:9). We can only 'become the righteousness of God' if God no longer counts our trespasses against us (cf. Rom. 4:6–8).[26] The logic of 2 Corinthians 5 is that God condemns our sin in the death of his sinless Son so that we might be justified and reconciled to him (cf. Rom. 8:1–4, 10). This 'great exchange' is a reality for all who are 'in him', that is, united to Christ by faith.

Paul's reference in 2 Corinthians 5:21 to the sinlessness of Christ and the justification that proceeds from his death recalls the portrait of the Suffering Servant in Isaiah 53:9–11. Isaiah's statement about the Servant making himself 'an offering for sin' (Gk. *peri hamartias*), is more explicitly echoed in Romans 8:3. Isaiah 53 is also alluded to in Romans 4:25; 8:32. The expression 'made him to be sin' in 2 Corinthians 5:21 more obviously refers to *punishment for sin* rather than

---

[26] R.P. Martin, *2 Corinthians*, WBC 40 (Dallas: Word, 1986), pp. 145, 158, combines what he terms the cosmic and the personal meaning of 'righteousness' in Paul's writings, arguing that it means 'to be given the salvific status as men and women rightly related to God' here.

to a 'sacrifice for sin'.[27] The image is forensic rather than cultic. Christ's death can be understood as atoning in the more general sense of a deliverance from the judgement of God by the payment of a ransom or price. But the cultic dimension will shortly be explored in connection with Romans 3:24–5.

In Romans 5:8, 10 it is clear that God has dealt with the trespasses that alienated us from him by 'removing from his side the obstacle to peace with him, his settled displeasure ("wrath") aroused by human sin'.[28] In other words, the process of reconciliation did not simply involve changing our attitude towards him. Reconciliation was accomplished *for us* through the death of Jesus, even though God himself was the aggrieved party. But it must still be proclaimed and received *by us* for its benefits to be enjoyed (Rom. 5:11; 2 Cor. 5:19–20). There is an objective, historical dimension to God's reconciling work on the cross and a subjective, personal dimension to the process whereby he enables us to respond to the 'message of reconciliation' with repentance and faith. Through his ambassadors, God himself invites us to 'be reconciled'. The particular appeal to the readers in 2 Corinthians 5:20 – 6:2 is 'to continue in what they have begun to be, a people forgiven by God, reconciled to God through Christ's sacrificial death for them'.[29]

Justification, redemption and atonement

R.P. Martin proposes that Paul moved from the theme of justification in Romans 1–4 to reconciliation in Romans 5 because he was dissatisfied with 'the forensic-cultic idiom that limited soteriology to covenant renewal for the Jewish nation'.[30] Paul preferred the

---

[27] Ibid., pp. 156–7.

[28] Barnett, *Second Corinthians*, p. 303. Cf. I.H. Marshall, 'The Meaning of Reconciliation', in R.A. Guelich (ed.), *Unity and Diversity in New Testament Theology: Essays in Honor of George E. Ladd* (Grand Rapids: Eerdmans, 1978), pp. 117–32 (123) ('in dying Christ exhausted the effects of divine wrath against sin').

[29] Barnett, *Second Corinthians*, p. 312.

[30] R.P. Martin, 'Reconciliation: Romans 5:1–11', in S.K. Soderlund and N.T. Wright (eds.), *Romans and the People of God: Essays in Honor of Gordon D. Fee on the Occasion of His 65th Birthday* (Grand Rapids: Eerdmans, 1999), pp. 36–48 (47).

reconciliation imagery as a tool of communication to the Gentile world because it related to a universal human need for forgiveness and personal relationship and could embrace personal and cosmic dimensions of the work of Christ (cf. Col. 1:15–23). Martin's approach doubtless appeals to many who are struggling to preach the gospel to a biblically illiterate culture. There are clear advantages in adopting the language of reconciliation to explain God's achievement in the death of Christ. But Martin has misread the significance and foundational importance of the previous chapters in Romans for Paul's gospel.

After all, Paul begins his letter with a statement about the universal relevance and power of the gospel, in which 'the righteousness of God is revealed through faith for faith' (Rom. 1:16–17). In 1:18 – 3:20 he deals with the problem of God's wrath and depicts God's impartiality in judging all people, both Jews and Gentiles. In 3:21 – 4:25 he proclaims God's impartiality in bestowing righteousness on all who believe in Christ, both Jews and Gentiles. The paragraph 3:21–6 repeats and expands some of the key ideas first announced in 1:16–17, highlighting the central thrust of Paul's argument in Romans 1–4 and preparing for the next main section of the letter (Romans 5–8).[31]

From the beginning of Romans 3, Paul considers 'the righteousness of God' in his dealings with Israel and, by implication, with the world. The righteousness of God appears to be a way of speaking about his covenant faithfulness.[32] However, this is not to deny that there is a judicial aspect to the righteousness of God. Romans 3:21–6 explains how God can be righteous in dealing with sin and, at the same time, faithful to his promises to save those who have faith in him. His righteousness is pre-eminently expressed in his justifying activity. This has been made possible because of the self-offering of Jesus in death as an atoning sacrifice, for the redemption of Jews and Gentiles alike.

---

[31] Contra R.N. Longenecker, 'The Focus of Romans: The Central Role of 5:1 – 8:39 in the Argument of the Letter', in Soderland and Wright, *Romans and the People of God*, pp. 49–61, Rom. 1–4 cannot simply be written off as material that Paul believed he had in common with his addressees and wrote merely as a preparation for Rom. 5–8. The polemical nature of the argument in these early chapters and the consistent development of the theme of God's righteousness speak otherwise.

[32] See S.K. Williams, 'The "Righteousness of God" in Romans', *JBL* 99 (1980), pp. 241–90 (265–80).

The *origin* of this justification is the grace of God (*dōrean* is used adverbially, meaning 'freely', 'as a gift'). The *basis* of this gift is 'the redemption which is in Christ Jesus'. Redemption is the process which makes justification possible. The Greek term *apolytrōsis* does not simply mean emancipation or deliverance. It is the language of the slave market, with a particular application in Jewish thinking to the great saving event of the exodus. Leon Morris argued that 'the LXX usage is such as to leave us in no doubt that *lytron* and its cognates are properly applied to redemption by payment of a price'.[33] Although his approach has been challenged by some, more recent assessments have confirmed that the note of 'ransom' and 'price' may rightly be discerned when such terminology is used in the New Testament (e.g. 1 Cor. 6:20; 7:23; Mk. 10:45; Acts 20:28).[34] In the flow of the argument in Romans 3:24–5, the price in view will be Jesus' death, freeing us from that death which is sin's penalty (cf. 5:12; 6:23). With his redemptive act in Christ, God has acted to free us from the penalty he himself imposed.

God is clearly the origin of the redemption accomplished by Christ, 'whom God put forward as a sacrifice of atonement by his blood, effective through faith' (3:25 NRSV).[35] The claim that Christ is 'our paschal lamb' in 1 Corinthians 5:7 suggests an act of salvation or redemption by means of his sacrifice, fulfilling the pattern of the exodus and Passover for Israel. The term *hilastērion* in Romans 3:25 more specifically has suggested to many an atonement for sin, fulfilling the pattern of the Day of Atonement ritual in Leviticus 16. The term has been taken to refer to the 'place of atonement' or 'mercy-seat' in the Holy Of Holies.[36] However, even if Christ is portrayed as

---

[33] Morris, *The Apostolic Preaching of the Cross* (Leicester: IVP, 1965³), p. 27.

[34] See J.D.G. Dunn, *Romans 1–8*, WBC 38A (Dallas: Word, 1988), pp. 169, 179–80; D. Moo, *The Wycliffe Exegetical Commentary Romans 1–8* (Chicago: Moody, 1991), pp. 229–30; W. Mundle, C. Brown, 'Redemption', pp. 189–200.

[35] It is possible to read the Greek *proetheto*, 'whom God *purposed to be*'. See C.E.B. Cranfield, *A Critical and Exegetical Commentary on the Epistle to the Romans*, ICC 1 (Edinburgh: Clark, 1975), pp. 208–10 (NEB, 'God designed him to be'). This is consistent with the emphasis of the three purpose clauses that follow in vv. 25b–26.

[36] This position is argued, for example, by D.P. Bailey, 'Jesus as the Mercy Seat: The Semantics and Theology of Paul's use of *Hilastērion* in Romans

the New Covenant 'place of sprinkling' by this language, the theological significance of the metaphor must surely be conveyed in translation. Given the widespread use of this term in Greek literature to refer to 'a propitiatory gift', many prefer to see *hilastērion* in Romans 3 as 'a general reference to the removal of the wrath of God, rather than a specific reference either to the mercy-seat, or to the Day of Atonement ceremonies'.[37] In other words, Jesus is described by this term as 'a propitiatory sacrifice' (the victim and not 'the place of sprinkling') or as 'a sacrifice of atonement'.[38]

The expression 'by his blood' is best connected with *hilastērion* (rather than with 'through faith') indicating that it was by the shedding of his blood that his death was an atoning sacrifice. This term enhances the cultic dimension to Paul's thinking at this point. The rest of Romans 3:25–6 then describes the purpose of God (Gk. *eis endeixin*) in ordaining that Christ should be such a sacrifice: it was with a view to showing God's righteousness. This was necessary 'because in his divine forbearance he had passed over the sins previous committed'. However, the *ultimate purpose* of God (Gk. *eis to einai*) in providing Christ as a propitiatory sacrifice was so that he could justify sinners rightly and still be just. Any view of God's righteousness which puts an emphasis on faithfulness to his covenant promises must reckon with the fact that, at the heart of Paul's exposition of this theme, the notion of Christ's death being a satisfaction of God's justice/wrath on the day of judgement is prominent in the context.[39]

---

[36] *(continued)* 3:25', *TynBul* 51.1 (2000), pp. 155–8 (an abstract of his PhD thesis), and by J.M. Gundry-Volf, 'Expiation, Propitiation, Mercy Seat', in Hawthorne, Martin, Reid, *Dictionary of Paul and his Letters*, pp. 282–3. *Hilastērion* is used of the 'mercy seat' in 21 out of 27 contexts in the LXX and in Heb. 8:5.

[37] Morris, *Apostolic Preaching*, p. 198. Cf. Cranfield, *Romans 1–8*, pp. 214–8; Dunn, *Romans 1–8*, pp. 170–1; Brown, 'Reconciliation', *NIDNTT*, vol. 3, pp. 151–66 (163–5).

[38] Moo, *Romans 1–8*, pp. 232–8, notes the work of Deissmann, who shows that *hilastērion* in ordinary Greek has the meaning 'means of propitiation', and argues that the Roman Christians would have been more familiar with this usage than the ritual of the Jewish Day of Atonement.

[39] Contra Travis, 'Christ as Bearer of Divine Judgement', pp. 31–2. It is totally inadequate to understand God's wrath in a non-retributive sense (p. 29), in view of Rom. 2:5–9.

Much debate has focused on whether Christ's death is viewed here as an expiation for sin or more specifically as a means of propitiating God's wrath. The issues are well reviewed by Douglas Moo. A good case can be made for finding some allusion to the notion of propitiation when the root *kpr* is used in the Old Testament in connection with the cult. It is the connotation of 'propitiate' that led the translators of the LXX to use words from the *hilask-* root to translate the Hebrew. 'This is not, however, to deny the connotation "expiation"; the OT cult serves both to "wipe away" the guilt of sin at the same time as – and indeed, because – the wrath of God is being stayed.'[40]

James Dunn translates *hilastērion* in Romans 3:24 as 'means of expiation' or 'medium of atonement'. Nevertheless, he argues that 'the logic of Paul's exposition is that the wrath of God (expounded in 1:18 – 3:20) is somehow averted by Jesus' death (cf. 2 Macc. 7:38)'.[41] Against the notion of propitiation, he insists that the passage portrays God as 'offerer of the sacrifice rather than its object'. But why cannot God be both offerer and object of the atonement? The idea of averting God's wrath in any *personal sense* demands that God be object (e.g. Num. 25:1–13). If we are not thinking of 'making God gracious', what is wrong with implying that God is both subject and object and that we have here a view of propitiation that differs from the pagan notions of the ancient world. There are many places in the Bible where pagan terminology is adapted in the light of God's self-revelation and distinctive way of dealing with us.

While 'propitiate' in ordinary usage may suggest a change from complete hostility to love, this need not be so. For example, loving parents may be angry with their children for a time and need to be 'appeased', but do not stop loving them in the process. From the earliest pages of Scripture it is clear that God can be both loving *and* wrathful towards his people, for example:

The LORD, the LORD,
a God merciful and gracious,

---

[40] Moo, *Romans 1–8*, p. 236. Cf. Brown, 'Reconciliation', pp. 151–60.
[41] Dunn, *Romans 1–8*, p. 171. Cf. C.K. Barrett, *The Epistle to the Romans* (London: Black, 1957), p. 78 ('expiation has, as it were, the effect of propitiation').

slow to anger,
and abounding in steadfast love and faithfulness,
keeping steadfast love for the thousandth generation,
forgiving iniquity and transgression and sin,
yet by no means clearing the guilty,
but visiting the iniquity of the parents
upon the children
and the children's children,
to the third and the fourth generation. (Exod. 34:6–7), NRSV

The question is always one of securing release from the consequences of sin, which include the expression of his wrath against sin (e.g. Exod. 32; Lev. 16; Dan. 9:16–19).

Of course the cross proceeds from God's grace and does not 'make God gracious'. But it is simplistic to argue that if God's attitude is one of unchanging love then it does not need to be changed, and if it is not changed then there is no need for propitiation. If God is wrathful against sinners, then his wrath somehow needs to be appeased and averted. If God in his love provides the way by which his own wrath is both expressed and satisfied, that is propitiation. As with the Old Testament provisions for atonement, God is both originator and recipient of the sacrifice that reconciles to him.

Judith Gundry-Volf makes the mistake of viewing 'the transformation of sinners' as the key to Christ's death and playing down any personal effect on God. She concedes that Paul probably thought of Christ's death as the anticipation of eschatological judgement and the outpouring of divine wrath. Thus the apostle probably also thought that those who are in Christ will be saved from God's wrath because Christ suffered it for them (Rom. 5:9). But this still does not mean that Christ's death propitiated God. Gundry-Volf interprets God's wrath in impersonal terms, as the judgement 'which destroys all unholiness and sin'.[42] Thus she concludes:

---

[42] Gundry-Volf, 'Expiation, Propitiation, Mercy Seat', p. 282. Green, 'Death of Christ', p. 206, similarly writes that 'for Paul divine wrath is not a divine property, or essential attribute, but the active presence of God's judgement toward "all ungodliness and wickedness" (Rom. 1:18)'. In this connection, he acknowledges his debt to Travis and also to A.J. Tambasco, *A Theology of Atonement and Paul's Vision of Christianity* (Collegeville: Liturgical, 1991).

In the light of the threatening wrath of God, the need of sinners can be said to be not *the transformation of God's attitude toward them* but the transformation of *their sinful existence before God* through its destruction and new creation. This transformation of sinners is precisely the significance Paul sees in the death and resurrection of Christ. And the notion of divine wrath as a judgement consisting in destruction fits well with such a view of the cross.

However, to separate God's wrath from his righteousness, as if one aspect of his dealing with us is impersonal and the other personal, is totally illegitimate. For example, in Romans 3:4–6, God's right-eousness and his judging the world are viewed together as inter-connected expressions of his relationship with Israel. Citing Psalm 51:4 in this context, Paul makes it clear that he holds a very personal view of the wrath of God. Restricting Christ's work to the transformation of our 'sinful existence before God', makes his atonement a mechanical operation that is far removed from the personal dynamic implied by the link between reconciliation and the wrath of God in Romans 5:1–11. There is also a subtle, but alarming shift in Gundry-Volf's argument, from the transforma-tion of our 'sinful existence before God' to the 'transformation of sinners'. Transformation of sinners flows from Christ's reconciling work of the cross (cf. Rom. 6; 2 Cor. 5:14–21), but it is not simply to be identified with God's action in making Christ 'sin for us' or putting him forth as 'a propitiatory sacrifice' through his blood.

Bearing the curse of God

Romans 8:1 proclaims that there is 'now no condemnation for those who are in Christ Jesus'. This is so because God has sent his Son to be 'a sin-offering' and thereby 'condemned sin in the flesh' (8:4). Apart from this passage and those examined above, the clear-est statement in Paul's writings that Christ bore the penalty for sin that was due to us is found in Galatians 3:13 ('Christ redeemed us from the curse of the law by becoming a curse for us – for it is written, "Cursed is everyone who hangs on a tree".'). Although it is true that Paul has left out the words 'by God' in his quote from Deuteronomy 21:23, it is odd to suggest that this was to avoid the implication that Christ in his death was cursed by God.[43] What is 'the curse of the law' if not the curse of God?

N.T. Wright has argued that in this passage Paul is echoing a widespread belief among his fellow Jews that Israel was still under the curse of Deuteronomy 29, the curse of exile.[44] Against this background, 'Christ redeemed us from the curse of the law' means that *Jews* who were under the curse of the law and alienated from God because of their sin have been redeemed from that curse by Christ. The removal of the curse which hung over Israel makes it possible for the blessing promised to Abraham to come to the *Gentiles* 'in Christ Jesus' (Gal. 3:14). Stephen Travis follows this line and concludes that

> Paul's argument is not a statement about atonement in general or about the salvation of individuals. His concern is not so much to explain how the death of Christ makes atonement for individual sinners as to show how it makes possible the coming of God's blessing to Gentiles.[45]

However, this line of interpretation can be challenged in several ways. Dunn disputes the evidence for Paul or his contemporaries viewing the exile as continuing.[46] Moreover, Paul's warning in Galatians 3:10 is that '*all* who rely on the works of the law are under a curse'. In the course of the argument, this must surely include Gentiles who were tempted to pursue a relationship with God characterized and determined by 'works of the law'. More generally, Paul assumes in Romans 2:12–16 that even Gentiles who do not possess the law will be condemned if they do not do what the law requires. Finally, the claim that '*we* might receive the promise of the Spirit through faith' (3:14) must include Jews and Gentiles together:

---

[43] See R.Y.K. Fung, *The Epistle to the Galatians*, NICNT (Grand Rapids: Eerdmans, 1988), p. 148.

[44] N.T. Wright, *The Climax of the Covenant: Christ and the Law in Pauline Theology* (Edinburgh: T. & T. Clark, 1991), pp. 141–2.

[45] Travis, 'Christ as Bearer of Divine Judgement in Paul's Thought about the Atonement', in J. Goldingay (ed.), *Atonement Today* (London: SPCK, 1995), pp. 21–38 (24).

[46] J.D.G. Dunn, *The Epistle to the Galatians*, BNTC (London: Black, 1993), pp. 171–2.

The curse which shut Gentiles out also prevented the Jews who lived 'from works of the law' from entering the full blessing of Abraham. The curse-bearing death of Jesus thus broke open that too restricted view of covenant righteousness for both Jew and Gentile to share in its eschatological fullness.[47]

Conclusion

What finally is the pastoral significance of the teaching about Christ being the bearer of our sin and its consequences? What is lost if this aspect of Paul's teaching is played down or ignored? Bishop Paul Barnett's assessment is simple but profound:

> The great doctrinal truth that 'Christ died in my place' joins the repentant sinner to his Saviour spiritually and emotionally. When through the gospel the lost soul 'sees' the Lord on the cross in *his* place for *his* sins he is overpowered with emotion and spiritual gratitude. Christ crucified is 'the bread that came down from heaven to give life to the world' and for the individual, and the drink that sustains the Christian throughout his earthly pilgrimage serving the Lord and sharing the gospel with others. Furthermore, how can one continue in sin in the face of such dying love?[48]

Atonement and Salvation in Hebrews

Atonement through the death of Christ is a more obvious and pervasive theme in Hebrews than in any other New Testament book. The writer soon alludes to Jesus' high-priestly work in terms of his having made 'purification for sins' (1:3, Gk. *katharismos*), using language that would have been familiar to his readers from the Greek translation of the Old Testament (e.g. Exod. 30:10 LXX). Sin is first viewed as a defilement which must be removed because it is a barrier to fellowship with God. The central chapters of Hebrews

---

[47] Ibid., p. 179. Cf. Fung, *Galatians*, pp. 148–50.

[48] This is part of a defence of the biblical doctrine of penal substitution in answer to challenges by Dr Peter Carnley, Archbishop of Perth and Primate of the Anglican Church of Australia, as found on www.anglicanmediasydney.asn.au/Carnley2.htm

recall the provisions of the Mosaic Law for cleansing and atonement through animal sacrifice and proclaim a definitive cleansing through the 'blood' of Christ (9:13–14, 22–3; 10:2, 22; cf. 2 Pet. 1:9; 1 Jn. 1:7, 9). Most importantly, this cleansing operates at the level of the conscience and not simply externally, as the Old Testament 'regulations for the body' did (9:9–10). In the perspective of Hebrews, the death of Jesus explicitly achieves a once-for-all atonement for sins (e.g. 2:17; 7:27; 9:25–6; 10:11–18), an 'eternal redemption' (9:12, 15) and a definitive sanctification (e.g. 10:10, 29; 13:12), that brings believers into a New Covenant relationship with God (Jer. 31:31–4; cf. Heb. 8:6–13; 10:15–18).

Atonement through the blood of Christ

When the writer first claims that Jesus was appointed to be 'a merciful and faithful high priest in the service of God' (2:17), he goes on to declare that the fundamental purpose of his calling was 'to make atonement for the sins of the people' (Gk. *eis to hilaskesthai tas hamartias tou laou*). This is consistent with the later assertion that the essential task of priests is 'to offer gifts and sacrifices for sins' (5:1). In 2:17, the writer uses the verb *hilaskomai*, which is regularly employed in the LXX in the compound form *exhilaskomai* to render the Hebrew *kipper*. The RSV translates the clause 'to make expiation for the sins of the people', following the view of many commentators that Christ's sacrifice is directed at removing sin and its effects (expiation), not at propitiating God.[49] However, the Greek construction can also be rendered 'to make propitiation with regard to the sins of the people',[50] and NRSV/NIV translate it, 'to make atonement for the sins of the people', thus allowing for the possibility of a propitiatory dimension.

---

[49] E.g. H.W. Attridge, *The Epistle to the Hebrews* (Philadelphia: Fortress, 1989), p. 96, n. 192. Cf. F. Büchsel, '*hilaskomai, hilasmos*', *TDNT*, vol. 3, pp. 301–18 (314–17); S. Lyonnet and L. Sabourin, *Sin, Redemption, and Sacrifice: A Biblical and Patristic Study*, AnB 48 (Rome: Pontifical Biblical Institute, 1970), pp. 120–48.

[50] W.L. Lane, *Hebrews 1–8*, WBC 47A (Dallas: Word, 1991), pp. 65–6, following Morris, *Apostolic Preaching*, pp. 125–60, 175–6. With this reading, if God is understood as the direct object of the verb, *tas hamartias* ('with regard to the sins') will be an accusative of respect.

As we have noted, the process of atonement in the Mosaic Law was ultimately concerned with the removal of that which offends God and brings down his wrath. Although purging is a fundamental notion, atonement is not simply a matter of removing guilt or defilement by cleansing but of averting the wrath of God by offering the life of an animal substitute to him. To determine whether any sense of propitiation is intended in Hebrews, it is necessary to discover what the writer has to say about the wrath of God and divine judgement.

The first warning about neglecting the salvation proclaimed in the gospel is based on that observation that, under the Old Covenant, 'every transgression or disobedience received a just penalty' (2:2). With a simple parable, the writer then warns those who harden their hearts against Christ in unbelief and apostasy that they will experience God's curse (6:8). This outcome is later expressed in terms of 'a fearful prospect of judgement, and a fury of fire that will consume the adversaries' (10:27). Of course, these passages are a warning about God's intention to judge those who claim to be his people, yet fall away (cf. 10:39). Nothing specifically is said about the fate of those who have never heard the gospel, though God is described as 'the judge of all' (12:23) and Hebrews insists that 'it is appointed for mortals to die once, and after that the judgement' (9:27). It is surely therefore valid to apply quite generally the warning that 'it is a fearful thing to fall into the hands of the living God' (10:31). Salvation in Hebrews thus appears to be deliverance from the wrath of God in order to enjoy the life of God in his presence for ever (cf. 9:28; 12:25–9).

In the writer's vision of the heavenly Jerusalem it is 'Jesus the mediator of a new covenant' who makes it possible for the redeemed to approach 'God the judge of all' and it is 'the sprinkled blood' of Christ that cries out for acceptance in this context (12:22–4). It is hard to avoid the conclusion from such a passage, and from the writer's general portrayal of Christ's work as a fulfilment of the Day of Atonement ritual (e.g. 9:11–15), that the blood of Christ functions in some sense to avert the wrath of God for those who are cleansed, sanctified and perfected by him. We become acceptable to God, not simply because of his work *in us*, but because of his work *for us*. The crucified and glorified Christ 'entered into heaven itself, now to appear in the presence of God on our behalf'

(9:24, Gk. *hyper hēmōn*). The representative nature of Jesus' work is certainly highlighted in Hebrews (cf. 6:20; 7:25), but is there any indication that he died as a substitute for us, to pay for our sins?

Redemption through the blood of Christ

The claim that Jesus 'tasted' or experienced death 'for everyone' (2:9, Gk. *hyper pantos*), is followed by the insistence that he was perfected as 'the pioneer of their salvation' through sufferings and that by this means God brings 'many sons to glory' (2:10).[51] In other words, Jesus' death uniquely qualifies him to save others from death and from the judgement of God that follows (9:27). Jesus' death is also said to be the means by which 'he might destroy the one who has the power of death, that is, the devil, and free those who all their lives were held in slavery by the fear of death' (2:14–15). There is a *redemptive* aspect to Jesus' death that liberates believers from the power of death and the devil.

The background to Hebrews 2:5–17 is Genesis 1–3 and the teaching of prophetic and apocalyptic writers about the restoration of paradise in the End time. Implicit in this context is the assumption that death is the divine penalty for sin, which Satan wields as a power over human beings within the divine economy, hindering them from sharing in 'the coming world' (2:5). The devil is deprived of that power because Jesus dies as the perfectly innocent one (4:15; 7:26–7) and opens the way to 'the promised eternal inheritance' (9:15) for all who trust in him. People are released from 'fear of death', and thus from Satan's power, by coming to experience the redemption achieved by Christ. Hebrews is more interested in the result of Christ's sacrifice than in the theory or doctrine behind it. Nevertheless, the progress of the argument in 2:5–17 suggests that his atoning work involves paying the penalty for sin by means of his death, thus liberating his people from all the consequences of

---

[51] Although the expression 'the pioneer of their salvation' could be taken to mean that Jesus goes ahead as leader in a journey where others may follow, the context implies a unique achievement by which he makes salvation possible for others. The expression thus captures the sense of 5:9 ('source of eternal salvation for all who obey him') as well as 6:20 ('forerunner on our behalf'). See D.G. Peterson, *Hebrews and Perfection*, SNTSMS 47 (Cambridge: CUP, 1982), pp. 57–8.

sin. Dealing with sin and its penalty is the focus of his high-priestly work.

It is interesting to observe the same theological sequence in Hebrews 2:14–17 as in Romans 3:24–5. The redemption which Christ achieves is grounded in the 'sacrifice of atonement' or *propitiation* he makes 'for the sins of the people'. Christ as redeemer and saviour can only truly be understood and appreciated when the high-priestly or sacrificial dimension of his work is made clear.

Again, in 9:11–12, having portrayed Christ's death and heavenly exaltation as the fulfilment of the Day of Atonement ritual, the writer proclaims that he has secured 'an eternal redemption'. Redemption from the power and consequences of sin is meant. Indeed, in 9:15 it is specifically declared that his death has made possible a 'redemption' from 'the transgressions under the first covenant'. This suggests that the sacrifice of Jesus actually makes effective the atonement promised to those who engaged with repentance and faith in the sacrificial rites given to Israel. Furthermore, picking up the wider implications of redemption from Exodus, Hebrews goes on to show how Jesus as 'mediator of a new covenant' by his blood has made it possible for 'those who are called to receive the promised eternal inheritance'. With the big sweep of Biblical Theology in mind, the writer envisages Christ bringing believers into the enjoyment of everything anticipated by the exodus under Moses and the conquest under Joshua. Christ's sacrifice rescues from condemnation and death as the Passover sacrifice did, thus initiating 'those who are called' into the benefits of the New Covenant. At the same time, his sacrifice and high-priestly work fulfil the provisions of the Law for sustaining God's covenant people in a relationship with him.

At first sight it is puzzling to see how Hebrews lumps together the daily sacrifices of Judaism (7:27; 10:5, 6, 8), the annual Day of Atonement sacrifices (9:6, 7, 12, 21, 23, 25; 10:1–3), the sacrifices inaugurating the Sinai covenant (9:18–20) and allusions to the red heifer ceremony (9:13; 10:22). However, what all these sacrifices have in common is the single point of blood. Without blood there is no access to God, no inauguration of the covenant and no forgiveness (9:22; cf. Lev. 17:11). In the writer's thought-world, sacrificial blood has a direct, immediate potency. The blood of Christ is the most powerful of all, because he offered himself without blemish to

God, as the true and final offering for sin ordained by God (10:5–10).[52] His blood cleanses from the defilement of sin and sets people free to serve God 'with reverence and awe' (12:28; cf. 9:13–14). Jesus' blood enables us to find acceptance before 'God the judge of all', to escape the judgement of death, and to live in his presence for ever (12:22–4).

Hebrews 9:26–8 significantly links the notion of Jesus as high priest with that of the Suffering Servant.[53] The eschatological significance of his self-sacrifice is indicated by the fact that he appeared 'once for all at the end of the age to remove sin by the sacrifice of himself' (9:26). The parallel expression in verse 28 speaks of his having been offered once 'to bear the sins of many' (Gk. *eis to pollōn anenengkein hamartias*), recalling the words of Isaiah 53:12 (*hamartias pollōn anēnegken*) about the vicarious suffering of the Servant of the Lord. In Hebrews, although suffering retains a role in the redemptive process (2:9–10; 5:7–9), it is Jesus' death which is paramount, because his 'blood' makes possible his entrance into the heavenly sanctuary, there to 'intercede' for 'those who approach God through him' (7:25).[54]

As we have previously noted, bearing the sins of others in Isaiah 53 must refer to the punishment of the Servant for the sins of others.

---

[52] Note the range of technical terms used in the citation from Ps. 40:6 (LXX 39:7) in Heb. 10:5–7. *Thysia* ('sacrifice'), while capable of referring to any kind of animal sacrifice, is used in the Old Testament with more special reference to the peace-offering. *Prosphora* ('offering'), while also used in a general sense, is restricted in the Levitical terminology to the 'cereal offering'. *Holokautōma* is the standard Greek term for the 'holocaust' or 'burnt offering' and *peri hamartias* is the usual technical translation for the 'sin offering'. See F.F. Bruce, *The Epistle to the Hebrews*, NICNT (London: Marshall, Morgan & Scott, 1964), pp. 233–4.

[53] It is possible that the Servant Christology, which was already current in early Christian circles, was one of several converging elements that actually brought the author of Hebrews to see Jesus' death as a priestly act in the first place. See J.R. Schaefer, 'The Relationship between Priestly and Servant Messianism in the Epistle to the Hebrews', *CBQ* 30 (1968), pp. 359–85.

[54] The idea that the Servant 'made intercession for the transgressors' is clear in the Hebrew of Isa. 53:12. On the relationship between Christ's intercessory work and his once-for-all atonement for sins, see Peterson, *Hebrews and Perfection*, pp. 114–16.

The prophet is clear about the Servant's innocence and the guilt of those for whom he is wounded. Hebrews similarly insists on the sinlessness of Jesus (4:15; 7:26) and the fact that he has no need to offer sacrifices for his own sins (7:27). Servant Christology makes it possible for the writer to combine the images of Jesus as victim and priest. By his willing self-offering in death, Jesus offered the perfect sacrifice (9:14, 26), thus fulfilling and replacing every aspect of the sacrificial system provided under the Mosaic Law (10:5–10), and making him the eternally effective high priest of the New Covenant (10:11–18).

Sanctification through the blood of Christ

The teaching about Christ's atoning work in Hebrews encourages us to believe that God will maintain us in a New Covenant relationship with himself. This is the logic of making the Day of Atonement ritual a key to understanding the significance of Jesus' death and heavenly exaltation. We have continuing right of access to 'the sanctuary' of God's presence, 'by the blood of Jesus' and because of his ongoing priestly rule 'over the house of God' (10:19–21; cf. 7:25). The challenge is therefore to keep on approaching God 'with a true heart in full assurance of faith, with our hearts sprinkled clean from an evil conscience and our bodies washed with pure water' (10:22; cf. 4:14–16). However, the writer also shows how the death of Jesus is the means by which we come to share in the benefits of the New Covenant in the first place.

The notion that God sanctifies or consecrates a people to himself through Jesus' once-for-all sacrifice for sins is stressed by the words 'we have been sanctified' in 10:10 (Gk. *hēgiasmenoi esmen*). The Greek indicates a state or condition made possible by the self-offering of Christ in death. No further sacrifices or rituals are required to keep us in that sanctified condition. The preceding context suggests that this involves a once-for-all cleansing from sin that the law of Moses could not provide (10:1–4). As in Old Testament teaching, purification and sanctification are closely related in the argument of Hebrews (cf. 9:13–14). Purification is the basis of sanctification. By his sovereign action in Christ, God sets apart and binds to himself those who have been purified from the defilement of sin.

In 10:11–18 the writer goes on to show how Jesus' perfect sin offering inaugurates the New Covenant promised in Jeremiah 31:31–4. Under the terms of that covenant, God writes his law in the hearts and minds of all his people, enabling them to know him and serve him in a new way. Such dedication to God is made possible by the sacrifice which allows him to 'remember their sins and their lawless deeds no more' (cf. Heb. 10:17–18). As in Jeremiah's promise, so also in Hebrews, a once-for-all forgiveness of sins is the basis of a new commitment to God on the part of his people.

Hebrews 10:10–18 suggests that the verb 'to sanctify' is primarily employed in a *covenantal* sense. Christ's sacrifice binds men and women to God in a new relationship of heart-obedience. The covenantal dimension is highlighted again in 10:29, where we are told that the readers were sanctified by 'the blood of the covenant'.[55] The writer recalls the language of Exodus 24:1–8, where the relationship between God and Israel was confirmed as Moses poured 'the blood of the covenant' on the altar and on the representatives of the people gathered with him on Mount Sinai. Hebrews 9:18–21 actually speaks about the first covenant being 'inaugurated' by Moses on this occasion. By implication, the New Covenant was inaugurated by the shedding of Jesus' blood. This also appears to be the message of 13:12, where we are told that he suffered outside Jerusalem, 'to sanctify the people by his own blood'.

The *cultic* dimension to the sanctifying work of Christ is more specifically developed in other passages. Those who come to him as 'the mediator of a new covenant' and trust in the cleansing power of his 'sprinkled blood' experience the benefits of his sanctifying death (12:24; cf. 9:13–14; 10:19–22). As the eternal high priest 'according to the order of Melchizedek', Jesus offered himself as a holy, blameless and undefiled sacrifice for sins (7:17–28). He entered once for all into the heavenly sanctuary for us, having obtained 'eternal redemption' (9:12). By the single offering of himself in death, 'he has perfected for all time those who are sanctified' (10:14).

---

[55] The Greek aorist passive participle *hēgēsamenos* is used in a summary way, to indicate how the readers came to share in the benefits of Christ's sacrifice.

Conclusion

Hebrews consistently portrays the atoning work of Christ as the fulfilment of the Day of Atonement ritual. At the heart of this portrayal is the presentation of Christ as the sinless saviour, who 'bears the sins of many' in his death, and delivers those who are cleansed and sanctified by his 'blood' from the awesome judgement of God. Allusions to the fulfilment of other blood rituals help to expand the picture. Jesus' death and heavenly exaltation accomplish an eternally effective redemption from sin and its consequences, inaugurating all the benefits of the New Covenant. Since he continues for ever as a heavenly high priest, he is always able to apply the benefits of his once-for-all sacrifice to those who draw near to God through him. One sacrifice replaces the many sacrifices of the Old Covenant used to maintain people in a relationship with God.

Atonement Teaching in 1 Peter and 1 John

Space does not permit a more extensive examination of New Testament teaching about Christ's atoning work. However, a survey of 1 Peter and 1 John affords the opportunity to draw some parallels with passages and perspectives already discussed.

1 Peter

The theme of eschatological salvation is introduced in Peter's opening paragraph, where an inclusion is actually formed by the use of the word 'salvation' (1:5, 9). Christ's resurrection is first identified as a cause of this salvation (1:3), which is then specifically defined as 'an inheritance that is imperishable, undefiled, and unfading, kept in heaven for you' (1:4). Old Testament terminology is adapted to compare and contrast Israel's experience of being brought into the inheritance of Canaan with the Christian hope of being part of God's new creation. Peter continues to focus on the importance of Christ's resurrection as the basis for Christian faith and hope (1:21). It is therefore the basis of salvation, because it makes possible an effective 'appeal to God for a good conscience' in baptism (3:21).[56] Peter also

---

[56] The Greek (*syneidēseōs agathēs eperōtēma*) can also be rendered 'a pledge to God from a good conscience'.

highlights the importance of Jesus' ascension in the securing of this eternal inheritance for believers (3:19, 22). In fact, the whole sequence of suffering, death, resurrection and ascension is necessary for our salvation. But, for our purposes, it is Peter's teaching about the achievement of Jesus in his death that is of particular interest.

Peter's second paragraph goes on to specify that the means of this salvation was announced long ago by the prophets as 'the sufferings destined for Christ and the subsequent glory' (1:11–12). The 'sufferings' are then described in terms of their redemptive outcome in 1:18–19 and the glory is mentioned again in 1:21. There is an echo of Isaiah 52:3 LXX in the claim that Christians were redeemed without 'perishable things like silver or gold' (1:18). This echo is significant because the verb *lytroun* is used in both texts to mean 'ransom' or 'redeem at a price' (cf. Tit. 2:14). But it is highly likely that Peter is also recalling the teaching of Jesus about his death being 'a ransom for many' and working with a long-established Christian tradition in this connection.[57] God has ransomed a people for himself, at the cost of 'the precious blood of Christ, like that of a lamb without defect or blemish' (1 Pet. 1:19). Moreover, Christ was destined by God for this purpose 'before the foundation of the world' (v. 20).

Passover allusions can be argued from the terminology in verse 19 (cf. Exod. 12:5), though there is not a precise parallel with the LXX. Peter's thought more generally seems to parallel the Old Testament pattern of redemption from bondage in order to serve God and enter his appointed inheritance.[58] But there is also a possible allusion to the silent and faultless lamb of Isaiah 53:7–9, especially in view of the argument to come in 1 Peter 2:21–5. As in the writings of Paul and in Hebrews, there is a blending of several strands of thought in 1 Peter to proclaim the significance of the cross.[59] Jesus

---

[57] The related noun *lytron* is used in Mt. 20:28 / Mk. 10:45. Paul uses the noun *apolytrōsis* in Rom. 3:24; 8:23; 1 Cor. 1:30; Eph. 1:7, 14; 4:30; Col. 1:14; see also Heb. 9:15; 11:35. See W. Mundle, C. Brown, 'Redemption', *NIDNTT*, vol. 3, pp. 189–200, on the meaning and use of this terminology.

[58] See P.H. Davids, *The First Epistle of Peter* (Grand Rapids: Eerdmans, 1990), pp. 72–3.

[59] Sprinkling with the blood of Christ is another image in 1 Pet. 1:2. This may echo the rite in Num. 19, but it is likely in the framework of Peter's redemption-inheritance thinking that the parallel is more specifically with the covenant affirmation ceremony in Exod. 24:3–8 (cf. Heb. 9:18–21).

the Suffering Servant offers a redemptive sacrifice that pays the price for sin and liberates those who believe from the 'futile ways' inherited from their ancestors (1 Pet. 2:18). This enables them to live for God with the sure and certain hope of entering the glorious inheritance already secured by Christ in his death and resurrection. The implications for Christian living are clearly set out at the beginning and end of this passage (1:17, 21–2).

Peter returns to the theme of Christ's sufferings in 2:18–25, where a pattern for discipleship is said to have been established by Christ in his pathway to glory (cf. 3:9; 4:12–19; 5:10). Christ's example is an encouragement to 'endure pain while suffering unjustly' (2:19–21), not retaliating but entrusting oneself 'to the one who judges justly' (2:22–3). However, even such a focus on the exemplary dimension of Christ's sufferings leads Peter back to the redemptive heart of the cross and its potential to transform the human situation (2:24–5). Isaiah 53:9 is cited in verse 22, to stress the sinlessness of Jesus and thus the injustice of his suffering. The allusion in verse 24 is to Isaiah 53:11–12, where the prophet declares that the Servant of the Lord will 'bear' the sin of others. Indeed, much of Peter's argument in verses 21–5 can be regarded as midrash or a paraphrase of Isaiah 53:4–12 LXX.[60]

With the words 'he himself bore our sins in his body on the cross' (v. 24), we have an assertion from Isaiah 53:12 ('he himself bore the sins of many'), modified with words from Isaiah 53:4 ('he has borne our sins'), interpreted in the light of its fulfilment ('in his body on the cross'). The word translated 'cross' is literally 'tree' (Gk. *xylon*) and recalls Deuteronomy 21:22, with its claim that 'anyone hung on a tree is under God's curse' (cf. Gal. 3:13). Without explicitly noting this connection, Peter points out that Jesus' death was penal and substitutionary. He was not a passive victim, nor executed for his own sins, but an active sin-bearer. The Greek word *anēnengken* which Peter uses can mean 'bore' in the sense of 'carried away'. Thus it is true to say:

---

[60] See J.R. Michaels, *1 Peter*, WBC 49 (Waco: Word, 1988), pp. 136–7, who argues that there is no need to posit an early Christian hymn behind these verses.

Sin in 1 Peter is not simply 'atoned for' or 'forgiven' with the tacit implication that if remnants of it persist they will be overlooked, and forgiveness guaranteed in any case. Rather, sin is literally taken away, carried to the cross and left there. It is assumed that the redeemed have 'parted with those sins' and are ready to 'live for what is right'.[61]

But in what sense is sin 'carried to the cross and left there'? The Greek in Isaiah 53:12 renders a form of the Hebrew expression *nāśā' ḥēṭ*, which is widely used in the Old Testament, as is the parallel expression in Isaiah 53:11 (*sābal 'āwōn*). When various combinations of these words are applied to persons or animals, and when their meaning is clear, the normal sense is that the subject bears guilt and punishment.[62] In the previous chapter, I argued that *nāśā' 'āwōn* in Leviticus 16:22 specifically means that guilty Israel is freed from the punishment of sin when the scapegoat symbolically bears the punishment in their place. The context in Isaiah 53 confirms that *sābal 'āwōn* and *nāśā' ḥēṭ* must be taken in their normal sense of bearing punishment. The Servant is punished for the sin of others, and that punishment is atoning, since it brings them wholeness, healing and righteousness. It is this perspective that Peter reflects when he employs the language of Isaiah 53 so precisely.

Like Isaiah, Peter uses the metaphor of healing to describe the effect of this sin-bearing work ('by his wounds you have been healed'). This healing has important lifestyle implications. Those who have 'died to sins' (Gk. *tais hamartiais apogenomenoi*, lit. 'parted with sins') can now 'live for righteousness' (2:24). The verb here means literally 'to be away' or 'parted from', but it is used by classical Greek writers to describe the dead as 'the departed'.

The idea is that, Christ having died for sins, and to sin, as our proxy or substitute, our consequent standing before God is that of those who have no more connection with our old sins, or with the life of sinning.

---

[61] Michaels, *1 Peter*, lxxi. Cf. pp. 148–9.

[62] See Garry Williams's extensive examination of the use of this terminology in ch. 3 of this volume. Both verbs are often paired with either noun, so that there are four possible combinations to investigate.

Henceforth we are free, and are intended, to live unto righteousness (cf. iv.2; Rom. vi. 11–13, 18).[63]

Put another way, the atoning work of Christ makes it possible for those who were 'going astray like sheep' (Isa. 53:6) to return to the shepherd of their souls (2:25). As in the Pauline writings, atonement makes reconciliation with God a possibility and leads to a new life of faith and obedience.

A further critical passage about Christ's redemptive work in 3:18–22 flows out of another exhortation to suffer for doing what is right (3:13–17). This passage makes Jesus an 'example' to the readers in a broader sense than 2:21–5. With reference to his death, resurrection and ascension, it makes him 'an example not merely of suffering for doing good, but of suffering followed by vindication, the single dominant theme of the last half of 1 Peter'.[64] Whatever the prehistory of the creedlike statements in 3:18, Peter uses these affirmations to confirm some of the teaching already given and to set the stage for what follows in verses 19–22. Beyond that, he also uses these affirmations as the basis for an exhortation to finish with sin in 4:1–6.

The introductory words in 3:18 are similar to the words that introduce Christ as an example of suffering in 2:21 (Gk. *hoti kai Christos epathen*).[65] However, addition of the phrase 'for sins once for all' (Gk. *hapax peri hamartiōn*) limits the analogy immediately. Christ's

---

[63] A.M. Stibbs, *The First Epistle General of Peter* (London: Tyndale, 1959), p. 121. Michaels, *1 Peter*, pp. 148–9, follows J.N.D. Kelly, *The Epistles of Peter and of Jude* (London: Black, 1969), p. 123, in arguing for the sense 'having broken with our sins'. But Davids, *First Epistle of Peter*, p. 113, is less troubled with the idea of a Pauline parallel here and argues like Stibbs for the translation 'having died to sin'.

[64] Michaels, *1 Peter*, p. 197.

[65] Although some manuscripts read 'died' (Gk. *apethanen*) instead of 'suffered' (Gk. *epathen*) in 3:18, the latter is used elsewhere in 1 Peter 11 times and sustains the argument from the preceding paragraph more naturally. Christ's death or blood-shedding is clearly the heart and climax of his suffering (cf. 1:18–19; 2:23–4), but 'suffered' is more probably the original reading in 3:18. Kelly, *Epistles of Peter and of Jude*, pp. 147–8, argues that 'died' is the more difficult reading and therefore more likely to be the original.

suffering is unique with respect to its timing and the fact that its purpose is fully accomplished (cf. *hapax* in Heb. 9:26, 28 and *ephapax* in
Rom. 6:10; Heb. 7:27; 9:12; 10:10). Moreover, Christ's suffering is
sacrificial and deals with the problem of human sin definitively.[66] The
significance of his self-offering 'for sins' is then further explained.
With the phrase 'the righteous for the unrighteous' Peter reaffirms
the innocence of Jesus (cf. 1:19; 2:22–3) and once more asserts the
penal and substitutionary nature of his suffering (cf. 2:21 [*hyper
hēmōn* as in 3:18], 24). The outcome of all this is reconciliation
to God ('in order to bring you to God'), and newness of life in
obedience to his will (4:1–6).[67]

1 John

After a brief preface (1:1–4), the first main section of 1 John begins
with the affirmation that 'God is light and in him there is no darkness at all' (1:5). With such imagery, John asserts the absolute holiness and moral purity of the God who has revealed himself in Jesus
Christ. This understanding of God is at the heart of the apostolic
gospel. The argument that extends at least to 2:2 spells out what it
means to be in fellowship with such a God and to 'walk in the light'.
As in the Old Testament, cleansing from sin (1:7, 9) and atonement
(2:2) are seen to be essential for those who would be in an authentic
relationship with the Holy One. Holiness, cleansing from sin and
atonement are intimately related concepts.

Each of the subdivisions in this passage commences with the
words 'if we say . . .' (1:6, 8, 10) and responds to the errors of certain

---

[66] The phrase 'for sins' (Gk. *peri hamartiōn*) is used with a sacrificial reference in Heb. 5:3; 10:26 (cf. 1 Jn. 2:2), along with *hyper hamartiōn* (Heb. 5:1;
10:12) and *peri hamartias* (Heb 10:6, 8, based on Ps. 40 [LXX 39]:7; also
10:18; 13:11; cf. Rom. 8:3). The last of these expression is the most
frequent in the LXX and occurs in Isa. 53:10 for Heb. *āšām*, presumably
with the meaning 'guilt offering'.

[67] There is some textual uncertainty about whether 'you' or 'us' should be
read in this clause. But 'you' is most probably the original reading. The verb
'to bring to' in 3:18 (Gk. *prosagagē*) implies introduction or access to God's
presence. Although it is not strictly a term for reconciliation, the related
noun *prosagōgē* is used in contexts where reconciliation is in view (e.g.
Rom. 5:2; Eph. 2:18; 3:12).

persons known to the author and his readers.[68] The practical behaviour or 'walking' of these false teachers gives the lie to their claim that they have fellowship with God and truly know him. Rhetorically, John also uses this formula ('if we say . . .') to warn the readers not adopt such an approach. Each error is opposed with the challenge of an alternative pattern of behaviour, reflecting certain fundamental beliefs about Jesus Christ (1:7; 1:9; 2:2–2). However, the structure of the argument changes somewhat in the last case.

'Walking in the light' actually achieves the goal of fellowship with God since it involves responding faithfully to the revelation that God has given of himself. This means believing the right things and putting them into practice. Specifically here it means being part of the true community of Christ (1:7, 'we have fellowship with one another'), since that is where Christ's message is preserved and lived out (cf. 1:3; 2:19–21). But John recognizes that no Christian can claim to be practically without sin: all will fail and be disobedient. The reassuring promise for those who walk in the light is that 'the blood of Jesus his Son cleanses us from all sin'. The verb 'cleanses' (Gk. *katharizei*) is in the present tense. This suggests that the sacrificial death of Jesus ('the blood of Jesus'), though a unique, once-for-all event, has an ongoing effect.[69] A link with the argument of Hebrews is obvious here (e.g. Heb. 9:14, 22–3, 10:22; cf. Eph. 5:26; Tit. 2:14) and a contrast with repeated Old Testament rites of cleansing may be implied.

John further pursues the matter of sin and divine cleansing when he attacks another slogan of his opponents in 1:8. Their claim to 'have no sin' sounds like 'the gnostic conviction that pneumatics cannot be defiled by the material world and its impurities'.[70] John

---

[68] Most commentators view the false teachers as representative of an incipient or developing Gnosticism, with a perverted Christology and a false ethic (e.g. S.S. Smalley, *1,2,3 John*, WBC 51 [Waco: Word, 1984], xxiv–xxvii, 21). However, R. Schnackenburg, *The Johannine Epistles: Introduction and Commentary* (ET Tunbridge Wells: Burns & Oates, 1992), pp. 17–24, warns that the heresy cannot simply be paralleled with any other manifestation of heresy known from the late first century or early second century AD. 'Yet it has affinities with more than one such movement' (p. 23).

[69] See Smalley, *1,2,3 John*, pp. 24–5, for the argument that 'the blood of Jesus' refers to his death as a sacrifice for sins.

[70] Schnackenburg, *Johannine Epistles*, p. 80.

views this as a dangerous lie ('we deceive ourselves and the truth is not in us') which obscures the need for redemption through Christ. Fellowship with God requires a life without sin, but this is only possible 'if we confess our sins', so that he who is 'faithful and just' might 'forgive us our sins and cleanse us from all unrighteousness' (1:9).[71] Confession of sins (Gk. *homologōmen*) implies some outward expression and not just an inner attitude of contrition. In Judaism it was particularly associated with the Annual Day of Atonement (Lev. 16:21) and with sin-offerings more generally (Lev. 5:5). John identifies God's willingness to 'forgive' or cancel the debt of sin (Gk. *aphē*) and to 'cleanse' or wash away its impurity (Gk. *katharisē*) with the sacrifice of Jesus in this context (cf. 1:7, *katharizei*).

John finally warns about any claim to be sinless, asserting that this makes God a liar and proves that 'his word is not in us' (1:10). Once more, he outlines the positive alternative, showing precisely how Jesus can help those who struggle with sin (2:1–2). Using the Greek title *paraklētos*, familiar from the Fourth Gospel in connection with the Holy Spirit, he describes Jesus as an 'advocate with the Father' (cf. Jn. 14:16, 'another Advocate', implying that Jesus already had this role in his earthly ministry). 'Intercessor' might be an appropriate rendering here (cf. Exod. 32:30–2; Job 42:7–10, and the use of different terminology in Rom. 8:34; Heb. 7:25). The high-priestly dimension to this activity is suggested by the cultic terminology in the following verse.[72] Describing him as 'righteous' (Gk. *dikaios*), John recalls the term used of the Father in 1:9 and implies that Jesus is supremely qualified to act as advocate/intercessor on our behalf because of who he is and what he has accomplished.

Christ's present work as advocate in heaven depends on the effectiveness of his atoning work on the cross. He remains 'the atoning sacrifice for our sins' (2:2, Gk. *estin*). His blood retains its redeeming and cleansing power because he is alive and remains 'with the Father' (2:1, Gk. *pros ton patera*), always able to apply the

---

[71] Smalley, *1,2,3 John*, p. 32, noting that there is no sharp dividing-line in Semitic thought between intention and consequence, rightly observes that 'The faithfulness and righteousness of God are such "that" he *will* forgive/purify (purpose), and *does* so (result).' This is because of the divine *promises* and the divine *provision* in Christ.

[72] Ibid., pp. 36–7; Schnackenburg, *Johannine Epistles*, p. 87.

benefit of his once-for-all sacrifice to 'those who approach God through him' (Heb. 7:25). As in Hebrews, Jesus is effectively both priest and victim in the divine provision for atonement under the New Covenant. The Greek word *hilasmos*, which occurs only in 2:2 and 4:10, is a verbal substantive formed from *hilaskomai*. In ordinary Greek usage, *hilasmos* denoted 'the action by which a deity is to be propitiated'.[73] In the LXX, such terminology translated derivatives of the Hebrew verb *kipper* (piel), describing the process of sacrificial atonement effected in the Israelite cult (e.g. Lev. 25:9; Num. 5:8). Such terminology belongs with words like blood, cleansing and sin.

In John's perspective, sin hinders a relationship with God and needs to be dealt with *for God's sake* as much as for ours (cf. 1:5–10; 4:7–21). Smalley weighs up the arguments for and against regarding God as the object of Christ's atoning work. He rightly concludes that God is both subject and object of sin offering in the Old Testament and that both senses of *hilasmos* are present in 1 John. As heavenly intercessor, he pleads the cause of the sinner because he is righteous and the perfect offering for our sins (2:1–2).

To this extent God is the *object* of the saving action. But he is also the *subject*, since in verse 9 we learn that the forgiveness and purification of the sinner ultimately stem from the Father: *he* is righteous, and on the basis of the Son's offering he will forgive our sins. Here, then, is not contradiction but complementarity.[74]

In summary, the teaching of 1:5 – 2:2 about atonement is this: Jesus suffered for our sin historically when he shed his blood on the cross, thus making it possible for us to experience fellowship with the Holy One. But the benefit of his atoning work needs to be appropriated by confession of sin and ongoing confidence in Christ as 'advocate' and 'atoning sacrifice for sins'. Walking in the light involves such honest confession of sin and the expression of our need for forgiveness and cleansing through 'the blood of Jesus'. Walking in the darkness involves a denial of sin and the need for continual application of Christ's atoning work to our lives.

---

[73] H.-G. Link, 'Reconciliation, Restoration', p. 149.

[74] Smalley, *1,2,3 John*, p. 40. Cf. I.H. Marshall, *The Epistles of John* (Grand Rapids: Eerdmans, 1978), pp. 117–19.

In 3:5 John affirms that the Son of God was revealed 'to take away sins' (Gk. *arē*) and in 3:8 he adds that the purpose of the incarnation was 'to destroy the works of the devil'. This is said within the context of affirming that 'no one who abides in him sins' (3:6). John holds out the possibility of profound change in the lives of those who belong to Christ and have been 'born of God' (3:9). This passage clearly needs to be held in tension with the warnings encountered in 1:5 – 2:2.

In 4:10 we learn again that Christ takes sin away by being 'the atoning sacrifice for our sins'. It is the ultimate manifestation of the love of God that he provides his only Son as the means of atonement, so that we might 'live through him' (4:9). John says little about the judgement of God against sin (cf. 2:17–18, 28; 4:17), but Christ's incarnation and atoning death are clearly necessary to enable us to pass from death to life (3:14; 5:6–12). The penal and substitutionary dimension to Christ's death is essentially conveyed in 1 John by the use of atonement language (2:2; 4:10). But there is also an exemplary and a re-creational dimension to Christ's death. Loving one another as God has loved us is a sign of the new life in Christ already at work in those who believe (3:11–17; 4:7–12).

Conclusion

It has not been possible to investigate all the relevant verses in the New Testament or to address adequately all the issues raised by scholars in connection with this subject. But the following conclusions are offered on the basis of what has been discussed.

There is evidence in the Synoptic Gospels that Jesus saw himself called to fulfil the role of the Servant of the Lord in Isaiah 53, paying the ransom to liberate 'the many' from the consequences of their sin by his death. This ransom was designed to rescue from the impending judgement of God those who trust in him. In so doing, Jesus also saw himself inaugurating the New Covenant promised in Jeremiah 31, making possible the forgiveness of sins, the restoration of relationships and the new life foretold by the prophets in a variety of contexts. These two strands of teaching profoundly influenced the thinking of his followers, enabling New Testament writers to understand the significance of his death essentially in sacrificial and atoning terms. They pointed back to the Pentateuch and to the need for the pattern of salvation and covenant continuance revealed there to be fulfilled in Christ.

Paul's teaching about Christ suffering the judgement of God against sin in our place is fundamental to his other claims about the outcome of Christ's sacrifice, such as reconciliation and justification. The logic of the argument in passages like Romans 3 and 2 Corinthians 5 is that all the benefits of Christ's death depend upon his sin-bearing as the innocent substitute. Those who wish to play down or deny this foundational aspect to Paul's theology often do so by propounding an impersonal view of the wrath of God. But this attempt to avoid any notion of propitiation leaves us with a strangely mechanical view of atonement. Furthermore, it is neither consistent with Paul's own teaching nor the perspective of Scripture as a whole to divorce God's wrath from his righteousness and justice and view it as an impersonal force which Christ must meet on our behalf.

Hebrews and 1 Peter give a broad biblical perspective on Christ's sacrifice, viewing it as redemptive in the sense of being a payment for sin and the means of liberation from sin's dominion and its consequences. Christ's sacrifice is also the means by which the benefits of the New Covenant are made available, supremely life in God's presence for ever. Both documents present Jesus as the sinless saviour, who 'bears the sins of many' in his death, and delivers those who trust in him from the judgement of God. 1 John joins with Hebrews in focusing on Jesus' death as the eternally effective sacrifice for sin and the basis on which he continues to intercede with the Father on our behalf. For John as for Paul, the propitiatory death of Jesus is the ultimate manifestation of the love of God for sinners (1 Jn. 4:9–10; Rom. 5:8–10; 2 Cor. 5:14–21).

Questions for Further Study

1. In what ways do the Synoptic Gospel writers portray the unjust nature of Jesus' suffering and suggest that it is an experience of the judgement of God for the sins of others?
2. What indications do you see in John's Gospel that Jesus saw his death as an atoning sacrifice for sin?

3.   How would you answer the charge that the penal aspect of the cross is only one among many perspectives on the death of Jesus in the teaching of Paul?

4.   What evidence do you find in the New Testament for the view that God is both 'the offerer' of atonement in the death of Jesus and 'the object' of Jesus' sacrifice (ie. propitiation)?

5.   How do New Testament writers use the teaching about Christ's atoning work as a motivation for obedience and godly living?

Select Bibliography

Bellinger Jr., W.H., and W.R. Farmer (eds.), *Jesus and the Suffering Servant: Isaiah 53 and Christian Origins* (Harrisburg: Trinity Press International, 1998)

France, R.T., *Jesus and the Old Testament* (London: Tyndale, 1971)

Hengel, M., *The Atonement: The Origins of the Doctrine in the New Testament* (Philadelphia: Fortress, 1981)

Morris, L., *The Apostolic Preaching of the Cross* (Leicester: IVP, 1965[3])

–, *The Atonement: Its Meaning and Significance* (Leicester: IVP, 1983)

Stott, J.R.W., *The Cross of Christ* (Leicester: IVP, 1986)

3

The Cross and the Punishment of Sin
Garry Williams

Introduction

In the preceding chapters, David Peterson has outlined a biblical theology of the atonement, ranging across the breadth of the Canon to show that penal substitution is an indispensable part of the scriptural revelation. Now the focus narrows, first to a more detailed examination of a single strand of the biblical evidence for penal substitution, and secondly to a biblical and systematic exploration of the nature of the punishment involved in the atonement. This latter exploration is intended primarily to provide a close account of the penal aspect of the atonement, but in so doing it will also serve to answer a widespread criticism levelled at penal substitution.

This criticism, that the doctrine reduces the atonement to an impersonal mechanism, will be taken as the starting point for the exposition, but it will not govern it. The need at the present time is for faithful theological reflection on penal substitution itself, and it is important that this should proceed by its inner logic, and not just by the logic of apologetics or polemics, let alone the logic dictated by its opponents.

If the mechanistic criticism of penal substitution is true, it suggests that the proclamation of the cross in much classical evangelical preaching and evangelism is untenable, and that it contradicts the broader teaching of the New Testament. Its relevance to the message we proclaim today is transparent.

The Biblical Evidence for Penalty Bearing

From 1 Peter 2 to Isaiah 52–3

The single strand of biblical evidence to be pursued begins with the description of the death of Jesus Christ in 1 Peter 2:24–5 (RSV):

> He himself bore our sins in his body on the tree, that we might die to sin and live to righteousness. By his wounds you have been healed. For you were straying like sheep, but have now returned to the Shepherd and Guardian of your souls.

We have here an explicit New Testament identification of Jesus with the Servant of Isaiah 52–3, which for any theologian who stands under 'God's word written' is sufficient reason to bring Isaiah 52–3 to centre stage in the doctrine of the atonement. It is true, of course, that Peter uses the material from Isaiah for a moral purpose – to exhort his readers to follow the example of Christ. Nonetheless, he is clearly moved by the magnitude of the death of his Master to go beyond this immediate aim in providing a concise statement of his doctrine of the atonement. What exactly would this statement have meant?

The phrase 'he bore the sin of many' in Isaiah 53:12 is the only place in the Septuagint where the noun *hamartia* and the verb *anapherō* are used together in the sense in which Peter uses them here. This, together with the other clear references to the Servant and his work made by Peter in verses 24–5, shows that the meaning of Isaiah 53:12 is determinative for the view of the death of Jesus found in 1 Peter 2:24.

What did Isaiah 53:12 imply about the meaning of the suffering of the Servant? Turning to the chapter, we see that the question can actually be widened slightly since Isaiah 53:11 also contains another statement which in the Hebrew vocabulary was often interchanged with the phrase used in verse 12. Thus in verse 12 we find the claim that 'he bore the sin [of many]' (where the essential Hebrew expression is *nāśā' ḥēṭ'*), and in verse 11 we find the parallel idea that 'he shall bear their iniquities' (where the essential Hebrew expression is *sābal 'āwōn*). As many commentators recognize, the parallel between these two statements here and in their usage elsewhere suggests that they may safely be taken to mean the same thing.[1] In fact, both verbs are often paired with either noun, so that we have four possible combinations to investigate. The basic elements of the meaning of these words can be sketched by offering a representative taxonomy of their use throughout the Old Testament.

The language of Isaiah 53:11–12 in the Old Testament

It is immediately clear that when the phrases are used with God as their subject they refer to the forgiveness of sins, as in the *locus classicus* of Exodus 34:6–7 (cf. Num. 14:18; Ps. 32:5; 85:3; Isa. 33:24; Hos. 14:3; Mic. 7:18):

> The LORD, the LORD,
> a God merciful and gracious,
> slow to anger,
> and abounding in steadfast love and faithfulness,
> keeping steadfast love for the thousandth generation,
> *forgiving iniquity* (Heb. *nāśā' 'āwōn*) and transgression and sin . . . (my emphasis)

When, however, the phrases are used of a person or animal, and when their meaning is clear, the normal sense is that the subject bears guilt and punishment. A few of the many examples will suffice to make the point. In Genesis 4:13–14, when Cain has just been cursed for killing Abel, he complains to the Lord:

> My *punishment* is greater than *I can bear*! Today you have driven me away from the soil, and I shall be hidden from your face; I shall be a fugitive and a wanderer on the earth, and anyone who meets me may kill me. (My emphasis.)

It is obvious from Cain's words about his sentence that it is the punishment imposed upon him which he thinks he cannot endure, so that a form of the expression *nāśā' 'āwōn* here refers to bearing the punishment inflicted by God.

In Leviticus 24:14–16 the words of Yahweh to Moses concerning a case of blasphemy use the combination found in Isaiah 53:12 (*nāśā' ḥēṭ'*):

---

[1] E.g. R.N. Whybray, *Thanksgiving for a Liberated Prophet: An Interpretation of Isaiah Chapter 53* (Sheffield: JSOT, 1978), p. 31.

Take the blasphemer outside the camp; and let all who were within
hearing lay their hands on his head, and let the whole congregation
stone him. And speak to the people of Israel, saying: Anyone who
curses God *shall bear the sin*. One who blasphemes the name of the
LORD shall be put to death; the whole congregation shall stone the
blasphemer. (My emphasis.)

This law, arising from the specific incident of blasphemy recorded
in verses 10–12, again indicates that the expression refers to the
bearing of punishment by drawing a parallel between the two pairs,
cursing and sin-bearing in verse 15, and blaspheming and death in
verse 16, thus linking sin-bearing and the punishment of death.
Hence the expression refers to bearing the punishment for sin, a
punishment which is inflicted by the people at the command of
God himself in the law.

In Numbers 14:34 the Hebrews in the wilderness have just rebelled against God, having heard the spies' reports of the formidable
Canaanites. God condemns the wilderness generation to a further
forty years of wandering in the wilderness, to match the forty days
during which the spies were active. The Lord speaks to Moses and
uses a version of the expression *nāśā' 'āwōn*, with a clear reference to
the punishment inflicted on the Hebrews by God and to be borne
by them during the further years of wandering: 'According to the
number of the days in which you spied out the land, forty days, for
every day a year, *you shall bear your iniquity*, forty years, and you shall
know my displeasure' (my emphasis).

Isaiah 64:6 provides an especially interesting example with its
statement that '*our iniquities*, like the wind, *take us away*', an important instance in that it is from the same mind as the statement about
the Servant in chapter 53 (and even on the basis that there were
multiple authors it is from the same final redactor). Here the iniquities are themselves the subject of the verb: they do the carrying
away. The image of being blown away by the wind describes the
process of punishment, and in the subsequent verses it is clear that
this punishment is the exile (vv. 10–11). Here then we find the
phrase *nāśā' 'āwōn* connected with the punishment meted out by
God upon Israel in the exile.

This is also the sense of the language used in Lamentations 5:7.
Here a version of the expression used in Isaiah 53:11 (*sābal 'āwōn*) is

part of the complaint uttered by the exiles: 'Our ancestors sinned; they are no more, and *we bear their iniquities.*' Again, the reference is to the punishment imposed on Israel by God as the result of her sin.

It should be noted that in some instances of the various expressions the context shows it is more specifically the bearing of guilt and liability to punishment that is in mind, and that there is at least a separation implied between guilt and actual punishment. This is evidently the case with the use of *nāśā' 'āwōn* in Leviticus 5:17–19, the description of the sacrifice for sin committed in ignorance. Moses is told, 'If any of you sin without knowing it, doing any of the things that by the LORD's commandments ought not to be done, you have incurred guilt, and *are subject to punishment*' (my emphasis).

The provision for such cases of guilt and liability is the sacrifice of a ram without blemish. If the sacrifice is made, then the guilty person will be forgiven. This shows that the expression cannot here be taken to describe the actual bearing of punishment, but only the liability to punishment, since the point is that the person who has borne the guilt is spared the punishment on account of the sacrifice.

The same pattern is found in Leviticus 22:15–16, where if someone profanes the donations made by the people of Israel he incurs guilt (*nāśā' 'āwōn*) and then requires a guilt offering. Nonetheless, we should not read too much into this separation of guilt and punishment, for even in such instances it remains true that the consequence of the guilt-bearing described by the expressions in these verses would have been the bearing of punishment, had the sacrifice not been interposed. Thus, even where the sense is limited to guilt-bearing, the notion of following punishment is never far away.[2]

---

[2] Many Old Testament scholars agree on the unity of the concepts of guilt and punishment, e.g. G. von Rad, *Old Testament Theology* (ET London: SCM, 1975), vol. 1, p. 266: 'there is absolutely nothing in the thought of the Old Testament which by and large corresponds to the separation which we make between sin and penalty'. This is not an instance of illegitimate totality transfer, that is, the error of importing all the possible meanings of a phrase into a single occurrence (here the idea of punishment into the mention of sin). Rather, the examples show from their contexts that guilt entails punishment unless there is a dramatic intrusion on the inevitable process.

In its use of the *nāśā' 'āwōn* formula, Ezekiel 4 provides a particularly good example of how guilt can be distinguished from punishment without altogether removing the latter notion from the context. The prophet is instructed to lie on his left side for 390 days in order to symbolize bearing the iniquity of the 'house of Israel' (vv. 4–5), and then to lie on his right side for forty days to symbolize bearing the punishment of the 'house of Judah' (v. 6). The figures given in the Hebrew (which have been changed in the Septuagint) require the distinction between guilt and punishment if they are to make sense. The figure of 390 days is comprehensible if it represents the time during which Israel sinned and was guilty, namely the time from the exile back to the founding of the Temple. If it is taken to refer to the period of punishment it is hard to see how it can be in any way accurate.[3]

Conversely, the period of forty years makes no sense if understood as the period of sin, since the sin of Judah was far more ancient. Unlike the first use of *nāśā' 'āwōn* in verses 4–5, the use in verse 6 must therefore refer to punishment. Here Ezekiel echoes the passage discussed above from Numbers 14 in that his action alludes to another great punishment in the history of Israel, the period of the wandering in the wilderness. As in Leviticus 5:17–19 and 22:15–16, we find here an example of the limited sense of guilt-bearing, but it is again notable that this is connected to the idea of punishment. Indeed, the connection between the 390 years of guilt and the 40 years of punishment is deliberately made by Ezekiel. Thus in some cases where there are obvious contextual limitations, we may read the phrases as speaking of guilt, but even then the idea of punishment is implied as the inevitable consequence of that guilt.

One final and crucial element must be drawn out from these examples and bolstered, namely the fact that our expressions often indicate that the punishment will be proportioned and imposed by

---

[3] There is much dispute about the numerical calculations. It is possible that the period of the monarchy rather than the Temple may be in focus here if the 40 years are to be taken as running concurrently with the 390, thus reducing the total to 350 and giving a later starting date. But as Thomas Renz points out, at this stage it is the temple that consumes Ezekiel's attention. See T. Renz, *The Rhetorical Function of the Book of Ezekiel* (Leiden: Brill, 1999), pp. 180–1.

God alone. This was the case with the various passages concerning Cain, the wilderness wandering, and the exile. It emerges especially clearly at the end of the procedure set out for a husband who suspects his wife of adultery in Numbers 5:11–31. The suspected adulteress is to be presented before the priest who will bring her before the Lord to drink the 'water of bitterness' (v. 23). If she is guilty, the water will 'cause bitter pain, and her womb shall discharge, her uterus drop, and the woman shall become an execration among her people' (v. 27), but if she is innocent she will be unaffected and will be able to conceive children (v. 28). The passage ends with the statement that a guilty woman will bear her punishment (v. 31, a form of *nāśā'* *'āwōn*). The mechanism for the punishment is clearly supernatural. There is no magical property in the water, which contains only dust from the floor of the tabernacle and the ink of a written curse which the woman has sworn (vv. 17 and 23). It is specifically in the presence of Yahweh that the guilt or innocence of the woman is to be determined, and it is thus he who will implement the punishment if according to his knowledge she is guilty.[4]

What can we conclude from this setting out of the use of these critical terms? In instances where their meaning is apparent from the context, the normal sense is 'to bear punishment'. In some cases, where there are obvious limitations to the meaning in the context, we may translate 'to bear guilt', but even in these cases the idea of subsequent punishment is implied. Frequently, the punishment is understood to be imposed directly by God.

Many of the examples we have seen speak plainly of *punishment*, but do not necessarily entail the idea of penal *substitution*. They speak of a sinner bearing punishment. This is sometimes the punishment for his own sins (for instance with Cain), or it might be that he shares in the punishment of another. This idea of shared punishment is evidently implied in the passage discussed from Numbers

---

[4] T. Frymer-Kensky emphasizes this point in 'The Strange Case of the Suspected Sotah (Numbers V 11–31)', *VT* 34 (1984), pp. 11–26 (24): 'Not only does God decide whether she is guilty, but even the right of punishment is removed from society and placed in the hands of God'. This reservation of punishment to imposition by Yahweh may explain the fact that in the law the punishment is often unspecified, as for example in Lev. 20:19–20.

14. Those under twenty who would later enter the Promised Land nonetheless shared in the punishment of their parents during the extended wilderness wandering. They were not substituted for their parents, since their parents themselves still suffered, but they did share in the punishment for their sin. Thus, the sharing of punishment is not the same as substitution, since in substitution the guilty one goes free from the punishment and another suffers it for him.

Substitutionary punishment in the Old Testament

There are, however, examples of substitutionary punishment in the use of our expressions in the Old Testament. One striking case is the passage cited above from Lamentations 5:7, where the punishment of the ancestors is shared by the exiles, but the ancestors themselves did not bear it: 'our ancestors sinned; they are no more, and we bear their iniquities'. Here the sin of the dead ancestors is borne by the generation in exile. This is not to say that those punished were themselves innocent. The author of Lamentations recognizes that his people are guilty with the words 'woe to us, for we have sinned!' (5:16). But it is to say that one group of people was spared the full punishment for their sins which was transferred to another, later group.

This process makes perfect sense in the light of the understanding of the history of Israel found in the passage cited above from Ezekiel 4. It is evident that the sin of Israel is there thought to have extended back for 390 years through the entire age of the Temple, even though the punishment had been reserved for the prophet's own generation. This does not contradict the proposition set out in Ezekiel 18:20 that 'the person who sins shall die', since in context that proposition serves only to deny the substitution of the innocent for the guilty, not the guilty for the guilty. The people protest that they are innocent and so should not be suffering for their fathers' sins, but the Lord answers with the assertion of their guilt. Were they innocent, the Lord argues, they would not suffer: 'When the son has done what is lawful and right, and has been careful to observe all my statutes, he shall surely live' (18:19). The concern here is to deny that these people could be innocent and yet suffering for the guilty (which would be an injustice on the part of God), not to deny that the guilty can suffer for the guilty.[5]

The dynamic of the Old Testament histories is also one of substitutionary punishment, that is, punishment where the guilty are spared the full penalty which is instead borne by others who share their guilt. The principle is established in Deuteronomy 5:9 with the warning against idolatry: 'I the LORD your God am a jealous God, punishing children for the iniquity of parents, to the third and fourth generation of those who reject me.' Here again we see not the idea of the innocent being substituted for the guilty, but of the guilty, 'those who reject me', being substituted for the guilty.

Whatever one thinks of the hypothesis of the 'Deuteronomistic historian', this principle is then undeniably spelled out in the narratives of the historical books, for example 1 and 2 Kings. In 1 Kings 9:6–7 King Solomon is given a warning by God:

> If you turn aside from following me, you or your children, and do not keep my commandments and my statutes that I have set before you, but go and serve other gods and worship them, then I will cut Israel off from the land that I have given them.

Despite the undoubted glory of his reign, Solomon is indeed seduced by his foreign wives into idolatry so that 'the LORD was angry with Solomon, because his heart had turned away from the LORD, the God of Israel' (11:9). Even in the face of his unfaithfulness, the threat of exile uttered in 9:6–7 is not fulfilled. Rather, Solomon is told, 'for the sake of your father David I will not do it in your lifetime' (11:12). The punishment for Solomon's sin is postponed until the time after his death and results in the division of the kingdom when his son Rehoboam loses the northern tribes.

This pattern of postponed punishment is found again at other points in the narrative of 1 and 2 Kings. The destruction of the Northern Kingdom, for example, is explicitly said to be the result of sin stretching right back through its history. In the narrator's explanation of the Assyrian conquest, the capture of King Hoshea, and

---

[5] This obviously raises the question of how it was just for the innocent Jesus to suffer in place of the guilty, a question Michael Ovey addresses in the next chapter.

the exile of the Israelites, we read that 'this occurred because the people of Israel had sinned against the LORD their God' (2 Kgs. 17:7). When the sin is detailed in the rest of the explanation, it includes instances from the reigns of earlier kings. Thus we read that the people made two images of calves to worship and served Baal: the first is a reference to the reign of Jeroboam (cf. 1 Kgs. 12:25ff.), and the second to the reign of Ahab (1 Kgs. 16:31ff.).

Hence, the destruction of the Northern Kingdom is a punishment not only for the sins of the generation destroyed, but for the sins of previous generations as well. Indeed, we are told that King Hoshea himself was actually less evil than his predecessors (2 Kgs. 17:2), and yet he still suffered captivity. By contrast, his evil predecessors had often lived far longer than the righteous kings; Ahab reigned for 22 years (1 Kgs. 16:29) and Jeroboam II for 41 years (2 Kgs. 14:23). As T.R. Hobbs comments, 'it is clear that the writer offers a much more complex interpretation of the history than a simplistic "sin and judgment" model'.[6] The principle forming the complexity is the principle of mercy, the withholding of punishment until the opportunity for a righteous response to God has been exhausted. Then, and only then, is the full punishment for the previous generations of sins poured out on a single guilty generation. As the rulers of Israel deteriorated, so the anger of Yahweh built up against them, but he repeatedly refrained from punishing them with destruction and exile.

This is also the case in the history of the Southern Kingdom, Judah. Near the end of her pre-exilic history she is ruled by the righteous Josiah who enforces the teaching of the recently discovered Book of the Law (2 Kgs. 22–3). But even his righteousness is insufficient to save the nation because of the sin of his predecessor but one, Manasseh. Thus we read after a eulogy to Josiah's righteousness that 'still the LORD did not turn from the fierceness of his great wrath, by which his anger was kindled against Judah, because of all the provocations with which Manasseh had provoked him' (23:26). It is the sin of Manasseh, now long dead and gone, that causes the destruction of Judah, as the writer repeats in recording the campaign of Nebuchadnezzar against King Jehoiakim:

---

[6] *Word Biblical Themes: 1 and 2 Kings* (Dallas: Word, 1989), p. 25.

> Surely this came upon Judah at the command of the LORD, to remove them out of his sight, for the sins of Manasseh, for all that he had committed, and also for the innocent blood that he had shed; for he filled Jerusalem with innocent blood, and the LORD was not willing to pardon. (2 Kgs. 24:3–4)

This is not to say that the generation exiled was itself innocent; Jehoiakim himself 'did what was evil in the sight of the LORD' (23:37). But the sins of Manasseh were punished in the exile, and thus Manasseh was spared the full punishment of his sins which was taken by a later generation. The prophet Jeremiah also knew that Manasseh's sins would bring Judah down:

> I will appoint over them four kinds of destroyers, says the LORD: the sword to kill, the dogs to drag away, and the birds of the air and wild animals of the earth to devour and destroy. I will make them a horror to all the kingdoms of the earth because of what King Manasseh son of Hezekiah of Judah did in Jerusalem. (Jer. 15:3–4)[7]

Substitutionary atonement in the Old Testament

These examples of substitutionary punishment are not, however, examples of substitutionary *atonement*. By theological definition they could not be, since those punished could not atone for the sins of others, given their own guilt. They are examples of the guilty bearing the punishment of the guilty, not the innocent bearing the punishment of the guilty and so atoning for their sin. In the sacrificial system, however, we do find the idea of atonement by penal substitution.

The most famous example is the scapegoat described in the ritual for the Day of Atonement in Leviticus 16. As David Peterson noted in chapter one, the meaning of *nāśāʾ ʿāwōn* in verse 22 is disputed. Given its ambiguity in this passage, it should be read in the light of the other Old Testament passages where it means 'to bear

---

[7] It is notable that this argument from the dynamic of sin and punishment in Israel's history seems not to have been reckoned with by those who wish to expunge the idea of substitution in the Old Testament, e.g. Whybray, *Thanksgiving for a Liberated Prophet*.

punishment', especially since the immediate context makes sense in the light of this general usage. The banishment of the goat to the wilderness is best understood as banishment to death, suggested by its being sent to a place of 'cutting off' (v. 22, 'barren region' in NRSV) and to 'Azazel' (vv. 8, 10, 26).[8] This means that the guilty people of Israel are freed from the punishment of sin when the scapegoat symbolically bears the punishment for their sin in their place.[9]

We may now turn to consider the nature of the Servant's sufferings in Isaiah 53, having established that the expressions used in verses 11–12 imply the bearing of punishment, sometimes imply that the bearing is substitutionary in character, and can imply that the substitutionary punishment is a means of atonement. In the context, the repeated terrible descriptions of the suffering of the Servant show that this is an act of punishment. The appearance of the Servant is marred 'beyond human semblance' (52:14); he is 'despised and rejected' (53:3), he bears infirmities and carries diseases (v. 4); he is wounded and crushed and bruised (v. 5), oppressed and afflicted (v. 7); he is 'cut off from the land of the living' and stricken (v. 8); he is anguished (v. 11), and he pours himself out to death (v. 12). This context for the use of *sābal* '*āwōn* and *nāśā*' *ḥēṭ*' confirms that they must here be taken in their normal sense of bearing punishment.

Isaiah 53:10 plainly states that the crushing of the Servant was the 'will of the LORD', even though it was also a 'perversion of justice' (v. 8). The tension between these statements is hard to unravel unless we think of some kind of double agency whereby the Servant suffers by the evil will of men and also by the pure will of God. This type of double agency is already present in Isaiah's view of Israel's oppressors, especially Cyrus (44:28ff.). Furthermore, the idea that it is God who wills the punishment of the Servant fits with the wider

---

[8] The fact that both words can be read to imply death and thus be read consistently with one another is a strong argument for reading each of them in this particular way. If Azazel means either 'complete destruction' or 'rocky precipice' the idea of death is present. On these questions, see G.J. Wenham, *Leviticus* (Grand Rapids: Eerdmans, 1979), pp. 233–5.

[9] The symbolic nature of the Old Testament sacrifices is required by Heb. 10:4.

use of the expressions *sābal 'āwōn* and *nāśā' hēṭ'* from 53:11–12 to denote a punishment imposed by God himself, as we have seen with Cain, the woman guilty of adultery, or Israel in exile.

Further attention shows that we are dealing not just with a case of punishment imposed by God, but with penal substitution as a means of atonement. Some have argued that, as the children of the disobedient Hebrews in Numbers 14:34 merely *shared* in their parents' punishment, so the Servant is merely described as sharing in the punishment of the people.[10] This interpretation is held by those who deny any notion of substitutionary punishment in the Old Testament, that is, by those who have not grasped the pattern of substitutionary punishment implied by texts such as Lamentations 5:7 and Ezekiel 4, and by the pattern of the biblical histories. On this ground alone we should be suspicious of their argument, although it would of course be fallacious to think that they are therefore automatically wrong.

The case against the substitutionary sense of Isaiah 53:11–12 is wrong, however, because it fails to deal with the internal evidence of the Servant Song itself. That is, it fails to take due measure of the significance of the repeated contrast within the Song between what 'he' the Servant does or endures and the 'we', 'us' or 'their' group. This aspect is clearly brought out in John Oswalt's commentary on Isaiah 40–66. Oswalt provides a literal translation of verse 4 which highlights the force of the emphatic independent pronouns 'he' and 'we': 'our sicknesses *he* carried . . . but *we* considered him stricken'.[11] He explains verse 5 thus:

> What the Servant does in bearing the undeserved results of his people's sin brings about positive results for the people. He is not merely

---

[10] So Whybray: 'The Servant cannot be said to be suffering, or to have suffered, in place of the exiles in such a way that they escape the consequences of their sins, since, as in the case of the speakers in Lam. 5:7, it cannot be said that these have escaped punishment: they are all actually suffering the consequences of defeat and banishment', *Thanksgiving for a Liberated Prophet*, p. 30. Whybray is building on the work of H.M. Orlinsky in 'The So-called "Servant of the Lord" and "Suffering Servant" in Second Isaiah', in H.M. Orlinsky and N.H. Snaith, *Studies in the Second Part of the Book of Isaiah* (Leiden: Brill, 1967), pp. 1–133.

[11] *Isaiah 40–66* (Grand Rapids: Eerdmans, 1998), p. 386.

participating in their suffering, he is bearing it away for them so that they may not labor under its effects anymore.[12]

Accordingly, we must add the further evidence that the suffering of the Servant rescues the people from their plight. He makes the people whole and heals them (v. 5), he makes many righteous (v. 11), and he intercedes for the transgressors (v. 13). On verse 11, Oswalt points out that the words are again arranged to contrast the experiences of the Servant and the people, not to suggest that they are shared:

> The object, 'their iniquities', is placed at the beginning of the clause in the emphatic position, and 'he', the internal subject of the verb, is emphasized by the addition of the 3rd masc. sg. independent pronoun. The sense is, 'it is *their* iniquities that *he* carries'.[13]

In short, it is clear that the Servant is punished, that his punishment is substitutionary since it is the result of the sin of others, and that his punishment is atoning, since it brings them wholeness, healing and righteousness.

Returning *via* Isaiah 52–3 to 1 Peter 2:24, we may affirm that, as the Suffering Servant the Lord Jesus Christ bore the punishment for the sins of his people in their place, and that in so doing he wrought atonement for them as the punishment was poured out upon him by the hand of God himself.

The Nature of the Law and Punishment in Scripture

The mechanistic criticisms of penal substitution

Having argued for the biblical status of penal substitution, we turn now to a widespread *theological* (as opposed to exegetical) criticism of that doctrine, which avers that it describes the process by which God makes atonement for sin in too mechanistic or mathematical a fashion. Within the pertinent literature there are two versions of this criticism. The first asserts that penal substitution is too

---

[12] Ibid., p. 388.
[13] Ibid., p. 405 n. 60.

mechanistic because it is a purely objective account of the atonement which excludes *our* intimate involvement in the process. The atonement is conceived as an event *extra nos* which does not touch our lives. The second claims that penal substitution is too mechanistic because it is a purely objective account of the atonement which excludes *God's* intimate involvement. Salvation is purely a process involving law codes and penal systems in which he cannot be intimately involved. The first version of the criticism is important, but here I shall attend only to the second, the claim that penal substitution reduces the atonement to a legal mechanism in which God is not personally involved.

A brief statement of this criticism is found in the report of the Doctrine Commission of the Church of England, *The Mystery of Salvation*, when it discusses the teaching of the Thirty-nine Articles and the Book of Common Prayer. The report claims that the dominant view of the atonement in these texts is juridical, and that it 'is constructed in terms of the impersonal considerations of law and justice rather than the personal categories of relationship and response'. The criticism is then widened to juridical theories in general:

> Judicial theories of the atonement have often pictured God's law, God's wrath, and human sin and guilt not as aspects of the relation between God and humanity, but as though they were actual objects or things that had somehow to be dealt with.[14]

A more sustained and developed version of this criticism was earlier put forward by Paul Fiddes: 'When the death of Jesus is presented as a legal device for satisfying a divine justice which has been affronted by human sin, this can easily reduce the doctrine of atonement to a mere formula.'[15]

He later expatiates on this point:

> Theories of legal satisfaction set a law above the character of God. The theory runs that God cannot forgive us until the punishment

---

[14] *The Mystery of Salvation* (London: Church House Publishing, 1995), p. 211.
[15] *Past Event and Present Salvation* (London: Darton, Longman & Todd, 1989), p. 84.

demanded by justice is exacted. This conceives justice as law with ultimate authority; even when the law is said to be God's own law, the theory still requires God to act in a way which is confined by legal restraints. Law has ceased to be a useful guideline to the purpose of God for his creatures, and has become a supreme principle.[16]

Why might one be tempted to hold this negative view of penal substitution? The principal reason is surely the biblical language which is used to describe the process of reconciliation, which is inherently personalistic language concerned with the restoration of friendship between one party and another. We might think of 2 Corinthians 5:18–19, where Paul writes that God 'reconciled us to himself through Christ' and that 'in Christ God was reconciling the world to himself'. Or we might turn to Ephesians 2:17–19 to find Paul's discussion of how the cross brought reconciliation:

> He came and proclaimed peace to you who were far off and peace to those who were near; for through him both of us have access in one Spirit to the Father. So then you are no longer strangers and aliens, but you are citizens with the saints and also members of the household of God.

Lastly, we might be tempted to make the parable of the Prodigal Son the controlling paradigm for our soteriology, thus taking a free forgiveness indifferent to the law as the key to the atonement.[17] Do these passages leave us with a contradiction between penal substitution and the equally biblical belief in salvation by reconciliation and fatherly love? My argument in the rest of this chapter is that this contradiction disappears when the nature of the law and the punishment for sin are properly explained, that is, when we give a careful exposition of the inner logic of penal substitution itself.

Those who question penal substitution often criticize the use of the language of law on the ground that it is inevitably mechanistic because it originates from culturally bound and outdated human legal systems. Thus Fiddes:

---

[16] Ibid., p. 101.
[17] Ibid., pp. 101–2.

The doctrine of penal substitution relies even more strongly than Anselm upon a retributive view of penalty, and in this it is heavily conditioned by its social context. Calvin assumes that when law, whether human ('positive law') or divine, is broken punishment must always be inflicted. As a matter of fact this no longer seems as self-evident to us today as it did in past ages.[18]

Fiddes offers no evidence from the sixteenth century to substantiate this argument.

Can it really be claimed that the nations of sixteenth-century Europe knew nothing of clemency in their legal practice? In particular, we might remember that Calvin's own first-published work was a critical edition of Seneca's *De Clementia*, the philosopher's advice to the young emperor Nero advocating the merit of mercy rather than severity in his legal authority. For this reason Fiddes cannot be right in his view of Calvin's context in the sixteenth century. But even if he is, an *ad hominem* argument directed against Calvin and his formulation of penal substitution does not suffice to undermine the doctrine itself, especially since the doctrine pre-dates the Reformers.[19]

Fiddes seems to presume that penal substitution always operates according to the norms of one specific type of historical human legal process, rather than according to the eternal divine law itself. Attention to the way in which penal substitution is articulated would suggest another way of assessing it, in that its proponents – not least of all Calvin – hold it to be a biblical doctrine based on the biblical view of the divine law. This claim at least warrants careful attention. Regardless of the supposed sixteenth-century understanding, do the Scriptures encourage us to think that by casting the atonement in legal terms we have set the law itself 'above the character of God' in a formulaic fashion?

---

[18] Ibid., pp. 102–3.

[19] Here is a debate which must be left for another occasion, but in short the evidence of the primary texts from the Patristic era is clear. For a small selection of the many examples, see Eusebius, *Demonstratio Evangelica* 10.1; Athanasius, *Oratio contra Arianos* 1.60; Ambrose, *De Esau sive de fuga saeculi* 7; Augustine, *Contra Faustum* 14.6; Gregory the Great, *Moralia in Job* 3.14.

The relation between the law and God in Scripture

Put another way, what is the relation between the law and God in Scripture? Is it a detached and mechanistic relation such that atonement by legal means will inevitably be atonement by external mechanism separate from God himself? On the contrary, the consistent biblical understanding of the law is that it mirrors the very being of God, and is therefore inextricably related to his character.

Taking the law of the Old Testament as the law which best indicates the relation of God to moral laws in general, we find that it is a holy law, which is intended to maintain a holy people, so that they will be like their holy God himself. These three claims are respectively ontological (concerning the nature of the law), functional (concerning its role), and teleological (concerning its purpose).

The ontological claim is found in Romans 7, where, having discussed the role of the law in manifesting sin, the Apostle Paul is concerned to affirm that the law itself *is* holy:

> Sin, seizing an opportunity in the commandment (*dia tēs entolēs*), deceived me and through it killed me. So the law is holy (*nomos hagios*), and the commandment is holy and just and good (*entolē hagia kai dikaia kai agathē*). (Rom. 7:11–12)

The functional claim is prevalent in the Old Testament, which teaches that the law serves to maintain the covenant relationship between Yahweh and his people by setting out the requirement of holiness for the people.[20] When God speaks to Moses on Mount Sinai in Exodus 19:4–6, he sets out his purpose for the people he has rescued from slavery in Egypt:

> You have seen what I did to the Egyptians, and how I bore you on eagles' wings and brought you to myself. Now therefore, if you obey

---

[20] There is an extensive debate concerning the precise nuances of the idea of holiness in the Old Testament. My present purpose is the limited one of establishing a link between the law and the being of God in terms of holiness; the detailed discussion of the content of the idea of holiness may be noted but not pursued. For a slightly dated but useful introduction to that discussion see G.J. Wenham, *Leviticus* (Grand Rapids: Eerdmans, 1979), pp. 18–25.

my voice and keep my covenant, you shall be my treasured possession
out of all the peoples. Indeed, the whole earth is mine, but you shall be
for me a priestly kingdom and a holy (*qādôš*) nation.

It is in the context of this description of the people as a holy nation
that Yahweh gives the law, beginning with the Decalogue in Exodus 20. The covenant thus specifies that the response of the people
by which they will be the holy nation is a response of obedience to
the law.

Lastly, the teleological claim that the law conforms the people to
the likeness of God is 'one of the slogans of Leviticus', as Gordon
Wenham puts it.[21] There are repeated statements of the imitation
principle, for example:

I am the LORD your God; sanctify yourselves therefore, and be holy,
for I am holy. You shall not defile yourselves with any swarming creature that moves on the earth. For I am the LORD who brought you up
from the land of Egypt, to be your God; you shall be holy, for I am
holy. (11:44–5; cf. 19:2; 20:26; 21:8)

From this it emerges that the law, in its nature, role, and final purpose is intimately related to the being of God himself.

The model of relationship between the law and the divine Judge
which pertains in Scripture is thus crucially different from the
model which has long been the ideal in human legal systems. The
more just of these systems do require that the judge should sever
himself from personal interest in the process of law, that the law
should in this sense be an impersonal formulaic mechanism. Thus
the *Institutes* compiled under Justinian state that the very first care of
a judge 'ought to be, never to judge otherwise than according to the
laws, the constitutions, or customary usage'.[22]

This emphasis on detachment is alien to both the Old and the
New Testaments, where the divine law in its nature, role, and func-
tion is understood in terms of the holy being of God himself. For
God to relate to his creatures by means of the law (and here we think

---

[21] Ibid., p. 180.
[22] *The Institutes of Justinian*, trans. T.C. Sandars (London: Longmans,
Green & Co., 1948), p. 500 (Lib. 4, tit. 17).

more widely than the Old Testament law) is not for him to become subject to an alien code which operates apart from his most intimate nature and concerns. It is for him to relate through a law which takes every aspect of its definition from who he himself is.

At first glance, it might be thought that the personal interest of God in his law must entail injustice as it would for a human judge, since it is rightly observed that a human judge who makes himself the end of his judgements exalts himself beyond his place. The structure of reality, however, vindicates God when he does the same. For God to make himself the end of his judgements is for him to accord to himself the place he truly holds within – or rather over and above – the created order. The sovereignty of God as Creator establishes his claim over the whole of creation, and thus ensures the justice of his judgement when it is exercised in his own interest. Moreover, the perfection of his knowledge and his will ensures that his judgement is flawless. This is not to opt for a variety of naked, unconditioned voluntarism, which says that any action we ascribe to God in any possible world will automatically be just. Rather, it is to say that he will always judge justly, and that judging with his own glory as his goal does not, simply because of that goal, entail injustice.

The relation between punishment and God in Scripture

Law is not the only category relevant to the exposition of penal substitution. Another area relevant and susceptible to the mechanistic criticism is penal substitution's conception of punishment. When God punishes sin, be it on the cross or in the next life, is his penal action impersonal and mechanistic? Is Fiddes describing penal substitution when he makes the following charge? 'Some preaching thus reduces the event of the cross to a factor in an equation, formulated by a divine mathematician; a death is needed to balance the cosmic sum, and a death is provided.'[23]

As with the law, we must investigate the nature of divine punishment in the Scriptures. Both Testaments suggest that God is in fact so personally and intimately involved in the punishment of sin that we cannot speak of that punishment as if it takes place through a

---

[23] Fiddes, *Past Event and Present Salvation*, p. 83.

mechanism apart from the being of God. Many Old Testament passages show that it is in a personal confrontation with God himself that sin is punished. The clearest example is Isaiah 6:5, where the prophet spells out the connection between his destruction and his sinful presence before God: 'Woe is me! I am lost, for I am a man of unclean lips, and I live among a people of unclean lips; yet my eyes have seen the King, the LORD of hosts!'

This explains why in Exodus 3:6 'Moses hid his face, for he was afraid to look at God'; why in 19:21 God tells Moses to 'warn the people not to break through to the LORD to look; otherwise many of them will perish'; why in 33:20 he tells Moses, 'you cannot see my face; for no one shall see me and live'; and why in 1 Kings 19:11–13 Elijah 'wrapped his face in a mantle' when he heard that the Lord would pass by him at Horeb.

Further passages from Isaiah endorse the view that the presence of the Lord is instrumental in the punishment of sin. In 2:10 the people are urged to hide themselves in the rock and in the dust 'from the terror of the LORD, and from the glory of his majesty'. In 2:19 they are told to hide in 'the caves of the rocks and the holes of the ground', and in 2:21 in 'the caverns of the rocks and the clefts in the crags' away 'from the terror of the LORD, from the glory of his majesty, when he rises to terrify the earth'. Similarly, in Jeremiah 4:26 the prophet sees the fruitful land turned into a desert and the cities laid in ruins 'before the LORD, before his fierce anger'.[24]

The desire of God's enemies to hide from his punishing presence is also evidenced in Psalm 66:3, where the psalmist declares to God, 'Because of your great power, your enemies cringe before you.' Finally, the idea recurs in Hosea 10:8, where it is prophesied that the people of the Northern Kingdom 'shall say to the mountains, Cover us, and to the hills, Fall on us'.

---

[24] It is interesting that Charles Quarles uses this material from Isaiah and the other Old Testament texts (together with a range of extra-biblical evidence) to argue that 2 Thes. 1:9 speaks not of exclusion *from* the presence of God but *by* the presence of God, following John Chrysostom, Hugo Grotius and others in taking the *apo* phrase in a causal sense. See 'The 'APO of 2 Thessalonians 1:9 and the Nature of Eternal Punishment', *WTJ* 59.2 (1997), 201–11.

Jesus alludes to this last passage when he uses the judgement God passed on Samaria as a type for the judgement he will pass on Jerusalem. As he is led to Golgotha he turns to address with these words the women who are wailing for him:

Daughters of Jerusalem, do not weep for me, but weep for yourselves and for your children. For the days are surely coming when they will say, 'Blessed are the barren, and the wombs that never bore, and the breasts that never nursed.' Then they will begin to say to the mountains, 'Fall on us'; and to the hills, 'Cover us.' (Lk. 23:28–30)

In the Apocalypse the same language of the divine presence to punish is applied to the final judgement under the heading of the sixth seal:

I looked and there came a great earthquake; the sun became black as sackcloth, the full moon became like blood, and the stars of the sky fell to the earth as the fig tree drops its winter fruit when shaken by a gale. The sky vanished like a scroll rolling itself up, and every mountain and island was removed from its place. Then the kings of the earth and the magnates and the generals and the rich and the powerful, and everyone, slave and free, hid in the caves and among the rocks of the mountains, calling to the mountains and rocks, 'Fall on us and hide us from the face (*apo prosōpou*) of the one seated on the throne and from the wrath of the Lamb; for the great day of their wrath has come, and who is able to stand?' (Rev. 6:12–17)

Here we must speak of the terrible presence of God and the Lamb appearing to judge the world. To the natural mind this is an extraordinary thought, that the very Lamb who was slain so that his blood might wash the robes of those who survive the great ordeal (7:14) should also be the one by whose presence the damned are tormented. This same idea is reiterated in the message of the third angel in 14:9–10:

Those who worship the beast and its image, and receive a mark on their foreheads or on their hands, they will also drink the wine of God's wrath, poured unmixed into the cup of his anger, and they will be tormented with fire and sulphur in the presence of the holy angels (*enōpion angelōn*) and in the presence of the Lamb (*kai enōpion tou arniou*).

By itself this passage might suggest punishment *in* the presence of the Lamb rather than *by* the presence of the Lamb, but the instrumental meaning is suggested by the parallel vision of the Lamb's coming and wrath as the feared means of punishment in 6:12–17.

This biblical description of the act of punishment shows that it is as far as it could be from the idea of a mechanism which is external to the intimate personal involvement of God. The act of punishment entails a holy God directly confronting the sinner. At this juncture questions may arise from what might at first glance appear to be the contradictory idea of punishment – especially the punishment of Hell – as *exclusion* from the presence of God. As early as Genesis 3, which in any biblical theology must be taken as paradigmatic, we find that sin results in exclusion from fellowship with God in the Garden of Eden, later reflected in the exile from the Promised Land and especially away from the temple where God dwells. C.S. Lewis famously noted that such a view is also taught by Jesus in the Gospels as one of his 'three symbols' for Hell, punishment, destruction, and 'privation, exclusion, or banishment'.[25]

The language of exclusion is notably prevalent in the parables when Jesus speaks of the Last Day. In Matthew 7:21–3 he warns that he will declare to some who profess his Lordship and claim to have worked in his name, 'I never knew you; go away from me, you evil-doers' (v. 23). At the end of the parable of the wedding banquet he describes how the man caught without a wedding garment is thrown out of the banquet into 'outer darkness, where there will be weeping and gnashing of teeth' (Mt. 22:13). Similarly, the brides-maids who are unprepared for the arrival of the bridegroom are shut out from the wedding banquet because they are unknown to the Lord (Mt. 25:1–13); the wicked slave who buried his talent in the ground is thrown 'into the outer darkness, where there will be weeping and gnashing of teeth' (25:30); and the accursed in the parable of the sheep and the goats are to 'go away' (the verb is *aperchomai*) into eternal punishment (25:46). Luke records that when Jesus spoke of the heavenly banquet he warned that many

---

[25] *The Problem of Pain* (London: Geoffrey Bles, 1940), pp. 112–13.

would try to enter and would fail, being instead told by the owner of the house, 'I do not know where you have come from; go away from me, all you evildoers!' (Lk. 13:27).

In the light of the fact that Jesus bore the eternal punishment for sins deserved by sinners, his cry of dereliction is also to be read in this sense of abandonment and exclusion: 'My God, my God, why have you forsaken me?' (Mt. 27:46). Lastly, when the Apostle Paul longs for the salvation of the Jewish people, he goes so far as to say that he would be prepared to be 'accursed and cut off from Christ' for their sake (Rom. 9:3).

The first question arising from such teaching asks how this idea of punishment as exclusion *from* the presence of God can fit with the idea of punishment *by* the presence of God. Hence Kendall Harmon, who is concerned to stress the exclusion aspect of punishment, grants that it 'seems difficult to reconcile with Revelation 14:10 which speaks of those who worship the beast being tormented *in the presence of* the saints and the Lamb'.[26] This puzzle is surely best solved if we read the language of exclusion as speaking of exclusion from blessing by God, from loving relationship with him, while taking the language of confrontation to mean that it is the holiness of God which will in the end confront and punish the sinner. Thus, in so far as a loving relationship is concerned, the sinner is excluded, but at the same time he or she is confronted by the holy being of God. In this light the confrontation becomes the very means of the exclusion. It is as sinners are confronted by the holiness of God that, as sinners, they are excluded from the blessing of God.

This argument shows that the language of exclusion must not be taken to imply a view of the torment of the lost which is inherently impersonal with regard to the role of God. We cannot deduce from it the idea that God is removed from any personal relationship with the lost in a mechanistic fashion, as if the damned were punished without God's personal involvement. This may be a tempting path. Indeed, one may reasonably think that some modern constructions of Hell seek to emphasize this aspect principally for apologetic

---

[26] 'The Case Against Conditionalism: A Response to Edward William Fudge', in N.M. de S. Cameron (ed.), *Universalism and the Doctrine of Hell* (Carlisle: Paternoster; Grand Rapids: Baker, 1992), pp. 193–224 (p. 224 n. 70).

reasons. The problem of the justice of judgement does seem to be eased if we can say that it is something that sinners do to themselves apart from the involvement of God, that they close themselves in Hell and hold themselves there. As C.S Lewis puts it, 'the doors of Hell are locked on the *inside*'.[27] In so far as this statement is concerned to stress human responsibility for sin J.I. Packer agrees that it is 'evidently one aspect of the grim truth' since 'no one is in hell who has not chosen to be there'.[28]

Nonetheless, the removal of God from a truly personal involvement in the process of punishment on the basis of exclusion language cannot be maintained. First, the preceding arguments have shown that the exclusion of the sinner is actually by means of personal confrontation with God. Hence it is that at the Day of Judgement all people come before the throne of Christ and the wicked hear the terrible words 'go away' from his lips, and it is in and by the presence of the Lamb that their punishment is inflicted. The responsibility for sin rests with the human individual, but the act of condemnation and the imposition of the sentence is the work of God. In this sense Hell is emphatically locked from the *outside*. Even though the sinner is responsible for his isolation from the blessing of God, that isolation is personally willed and enacted by God himself in Christ.

By way of illustration we may remember that if a subject commits a crime, he may suffer certain natural consequences of his act, but when he is sentenced for it, the society itself – in the person of the judge – becomes responsible for the fixing and enactment of the punishment. Given the biblical picture of the Last Day in juridical terms, such a model of a proportioned sentence imposed *from without* is certainly appropriate (a claim to which I shall return below).

In this fashion Henri Blocher warns against emphasizing the idea that the damned are responsible for their own damnation to the point where God becomes no more than quiescent: 'the biblical picture of the wrathful Lord and Judge of all hardly suggests a mere

---

[27] *The Problem of Pain*, p. 115.

[28] 'The Problem of Eternal Punishment', *Orthos* paper 10 (Disley, UK: Fellowship of Word and Spirit, n.d.), p. 9, also published in *Crux* 26.3 (1990), pp. 18–25.

passive role'.[29] Likewise, K.S. Harmon reverses the argument for God's non-involvement and uses the personal role of God in the process of punishment to refute John Hick's criticism that the Augustinian theodicy has a 'tendency to view God's relationship to the world in subpersonal terms'. Harmon plausibly claims:

> Hick is reacting to the neglect in Western Christian thinking of the idea of God as the personal judge, an example of which would be the lack of reflection on this image of hell as being *personally* banished from Christ by Christ.[30]

Secondly, and in more metaphysical terms, we must understand that so long as God remains the sole Creator and Sustainer of his creation all that takes place within it is immediately kept in being by his own work. Thus Blocher explains that 'orthodoxy has to maintain that the lost, in the final state, still depend *metaphysically* on God, and have in him their being if they are to exist at all'. Behind this claim lies the Christological argument used by Paul in Colossians 1:16–17: 'all things have been created through him and for him. He himself is before all things, and in him all things hold together'.

While there will ultimately be those in the creation whom God does not bless with his love, there is no one and nowhere in creation that can continue without God's involvement. The damned cannot maintain a Hell without the active involvement of God. While God is absent from Hell in the sense that his love is withheld, he cannot be absent in every sense. If he were truly and completely absent in every way then Hell would cease to exist. Hence, even on a view of Hell which emphasizes the ending of any kind of loving relationship between the sinner and God, the punishment remains relational, but the relationship is now one where God continually sustains his own personal condemnation of the sinner. The relationship is one of curse rather than blessing, yet it still entails relationship.

We may thus conclude that those who criticize penal substitution have not taken full measure of significant features in the biblical

---

[29] 'Everlasting Punishment and the Problem of Evil', in Cameron, *Universalism and the Doctrine of Hell*, pp. 283–312 (p. 300).
[30] 'The Case Against Conditionalism', pp. 219–20 n. 64.

understanding of divine law and punishment. Instead, they have attacked penal substitution on the basis that it is bound in a culture that we have left behind and is mathematical or mechanistic. Against this, the close identification of God with the law and with the act of punishment made in Scripture shows that he is thoroughly involved in both, and thus proves that penal substitution, being formed by such categories, is not as a consequence impersonal or mechanistic.

The mechanistic criticism refutes itself

The irony is that it is often the critics of penal substitution themselves who introduce a mechanistic account of punishment. For example, if we endorsed the penology developed by Fiddes in *Past Event and Present Salvation*, then we would have to agree that in speaking of law and punishment the doctrine of the atonement becomes mechanistic. Fiddes affirms the statement that 'Jesus so completely identifies himself with sinful human beings that he shares their experience of standing under God's verdict upon distorted human life'. He is even prepared to grant that 'we may say that he dies under the "wrath" of God'.[31] By such expressions, however, he does not mean to affirm the idea of penal substitution. This he rejects because it describes the wrath of God as 'a judgement inflicted from outside human life' rather than as 'God's consent to the natural consequence of human sin from within'.[32]

Again, Stephen Travis thinks it important to say that Jesus 'was judged in our place', but means by this that 'he entered into and bore on our behalf the destructive consequences of sin. Standing where we stand, he bore the consequences of our alienation from God.'[33] Behind this lies Travis's rejection of what he understands to be retributive punishment, namely punishment '*inflicted from the outside, by someone's voluntary act*' and which '*operates on a less than fully personal level*' and '*deals with externals*'. Instead, he prefers to speak of intrinsic rewards and punishments that 'are not imposed

---

[31] *Past Event and Present Salvation*, p. 91.

[32] Ibid., p. 101.

[33] 'Christ as Bearer of Divine Judgement in Paul's Thought about the Atonement', in J. Goldingay (ed.), *Atonement Today* (London: SPCK, 1995), pp. 21–38 (37).

from outside, but are inherent in the acts to which they are attached, they are not strictly retributive at all'.[34]

Writing both before and after these British authors, Wolfhart Pannenberg similarly separates God from any immediate personal involvement with the moral law active in the process of punishment. He rejects the idea of punishment being the immediate local response of God in judgement, and redefines it as the outworking of sin through the natural process, principally in the death of the sinner. Although the connection of sin with death as its inevitable consequence is held in his earlier work *Jesus – God and Man*, this notion is clearest in his more recent *Systematic Theology*:

> God himself by means of the human judges not only made Jesus to be sin but also had him bear in our place (and not merely in that of his Jewish judges or the whole Jewish people) the penalty that is the proper penalty of sin because it follows from its inner nature, i.e. the penalty of death as the consequence of separation from God.[35]

The important statement here is that death results from the 'inner nature' of sin, rather than as an external sentence imposed by God. This is not to say that Pannenberg any more than Fiddes or Travis entirely divorces death from the wrath of God, since he explicitly states that the death of Jesus 'is rightly described as the vicarious suffering of the wrath of God at sin'.[36] It does, however, mean that, like them, he redefines wrath as the automatic outworking of sin in death.

The common core of the views set out by each of these authors is best understood as a form of moral naturalism in which God has created the world in such a way that sin has its punishment as a natural

---

[34] S. Travis, *Christ and the Judgment of God* (Basingstoke: Marshall Pickering, 1986), pp. 3, 5. It is important to note that the ensuing case against Travis's understanding of retribution undermines his exegetical arguments in *Christ and the Judgment of God* and his paper in *Atonement Today*, since those arguments depend totally on his definition of retribution.

[35] W. Pannenberg, *Systematic Theology*, vol. 2, trans. G.W. Bromiley (Edinburgh: T. & T. Clark, 1994), p. 426. The earlier discussion is in *Jesus – God and Man*, trans. L.L. Wilkins and D.A. Priebe (London: SCM, 1968, repr. 1992), pp. 264ff.

[36] *Systematic Theology*, vol. 2, p. 427.

consequence. This consequence occurs without any judicial act on the part of God after he has made the world and after the sin has been committed. In other words, for sin to receive its punishment, God has to do nothing other than sustain the existence of the world which he has created.

The striking feature of this moral naturalism is that it shows how it is not the proponent of penal substitution who reduces the atonement to a mechanism, but the very opponents like Fiddes and Travis who themselves level that criticism. As we have seen, a biblically conceived doctrine of penal substitution draws God and the processes of law and punishment together, but moral naturalism separates God far from both processes, which take place in a literally automatic fashion without God being involved. This moral naturalism is, when measured on its own terms, the truly mechanistic system, since it explicitly purports to exclude God from the punishment of sin. By embracing it Fiddes, Travis and Pannenberg leave themselves with an impersonal doctrine of the atonement.

Moreover, if moral naturalism succeeds in its aim, it clearly contradicts the teaching of Scripture, in that we have seen how Scripture sets out the personal involvement of God in punishing sin. It is true that there are natural consequences of sin, that sin has negative effects according to the laws of creation, but it is also true that God imposes further punishments on sin from outside the natural nexus.

The various passages discussed above from both Testaments, and from the Lord Jesus himself, suggest that God acts at a level beyond that of natural consequence, that in his holiness he acts to pursue and to confront sinners, and that they are then punished in his presence. Moreover, from the statement that 'it was the will of the LORD to crush him' (Isa. 53:8), which we read together with the expressions *sābal 'āwōn* and *nāśā' ḥēṭ'* (Isa. 53:11–12), the divine involvement in the atonement must be said to be direct, as direct as the imposition of the punishment on Cain, a woman guilty of adultery, or Israel in the exile.

We cannot, however, measure this moral naturalism on its own terms, since it actually fails to achieve its aim of reducing the process of sin and punishment to a natural mechanism. It holds that the relation between sin and punishment arises from the character of the creation God has chosen to make, which means that the relation still stems ultimately from the will of God himself. That is to say, God has decided to make the world in such a way that sin will lead naturally to punishment, so that this conception relies as much as any other on a decision, an external imposition or judgement, made by God. The only difference is that moral naturalism locates the act of judgement earlier in the divine economy, at the beginning of creation rather than at the Last Day, but proximity in time is no measure of the involvement of a lawgiver in punishment, particularly if all times are alike present to that lawgiver.

Moreover, as we saw above with the argument concerning Hell, the natural process depends on the immediate sustaining work of God for its continuance, so that he is not only its Creator but also the one who gives it its present effect. We cannot say that God established the law and left people to their own devices. It remains his law, and he is the one who sustains its outworking from moment to moment. Consequently, locating the relationship between sin and its punishment in the moral order of creation cannot be thought to exclude God from the process of punishment to the extent that he no longer needs to be personally reconciled in the atonement. Further, given that the being of God is not remote from the process of punishment, any satisfaction that takes the place of that punishment will have to take the form of directly reconciling God himself.

It emerges that moral naturalism is caught on one of two prongs. If it fails to reduce the process of punishment to a merely natural sequence, then it simply moves the moment of the imposition of the punishment to the time of creation. Yet if it succeeds in such a reduction, then it also reduces the atonement to a mechanism of natural consequences rather than an act of personal reconciliation.

Conclusion

It is the teaching of the Scriptures, shown sufficiently by a single but long strand of evidence, that Jesus did bear the punishment for sin, that in bearing it he made atonement, and that he bore it from the hand of God himself. Penal substitution is consonant with the language of reconciliation used elsewhere in Scripture. It does not entail a mechanistic view of the atonement, because in bearing the punishment of sin on the cross, the divine Word as a man endured the consequences of the personal confrontation between God and sinful men and women. This punishment involved the very being of God himself, since it was punishment on the basis of his holy law executed by the presence of his holy being, the punishment of exclusion from the relationship of love with God expressed by Jesus in his cry of dereliction, 'My God, my God, why have you forsaken me?' (Mt. 27:46).

So it was that the one who will himself be the acting subject in the Last Judgement became its object in the place of sinners. But as he stood in their place he exhausted the punishment due to them, and the presence of God to Jesus turned from curse to blessing. As the human life of Jesus was spent on the cross, so he rested in the grave only to be raised again under the blessing of God. Throughout, the Trinitarian God had been there, personally involved in the work of atonement, both as the Judge pouring out his cup of wrath, and in the one judged drinking that same cup. Here indeed is the glorious hope of our salvation which we must proclaim, that the punishment that brought us peace was upon God himself in his incarnate Son.

Questions for Further Study

1.   How would you answer someone who said that penal substitution entails a mechanistic view of the atonement?
2.   How would you relate penal substitution to the biblical language of reconciliation and the parable of the Prodigal Son?
3.   How does God relate to the moral law?
4.   How should we describe the process by which God punishes sin?
5.   How might the arguments of this chapter affect your preaching of the cross?

Select Bibliography

There are no sustained treatments of the specific issues dealt with in this chapter which affirm penal substitution, but on related issues the following are well worth considering.

On Isaiah 52–3

J.N. Oswalt, *Isaiah 40–66* (Grand Rapids: Eerdmans, 1998), pp. 373–410

On the death of Jesus as propitiating the wrath of God

L. Morris, *The Apostolic Preaching of the Cross* (Grand Rapids: Eerdman, 1992³), pp. 144–213

On the nature of the punishment for sin

H. Blocher, 'Everlasting Punishment and the Problem of Evil', in N.M. de S. Cameron (ed.), *Universalism and the Doctrine of Hell* (Carlisle: Paternoster; Grand Rapids: Baker, 1992), pp. 283–312

Harmon, K.S., 'The Case Against Conditionalism: A Response to Edward William Fudge', in Cameron, *Universalism and the Doctrine of Hell*, pp. 193–224

Packer, J.I., 'The Problem of Eternal Punishment', *Orthos* paper 10 (Disley, UK: Fellowship of Word and Spirit, n.d.), also published in *Crux* 26.3 (1990)

Quarles, C.L., 'The 'APO of 2 Thessalonians 1:9 and the Nature of Eternal Punishment', *WTJ* 59.2 (1997), pp. 201–11

4

The Cross, Creation and the Human Predicament

Michael Ovey

[T]he whole economy of salvation regarding man came to pass . . . in order that God might not be conquered, nor His wisdom lessened . . .[1]

Introduction: the Question of Sin

In September 1995 I stood looking at some documents in a museum. The museum was in the World War II death camp at Majdanek, on the outskirts of the city of Lublin, Poland. The documents showed reputable engineering firms from central Europe bidding to build the crematoria for the camp, crematoria whose design specifications were to be able to cope with hundreds of bodies per day. It confirmed the way that ordinary people were not simply aware of, nor indeed complicit, but actually involved in the Holocaust.[2] Repetition is apt: ordinary, professional people, with good qualifications.

It is almost *de rigueur* to say that our doctrine of God must be thought through in the light of the Holocaust, summed up in the phrase that all theology is post-Holocaust. Yet those engineering

---

[1] Irenaeus, *Against Heresies* (c. 185) (ET *Ante-Nicene Fathers*, vol. 1, ed. A. Roberts and J. Donaldson, rev. A. Cleveland Coxe 1867 [Grand Rapids: Eerdmans, repr. 1973]), 3.23.1.

[2] For further details of the building of Majdanek see J. Marzalek, *Majdanek: The Concentration Camp in Lublin* (Warsaw: Interpress, 1986), pp. 25–36.

tenders show that our doctrine of humanity equally needs to be post-Holocaust: those appalling events were not the exclusive preserve of the freak or the psychopath, but involved ordinary people.[3] The misgivings this prompts are confirmed by so much else in the history of the nineteenth and twentieth centuries: the ordinary Party officials who implemented Stalin's plans for the Ukraine in the 1930s, resulting in millions starving to death;[4] the civilized nations of former Yugoslavia involved in an ethnic bloodbath; some of our fellow Christians apparently deeply implicated in mass slaughter in Rwanda; and, lest we indulge in ethnocentric smugness, our own national history stained with ethnic cleansing in the settlement of Tasmania and the death of non-combatants in the bleak concentration camps of the Boer War. The conundrum these crimes present is not just about the goodness of God; it relates to the sinfulness of humanity.

To its credit, postmodernism in some of its darker moods starts to face something like this. Michel Foucault memorably observed that we should think of the relationship between the individual and the state as one of war, sometimes overt, sometimes covert.[5] Similarly, relations between social classes, and possibly relations between individuals too, are ultimately those of war.[6] The analysis is all the more sobering with war's connotations of brutality and ruthlessness and, notably, deception.[7] Such observations ought to make the question of human sinfulness central to our thinking, because it is so central to our lives. Hence a theology, let alone a theology of the cross, that fails to recognize this seems existentially irrelevant.

---

[3] Detailed by, among others, M. Gilbert, *The Holocaust: The Jewish Tragedy* (London: Guild, 1986).

[4] For Stalin's 'dekulakization' programme see R. Conquest, *The Harvest of Sorrow* (London: Hutchinson, 1986).

[5] E.g. M. Foucault, 'Two Lectures', in C. Gordon (ed.), *Power/Knowledge* (New York: Pantheon, 1980), pp. 78–108 (90).

[6] M. Foucault, 'Truth and Power', in Gordon, *Power/Knowledge*, pp. 109–33 (123). The explicit debt is to Nietzsche (see *Power/Knowledge*, p. 133), for Foucault has glossed Nietzsche's ideas of the centrality of power in terms of war: 'isn't power simply a form of warlike domination?' (*Power/Knowledge*, p. 123).

[7] The objectivity of truth is a notorious casualty here (*Power/Knowledge*, p. 133).

The claim of the Bible, of course, is that the salvation Jesus brings deals precisely with sin (e.g. Heb. 9:26; Jn. 1:29). This at once highlights the importance, biblically speaking, of analysing sin. In understanding sin we grasp more clearly both the nature of the salvation Jesus brings, and what that salvation must involve. This in turn makes us see that weighing up a particular view of salvation involves examining what account of sin that view deals with. A false view of sin may all too readily leave us with a false view of salvation. For, as the old adage has it, the nature of the disease determines the nature of the remedy. It is for these reasons that this chapter focuses so largely on the question of sin, which is central, both existentially and biblically.

It is also necessary, however, to say something about the overall debate to which this chapter contributes. The purpose of this book is to reassert the necessity of penal substitution. Naturally, penal substitution can be formulated in a number of ways, but for present purposes I adopt Packer's summary:

> [T]hat Jesus Christ our Lord, moved by a love that was determined to do everything necessary to save us, endured and exhausted the destructive divine judgement for which we were otherwise inescapably destined, and so won us forgiveness, adoption and glory.[8]

Such statements of Christ's work have come under attack for several reasons, some of which merit rehearsal here. Thus it is said that penal substitution is

1. *textually unfounded.* If true, this is a formidable criticism indeed. It is voiced for several reasons. It has been said that sin has no penalty; that the Bible does not deal with substitution; and that, while sin may have a penalty and there may be substitution within the pages of Scripture, the two ideas are not combined together to form the compound notion of penal substitution.
2. *mechanical.* It is argued that penal substitution offers a mechanistic or 'mathematical' model of relations between

---

[8] J.I. Packer, *Celebrating the Saving Work of God* (Carlisle: Paternoster, 1998), p. 105.

humanity and God, which is essentially impersonal. However, the biblical model of divine–human relations is personal, and, as it is those relations that need to be restored,
penal substitution offers an inappropriate model for
achieving this.

3. *immoral.* The point here is that if penal substitution were
    indeed in an absolute sense immoral, then God could
    not countenance it, for he is altogether righteous. Vari-
    ous immoralities have been suggested. Thus some
    would say it is simply barbaric for the Son to be substi-
    tuted, as in the Primate of Australia's recent comment
    that penal substitution is morally repugnant.[9] Here,
    however, I focus on a moral objection that can be put
    like this: penal substitution denies the principle that
    people are responsible for their actions. That principle
    requires that a person must bear the consequences of her
    or his actions, for better or worse. This means no person
    can be either condemned or acquitted for another's ac-
    tions, for there can be no transfer of positive merit or de-
    merit between persons. Passages like Ezekiel 18:20 are
    said to mandate it: 'The person who sins shall die . . . the
    righteousness of the righteous shall be his own, and the
    wickedness of the wicked shall be his own.' This argu-
    ment is of especial importance and I shall refer to it as the
    'no transfer of merit' argument.

4. *redundant.* This is asserted on the following basis. God's
    plan for his fallen creation is to renew or restore it, which is
    secured for us by our being in Christ and being raised with
    him in his resurrection life (Rom. 6 is sometimes cited in
    this connection). This argument focuses, then, on God's
    overall goal, a new heaven and a new earth, and asks how
    an atonement theory contributes to this. It recognizes the
    New Testament's language of participation by its stress on
    being 'in Christ' and suggests God's goal is met fully
    through our dying and rising with Christ. We have the

---

[9] In *Anglican Messenger*, July and November 1991, he argued that such a
theory produces an image of God 'of a morally repugnant kind, whose
Son becomes the hapless victim of his Father's righteous anger'.

new life of the new age in him.[10] Those who take this line argue that penal substitution does not contribute to the goal because the forensic category of penalty does not entail the kind of re-creation envisaged. Penalty aims simply at restoring the *status quo ante*, which does not extend as far as the new, better, re-created world. On this view penal substitution is redundant because what it demands is met, and more, by the logic of re-creation. Moreover, far from having an overzealous view of sin, penal substitution does not treat sin seriously enough. This significant argument is currently associated with Vernon White, who writes that 'a recreative logic actually does more justice, not less, to the wrath of God'.[11] I shall call this argument the 'exclusive re-creation' argument, because it stresses the goal of re-creation and its account of re-creation excludes penal substitution.

David Peterson and Garry Williams engage with the first two views in preceding chapters. Of course, justifying a biblically warranted view of the penal substitutionary death of Jesus is itself decisive. Yet it is still useful to examine the 'no transfer of merit' and 'exclusive re-creation' arguments since, if they are found plausible, that tends to render those exegetical answers to the first objection above (i.e. *textually unfounded*) less plausible. So in this chapter I shall examine the 'no transfer of merit' and 'exclusive re-creation' arguments, and conclude that the renewal of creation is not merely consistent with penal substitution, but actually requires it.

---

[10] These views are traced back notably to Irenaeus of Lyons. G. Aulén, *Christus Victor: An Historical Study of the Three Main Types of the Idea of the Atonement* (ET London: SPCK, 1953), argues that the classic or dramatic view of theologians like Irenaeus was displaced by 'Latin' views of the Atonement.

[11] V. White, *Atonement and Incarnation* (Cambridge: CUP, 1991), p. 102. Similar arguments appear in T. Smail, 'Can One Man Die For the People?', in J. Goldingay (ed.), *Atonement Today* (London: SPCK, 1995), pp. 73–92 (what is fulfilled and renewed in Smail's view is 'the covenant that we had broken', p. 87), and D. Atkinson, 'What Difference Does the Cross Make to Life?', in Goldingay, *Atonement Today*, pp. 253–71 (note p. 258).

Redemption as Re-creating Creation

One of the great strengths of the 'exclusive re-creation' argument lies in its stress on restoration. This usefully takes us back to biblical terms. It also helps to minimize an atomistic reading of texts on redemption because it attempts to take in the whole sweep of salvation history in biblical-theological concepts. After all, the Bible uses re-creation language (among other terms) to describe what salvation achieves in at least two important ways.

First, re-creation, or new creation, language is used of individual conversion. In 2 Corinthians 4:6, God's illuminating work of conversion is paralleled with his original creational command of Genesis 1:3 that there be light. In 2 Corinthians 5:17, the woman or man who comes to faith in Christ is a new creation.

Secondly, re-creational language is also applied to the cosmos itself at the fulfilment of all things. Thus Revelation 21 talks of a new heaven and a new earth, while the terms of Revelation 22:1–5 are those of a new Eden, in which the curse is conspicuous by its absence (v. 3). Even more remarkably, perhaps, human salvation is linked to a perfected and fulfilled cosmos in Romans 8:19–23. Behind this stands God's plan for the whole cosmos (Eph. 1:10ff. and Col. 1:15–20).

Now this emphasis of redemption as re-creation is thoroughly coherent *theologically*. It is worth seeing why. A basic principle is that God acts in all things for his glory, whether in creation, judgement or salvation. This is startlingly evident in certain statements about why God saves. It is for his glory and his name's sake (e.g. Pss. 79:9; 85:9; Isa. 43:7, 25; 48:9, 11; and Ezek. 20:9, 14) . This is also true in acts of judgement (e.g. Exod. 14:4, 17; Ezek. 28:22). As for the act of creating, it is clear that this was not out of need (Acts 17:25), but is something also linked with his glory. Thus in Psalm 19:1, the heavens tell of God's glory, while the song of Revelation 4:11 glorifies God because he has created all things.

Yet God's glory would be marred if he did not achieve his purposes, whether through inability or malice. This principle can be seen at work in incidents such as the golden calf. In Exodus 32:11–14 Moses' appeal touches on God maintaining his original promises of blessing under the Abrahamic covenant, rather than seeming to have an 'evil intent' (v. 12). Moses also comments later on the same incident in Deuteronomy 9:28, where he points out that if God does not bring his people into the Promised Land this raises the question of God's ability to keep those promises (cf. Ps. 115:1–2). Quite understandably then, achieving his purposes in creating pertains closely to God's glory. To this extent, salvation could well be described as ensuring God's creation purposes are after all fulfilled, to vindicate his glory and wisdom. Salvation may well be more than that, but it is at least that. If God did not achieve his creative purposes, it would look as though the creation project was beyond him. One is reminded of a graffiti riposte to Nietzsche's slogan that God is dead: 'God is not dead, but alive and well – although working on a much less ambitious project.'

However, this carries very important implications for our understanding of sin. If, first, salvation is to 'solve' the problem of sin, and if, secondly, salvation concerns the restoring of creation, that in turn suggests that sin 'de-creates' creation. This requires testing.

Sin and 'De-creation'

Sin no doubt has many facets – the sheer range of biblical terms to describe it testifies to this. Certainly the essence of sin has been put in a number of ways: pride; self-centredness, in the sense of regarding oneself and not God as the central locus for judgement and importance in the universe; rebellion, which is strongly flagged in many evangelistic presentations of the gospel; alternatively, gluttony and excess. Naturally, many of these suggestions take their cue from Genesis 3, and rightly so. For as far as human beings are concerned this is the first sin, the original sin in that sense. Furthermore, it is treated as having the most tremendous significance by Paul in Romans 5:12–21 in terms of its introduction of death to humanity. Jesus, too, seems in John 8:39–47 to treat Genesis 3 as archetypal. A consideration of Genesis 3 is therefore appropriate to see whether it suggests that sin 'de-creates' creation.

Genesis 3

Context
In terms of context, it is obvious, but important to note that the narrative of Genesis 1 and 2 focuses the reader on God rather than

humanity. Adam emerges as a centre of attention in the latter half of chapter 2. But primarily the actor in chapters 1 and 2 is God. God is seen, first, as a God whose word is effective. He speaks and it happens accordingly: 'it was so'.[12] Secondly, since his word is utterly effective, his word is truthful, in that it corresponds with reality, or more accurately reality corresponds with it.

Nevertheless, it must be added that, although God's word has emerged as utterly truthful and effective, there is one statement that has not yet received obvious fulfilment at the end of chapter 2. That statement, in 2:17, sets out the consequence of taking the fruit of the tree of knowledge. This consequence or sanction is unfulfilled because the condition that brings it into effect, the taking of the fruit, has not yet occurred. But this condition and sanction are set in a sea of statements where God speaks, and it is so. The narrative, therefore, leads the reader to expect strongly that the sanction of Genesis 2:17 will be fulfilled when the condition is met. It is an ordinance of the creator God.

As well as a God whose word is effective and truthful, he appears as a God who is good. For the cosmos he creates is both good (Gen. 1:10, 18, 21, 25, 31; v. 31 describes creation as 'very good'), and he is seen as a God who blesses (Gen. 1:22, 28; 2:3). That activity of blessing points to a fundamental benevolence towards that which he creates. Further, God is the creator of all, a fact brought out by the holistic pairings in creation language: heaven and earth; sea and dry land; day and night; height and depths. This thought of God as creator of all is developed elsewhere in terms of his lordship of all. He rules all because he made all. The relation between making and ruling is sometimes explained in terms of ownership. The universe belongs to God, since he made it. What is more, since the universe belongs to God, he rules it. The motif of ownership and belonging, based on creating, is present in passages such as Psalm 24:1–2 (see too, e.g., Pss. 89:5–14, esp. vv. 11–12; 95:3–5), and strongly evident in images such as God being the potter in Isaiah 45:9. To this extent, the biblical account of creation sets forth a Creator who is lord of all and legitimately so.

---

[12] Gen. 1:3, 6–7, 9, 11, 15, 20–1, 24, 26–7, and 30 either contain the formula 'it was so' or show things happening according to God's word.

However, that legitimate lordship establishes an ordered creation in which God is king of his universe, with humanity exercising
dominion under him and over the rest of creation. Crucially, we
must note that this order, far from being inherently exploitative, is
described as good, for God is benevolent.

The contribution of Genesis 3

Many commentators note the subtlety and deceptiveness of the serpent's approach in verses 1 and 4. First, he implies, or, more accurately, induces, a disbelief in those characteristics that the narrative
of Genesis 1 and 2 have been at such pains to outline. After all, he
implies that God's word of Genesis 2:17 will not be fulfilled. In doing so, he suggests that God's word is not effective and therefore not
truthful. Moreover, the tone of verse 5 is that God is oppressing
Adam and Eve by keeping them below the station to which they
could ascend, which in turn hints that the prohibition of Genesis
2:17 is self-interested, sprung from a fear of rivals. This, of course,
would mean that God is not benevolent towards the creatures he
has made.

There is, then, substantial disbelief behind the disobedient actions of verse 6. The serpent has induced disobedience to the one
who, on the basis of the creative work reported in chapters 1 and 2,
has the right to obedience. The sovereign ruler and owner of the
cosmos is defied by his human creatures, and this under the influence of one who should properly have been governed by those human creatures after the mandate of Genesis 1:28. Gordon Wenham
rightly points out that the order of relationships has been reversed,
and the created order of Genesis 1 and 2 is inverted.[13]

Sin considered after Genesis 3

This brings out a crucial point. Sin is shown to be profoundly
anti-creational. This disbelieving disobedience is a de-creating act,
because it picks away at and undoes the network of relationships
that God created. This, of course, helps to explain why dealing with
sin amounts to a re-creation, a fulfilling of creation's purpose.

Calvin sums matters up in this way:

---

[13] G.J. Wenham, *Genesis 1–15*, WBC 1 (Waco: Word, 1987), p. 75.

Yet it is at the same time to be noted that the first man revolted from God's authority, not only because of Satan's blandishments, but also because, contemptuous of truth, he turned aside to falsehood. And surely, once we hold God's word in contempt, we shake off all reverence for him. For, unless we listen attentively to him, his majesty will not dwell among us, nor his worship remain perfect. Unfaithfulness, then, was at the root of the Fall . . . Yet it was not simple apostasy, but was joined with vile reproaches against God. These assented to Satan's slanders, which accused God of falsehood and envy and ill will. Lastly, faithlessness opened the door to ambition, and ambition was indeed the mother of obstinate disobedience; as a result, men, having cast off the fear of God, threw themselves wherever lust carried them.[14]

Calvin here underlines three vital points. First, the appropriate attitude of the creature to the Creator has vanished ('we shake off all reverence for him' etc.). There is indeed an undoing of creational relationships.

Secondly, sin is not just rebellion. Instead, it has a belief dimension and involves what one thinks about a person. That belief dimension in turn has two aspects. On the one hand it involves a *disbelief* in the truth about a person, that is to say a denial of who that person really is. On the other hand it involves *belief*, but belief in falsehood about that person. Francis Turretin, Calvin's seventeenth-century successor at Geneva, catches this latter aspect in a brilliant phrase. He speaks of Adam 'engendering a *false faith* from [Satan's] lies'.[15] What this highlights so strikingly is that the distinction is not simply between those who have faith and those have not. Rather it is between those who have true faith and those who have false faith. Further, the truth or falsehood of the faith turns not on whether the person who has faith is sincere or not, but on whether the belief that person holds is true to the reality of the person of whom he or she believes it.[16] There is, after all, little to show that Adam and Eve were insincere.

---

[14] J. Calvin, *Institutes of the Christian Religion* (1559) trans. F.L. Battles (Philadelphia: Westminster, 1960), 2.1.4.

[15] F. Turretin, *Institutes of Elenctic Theology* (1688–90) trans. G.M. Giger and ed. J.T. Dennison (Phillipsburg: P. & R., 1992), Topic 9 Q. 6 IX.

[16] See Article 18 of the 39 Articles for a similar point.

The third point arising from Calvin, though, is that sin is not simply disbelief in the sense of chancing to think the wrong things or making a straightforward intellectual error. Genesis 1–3 shows that this false faith is ethically unjustified, both because it treats God as bad when he is shown to be good, and because God is treated as not having legitimate sovereignty when the process of creation shows that he does have such sovereignty, as Adam well knows.

At this point a strong nexus between New Testament and Old Testament emerges on the subject of sin. Genesis 3 gives us a picture of a disbelieving disobedience against God. The New Testament also sees sin in relation to questions of belief, specifically belief about Jesus. John's Gospel and letters focus on belief as believing that Jesus is the Son whom God has sent into the world. Thus John 3:36 states, 'Whoever believes in the Son has eternal life; whoever disobeys the Son will not see life, but must endure God's wrath' (NRSV). Here the positive, eternal life, rests on belief (*pisteuō*), in Jesus as who he truly is (v. 36a). The converse case appears in verse 36b. There is, though, an interesting variation of phrasing. The most obvious opposite of 'believe' is 'not believe'. But the contrasting verb used is not 'disbelieve', but 'disobey' (*apeitheō*). That nuances the contrast with belief, so that disbelief in Jesus is seen in disobedience terms: disbelief is not merely a mistake, a descent into error; rather, it is ethically unjustified and wrong. Moreover, this disobedience is not merely to the Son incarnate: it is disobedience to the Father who sent him, for it is the will of the Father that people believe in Jesus in this way (Jn. 6:29), and that Jesus be honoured as the Son (Jn. 5:22–3).

Nor is Johannine theology unique here. A similar strand is found within the Pauline corpus in 2 Thessalonians 1:6–10. This depicts the requital awaiting those who persecute God's people. Part of the criterion of judgement (vv. 8–9) is that of disobeying the gospel of Jesus. Here again the focus is on Christ, and the way his gospel calls humanity to belief as a matter of obedience. The divine reaction to such disbelief is punishment (Gk. *dikēn tisousin*).

Naturally, this Christological focus for belief and disbelief is quite consistent with what emerges from Genesis 3. For in Genesis 3 the truth of God's word is challenged. Jesus' case is parallel. For he is the creative Word (Jn. 1:1–3), yet the world sees him as untruthful. For example, in John 5:18 his claims to be God's Son are treated as blasphemy, while in John 7:12 some say he is a false teacher. In Genesis 3 God's word is seen as ineffective. In the New Testament Jesus is similarly seen as ineffective: as Son he claims to have life within him (Jn. 5:26) and to be one who will rise from the dead (Jn. 2:19). Yet the tone of mockery at the crucifixion (e.g. Mt. 27:39–44) shows a dismissal of Jesus' words as ineffective. Further, in Genesis 3, God's goodness is implicitly denied, while in the New Testament Jesus is seen as morally wrong.[17] Finally, of course, in Genesis 3, God's rightful claims are defied, while in Jesus humanity crucifies its king ('Pilate asked them, "Shall I crucify your King?" The chief priests answered, "We have no king but the emperor" ', Jn. 19:15).[18]

This correspondence between Old Testament and New Testament can roughly be tabulated:

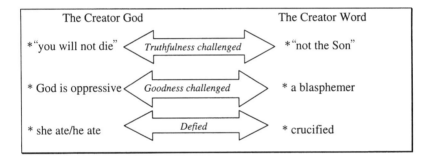

Sin's consequences: the frustration of creation

So far we have seen sin as involving a de-creation of creation by its inversion of creational relationships. We move now to the consequences for sin which God establishes in Genesis 3:14–24. A common thread here is the way these consequences are inimical to his original creation purposes. Indeed, they tend to frustrate them. In this way, 'de-creation' again enters the scene. This is signalled in a

---

[17] Strikingly, in Jn. 9:24, where this is the starting point, so to speak, for the reaction of the 'Jews' to the sabbath healing of the man born blind.

[18] Treating the chief priests as in some sense a representative corporate character. This is indicated by the summary statement of Jn. 1:10–11, where the events of the incarnation are treated as global rejection, rather than limited as merely that of Caiaphas and his associates.

number of ways. First, and most obviously, the God who has been so given to blessing in Genesis 1–2 now curses (Gen. 3:14, 17). Secondly, in Genesis 1 and 2, the multiplication of humanity was a joyful feature of the created order, but in Genesis 3:16 it is associated with pain. Thirdly, the co-operative relationship of Genesis 2:18 between man and woman has the shadow of conflict over it in Genesis 3:16b.[19] Fourthly, the relationship between the man taken from the earth and the earth that he tills is also altered. For the man now has to wrest his living from a grudging soil that perversely provides what he does not want (3:17–19). Fifthly, Genesis 3:19 brings us to death. It is worth noting, as one considers this whole sequence, that God actively imposes these dire consequences. These consequences of Adam's sin are not worked out mechanistically or impersonally but with God's direct intervention against Adam's sin. This is just the point that Garry Williams's chapter develops. Also, given this active intervention by God, it is extremely difficult not to see Genesis 3:14–19 as something like a judicial sentence.

The question of death is deeply significant. Death is first raised as an issue by Genesis 2:17 and the consequence of taking the fruit. Two questions arise:

- Is 'death' here more than physical death?
- Is 'death' a penalty?

Is 'death' more than physical death?

This is a highly important question. If the 'death' of Genesis 2:17 is only physical death, then it is obvious that Jesus has not delivered believers from it, and that the writers of the New Testament were well aware of this (e.g. 1 Thes. 4:13–18). It would mean that whatever Jesus saves from, it is not the consequence set out for the archetypal sin of Genesis 1–3. If physical death alone is at stake in Genesis 2:17, then while we can say that Jesus shares it, we cannot say his experience of it releases us from it, whether by penal or any other form of substitution. One can add here that a salvation that only dealt

---

[19] This seems to be so whether the desire of the woman in 3:16b is sexual or for control. The close parallel of Gen. 4:7 suggests the desire may be that for mastery. Wenham, *Genesis 1–15*, pp. 81–2, is cautious.

with deliverance from physical death, whether by resurrection or otherwise, also leaves unsolved questions such as the conquest of evil and the restoration of right relationships. This, of course, does not correspond with the view of the new creation in Revelation 22, where there is nothing accursed (v. 3).

Genesis 2:17 is eventually fulfilled at the straightforward level of the physical (5:5 specifically points out that Adam does die), but not immediately. At this purely physical level, the serpent's words have a ring of truth – 'you will not die' (Gen. 3:4). For Wenham, this suggests that the reader is being invited to look deeper at the notion of dying to see if more than the physical is at stake.[20] Contextually, it must be noted that the judgement of chapter 3 issues not just in physical death, but exclusion from the Garden.[21] Indeed, from the point of view of the narrative of Genesis 3, exclusion is strongly emphasized.

It is worth pondering the significance of exclusion. Within the terms of Genesis 1–3, Vos observes that life in the Garden was life in what might be called the loving presence of God.[22] Part of the horror of exclusion is being excluded from the place where Adam and Eve have enjoyed that loving presence. In a similar vein, Wenham cites Leviticus 13:45–6, where exclusion from the camp is again exclusion from the arena of God's fruitful presence and is associated with death.[23] Significantly, exclusion from the Promised Land is part of the covenant curse material of Deuteronomy 28:15ff., and the events of the exile are seen in terms of death in Ezekiel 37. Israel says, 'Our bones are dried up . . .' (v. 11), in the circumstances a strong image of death. Yet, of course, the exiles are physically alive, but in Babylon. God's response in verse 12 is to promise new life through his Spirit. In the New Testament, Paul comments that the wages of sin are death (Rom. 6:23), but the context shows that more than physical death alone is involved. 'Death' here is the opposite of 'eternal life'. Lastly, exclusion from

---

[20] Ibid., pp. 88–91.

[21] Cf. G. Vos, *Biblical Theology: Old and New Testaments* (Edinburgh: Banner of Truth, 1975), p. 40.

[22] *Biblical Theology*, pp. 37 ('fellowship with God') and 40 ('life consisted in communion with God').

[23] *Genesis 1–15*, p. 90.

God's loving presence[24] after judgement is put in terms of a second death in Revelation 2:11; 20:6, 14; and 21:8.

Conversely, 'life' in biblical terms may well include more than simply physical life. In the Old Testament this arises in various ways. Psalm 16:11 associates the path of life with the joy-giving presence of God, and this is perhaps all the more striking given the application of this psalm to Jesus in the New Testament (Peter applies Ps. 16:8–11 to Jesus in Acts 2:25–8). The psalm cannot be talking about the preservation of physical life *alone*, for Jesus endures physical death, even though he is not held by it. In Psalm 119, the psalmist longs for the life that comes through joyful obedience to the Law and the promises of God (e.g. vv. 37, 50, 93). This again points to something more than the physical life he already has. In the Wisdom literature, the way of Wisdom is a way that leads to life (Prov. 8:35) and although this does relate to physical preservation,[25] it also relates to a happiness of life with God's favour (8:34–6).

The New Testament similarly does not restrict 'life' simply to the physical. Jesus himself plays on the difference between full life and simply physical life in various sayings (e.g. Mt. 10:39). These depend for their effect on the point that life is more than preservation of biological life. Further, in Jesus' scale of values physical life is less important than spiritual life. This emerges in Matthew 10:28, as he says that those who bring physical death are less to be feared than the one who can cast into hell. Importantly, eternal life is described in relational terms in John 17:3. It is life when one 'knows' the Father and the Son.

Extended meanings of life and death are brought together in Ephesians, where the state of those who are not Christians is put in terms of those who are 'dead' (2:1), and this is a death that is not physical, but spiritual, dead in sins. Becoming a Christian means being made alive by God (2:5). Within Ephesians this new life is one with Christ, and one in which we are reconciled to God (2:16), and no longer strangers and aliens (2:19). This underlines the

---

[24] The emphasis here is on the loss of loving relationship, rather than any notion of geographical separation, developed by Garry Williams in chapter three of this volume.

[25] The adulteress of Prov. 6 seems to lead to a real physical peril (vv. 33–5).

observation that Old Testament and New Testament alike do not simply restrict life and death to the biological.

Physical death and exclusion from God's loving presence are 'de-creational' as they are not a feature of the creation order established by Genesis 1–2. However, the 'de-creational' aspects of Genesis 3:17ff. should not be overstressed. God has not, for instance, removed himself from his world entirely, but remains active within it, sustaining it through his Son (Heb. 1:3), maintaining humanity in its dominion status (Gen. 9:1–7), and remaining sovereign over its history (Dan. 2:20ff.). Having said that, the exclusion and curse of Genesis 3 show a creation at odds with the order its Creator originally established.

Given this, a fuller meaning for 'death' in Genesis 2:17 is to be preferred, a meaning including but going beyond the purely physical. The context prompts us to look deeper, and the logic of salvation history leads us to see the real death Jesus delivers us from as 'the second death' of Revelation, the 'death' of being judged to exclusion from God's loving presence. Such an interpretation of the biblical theological value of 'death' has, of course, been present since the early Fathers.[26]

Is 'death' a penalty?

We now move to the second question, whether Genesis 2:17 stipulates a penalty. This acquires particular importance after the conclusion that the death of Genesis 2:17 goes beyond the purely physical. For, if Genesis 2:17 entails 'second death' as well as physical death, and if it is a punishment, then a complete doctrine of salvation must have an answer to this punishment, or else humans are left to bear the punishment themselves.

The terms 'penalty', 'punishment', 'retribution' or their cognates are not, of course, found here. This is not a decisive argument, however, against seeing the prohibition as stipulating a punishment. For, as already observed, exclusion from God's loving presence is seen in express penalty terms in 2 Thessalonians 1:8–9. In addition, Ezra confesses of the conquest and exile explicitly that 'you, our

---

[26] E.g. Irenaeus, *Against Heresies* 2.33.5. and 5.27.2. Cf. Origen, *Dialogue with Heraclides* 168–72. So too, later, Augustine, *City of God* 13, esp. 2, 12; 19.28.

God, have punished us less than our iniquities deserved' (Ezra 9:13). The statement is significant on three counts. First, the use of punishment language. Secondly, the link here between punishment and a notion of moral desert ('less than [we] *deserved*').[27] Thirdly, in biblical-theological terms the exile is a counterpart of the exclusion from Eden.

One may ask, finally, if Genesis 2:17 and its implementation is not penal, what is it? Conventionally, questions one may ask of a sanction attached to a command or prohibition would run like this: is it deterrent, or rehabilitative, or protective, or penal/retributive? Naturally, a particular sanction may involve more than one of these elements. Now in this case the particular sanction as envisaged in its full form by 2 Thessalonians 1:8–9 is scarcely rehabilitative, for eternal exclusion is in view, which eliminates any prospect for rehabilitation. The Bible does not envisage a parole board in hell.[28] Nor, again, is it simply protective, for it goes beyond what is needed for simple protection of others. Nor does it easily fit primarily as a deterrent, for conventional deterrence depends on a basic rationality in decision-making. We decide to alter our conduct on the basis of the threat of sanctions. However, as Paul reminds us in Romans 5:12–21, Adam's sin is engulfing in its effects, including the decision-making faculties,[29] and this seems to weaken the basis on which deterrence could operate. If Adam's fall does indeed leave any given human being as a child of wrath, inclined to sin, then the deterrent value of Genesis 2:17 has long since withered. It is true that Genesis 2:17 may invoke dread, but seems unable to induce humans always to keep God's law. Penalty, however, fits the terms of Genesis 2:17 and the subsequent judgement section of Genesis 3 like a glove.

It is vital to grasp the significance of seeing Genesis 2:17 as involving a penalty that includes, but goes beyond, physical death. White traces penal views back to Augustine.[30] But this underplays

---

[27] For other strong uses of moral desert language see e.g. Rom. 1:32 ('deserve death'), Rev. 2:23 ('as your works deserve') and Rev. 16:6 ('It is what they deserve').

[28] Nor would it be rehabilitative if annihilation is preferred as the final punishment for sin. In that case too there is no scope for rehabilitation.

[29] See below on the captivating nature of sin.

[30] *Atonement and Incarnation*, pp. 87–106.

the fact that penal views of God's actions against sinners are present much earlier in the Fathers. In particular, they are there in Irenaeus,[31] whom White apparently envisages as advocating in 'embryonic form' the 'exclusive recreation' argument.[32] Even more seriously, White does not look at the biblical material on which Irenaeus and Augustine and so many others were building their views.[33] The vital point to be faced here is that if God has indeed set a penalty for sin, then what happens to that penalty in the salvation process? As long ago as 1946, H.E. Guillebaud drew attention to this, that a salvation that did not save from the penalty of sin would be but a 'dreadful mockery', for we would still bear the penalty ourselves.[34]

Genesis 3 in summary

In this way, Genesis 3 outlines a double problem: the sin we commit is de-creational, and the judgement sin calls forth after Genesis 2:17 also sees a destabilization of the original created order. We move now to examine the implications of those forms of de-creation.

The Implications of Sin as 'De-creation'

For us

To deal first with the consequences for humanity, sin has two characteristics we must stress. To begin with, sin is profoundly captivating. This arises from Turretin's description of sin as 'false faith'.[35] False faith involves treating God as other than he is and it is more

---

[31] E.g. *Against Heresies* 2.33.5.
[32] *Atonement and Incarnation*, p. 103.
[33] Space precludes a full consideration of the account of penalty and retribution in *Atonement and Incarnation*. Suffice it to say it is flawed by its failure to specify adequately what the particular penalty involved might be. That alone makes it impossible to determine whether exclusive re-creation produces a greater, lesser or the same result as a salvation including penal substitution.
[34] H.E. Guillebaud, *Why the Cross?* (London: IVF, 1946²), p. 101.
[35] *Institutes of Elenctic Theology*, Topic 9 Q. 6 IX.

than a merely 'rational' commitment. Disbelief is indeed a leap of faith. We inhabit a delusional framework of our own construction. Yet the captivating nature of this leap is not always readily seen. Paul points out in Romans 1:18ff. and Ephesians 4:17ff. that in our false faith we become futile in thought. Sin has a noetic effect, and this is compounded by the fact that God 'gives humans up' (Gk. *paradidōmi*, Rom. 1:24, 26, 28) to their error. The judicial connotations are hard to miss: God 'has consigned sinners . . .to sin'.[36] It is thus no easy matter to provide a rational correction of 'false faith'. Thus a mistake about the nature of sin may both make us understate what Jesus must do to save us, and overstate our unaided abilities to evaluate what he did.

But the captivating nature of sin is apparent in another way. This delusional framework, or false faith, is readily associated with idolatry. Idolatry at its most straightforward can simply be a false god, whether called Baal or National Socialism. Idolatry can also use the name of the true God but attach a lie to it. A crucial point here is the notion of exchange. Idolatry involves an exchange of the true God for something else. This is caught by Paul in Romans 1:25 ('they exchanged the truth of God for a lie').[37] In the false faith of sin we are left only with a 'counterfeit God',[38] for we have suppressed certain truths (e.g. his judgement) or distorted others (e.g. his love) to produce a designer deity out of our own imagination.

But the link with idolatry is perhaps especially illuminating in the sense that idolatry commits us to a lie and lies can be very difficult to penetrate. The celebrated satire on idolatry in Isaiah 44 draws this out. Verse 20 comments on the irrational blindness of the idolater. One would have thought he would see the folly of his actions but he does not (cf. Ps. 115:8). Part of the difficulty, no doubt, is the attachment one feels to one's idols. In this respect, there is an echo in some analyses of addiction, which draw attention to the addict's inclination to use denial. McCormick comments:

---

[36] C.K. Barrett, *A Commentary on the Epistle to the Romans* (London: A. & C. Black, 1957), p. 38.

[37] The exchange language also features in Rom. 1:23, and is present in the Old Testament too (cf. Ps. 106:20; Jer. 2:11).

[38] R. Keyes, 'The Idol Factory', in O. Guinness and J. Seel (eds.), *No God but God: Breaking with the Idols of our Age* (Chicago: Moody, 1992), pp. 29–48 (33).

Denial, projection and delusion constitute the unholy trinity of addiction. In order to justify irrational thought and behaviour it is necessary to block out painful information, create and maintain an unreal world, and affix blame for all bad news on any source except the self or the source of the addiction.[39]

Given this, it is little wonder that sin is associated so much with uncompromising language of helplessness: it enslaves (Jn. 8:34); it has a dominion or empire (Col. 1:13); it holds us in death (Eph. 2:1). No wonder McCormick finds a contemporary icon of sin in addiction, with all the horror that conveys: 'Sin, like addiction, seems to involve a progressive enslavement to our compulsions.'[40]

All this is essential for Christian practice. Such an understanding illuminates our apologetics and our evangelism, as well as our pastoral care for believers. Sin is captivating. It also impinges on our theology and the way we do it. It is for this reason, for example, that care is needed over some versions of the 'no transfer of merit' argument, which state that penal substitution is simply barbaric, or unacceptable to the modern mind. Romans 1:18ff. teaches that sin makes the modern mind unreliable when it comes to the things of God, and as needful of God's revelation as was the ancient mind, the medieval mind or the Reformation mind. On these grounds, what White says about testing propositions, not against the Bible but 'our natural moral intuition',[41] is highly problematic: caught in the delusional framework of false faith, our moral intuition seems unreliable. This problem is further exacerbated by the way that White applies this method inconsistently, conceding that some do hold to penal positions out of conscience,[42] but not allowing those particular moral intuitions the same role of adjudication.

As well as profoundly captivating, this false faith is a relational disaster. In this respect, this chapter, like the others in this book, reasserts the importance of the personal in penal substitution. Martin Buber famously used the term 'I–Thou'[43] to describe a particular

---

[39] P. McCormick, *Sin as Addiction* (New York: Paulist, 1989), p. 155.

[40] Ibid., p. 161.

[41] White, *Atonement and Incarnation*, p. 87.

[42] Ibid., p. 91.

[43] Notably in M. Buber, *I and Thou* (ET Edinburgh: T. & T. Clark, 1958[2]).

type of relationship, a relationship in which one encounters or meets another, and meets them as person, not merely as object to experience or sense. Yet false faith presents the difficulty of trying to meet a person who is not there. For the false faith of Eden dealt with a fictional God, not the one that Genesis 1–2 discloses. There is no real meeting because there is no meeting of the real person. We readily sense how disastrous this is in personal relations between humans. If I persist in treating people as other than who they are, and other than who they show and state themselves to be, then my relationship is illusory, and my treatment of them quite likely to be seen as demeaning. It would mean that I was defining them as I saw fit. In short, I would be refusing their identity.

Two consequences merit specific mention. The first is that, in the New Testament, God the Father regards false faith as an attack on himself and his character. After all, 1 John 5:10 observes that refusal to believe God's self-revelation through his Son makes the Father a liar, poignant indeed in view of the disbelief of Genesis 3. The second is that this non-relation with God results in a different understanding and knowledge of ourselves. For Buber, the 'I' of the 'I–Thou' relationship was in part shaped by the relationship. Thus if the relationship is altered, so is the 'I'. In a sense Calvin makes a parallel point: 'it is certain that man never achieves a clear knowledge of himself unless he has first looked upon God's face'.[44] It is perhaps unsurprising that a race characterized by false faith with respect to its Creator should wrestle with problems of self-identity.

The various features of sin can now be seen to combine with peculiar unhappiness. We have done wrong and need to deal with the damage our sin does to relationship with God, including its penal consequences. The problem is, our false faith eliminates the very relationship through which we would want to act. It has been suggested that the Old Testament system of sacrifice is like the giving of flowers from within an existing relationship.[45] Among other things, that simile would need amending at least in the following way to capture human relationships with God after Genesis 3. Sin means

---

[44] *Institutes* 1.1.2.

[45] Goldingay, 'Old Testament Sacrifice and the Death of Christ', in idem, *Atonement Today*, pp. 3–20 (3–4). The simile is in any case open to criticism.

fallen unredeemed humans are like people trying to deliver flowers at an out-of-date address to a person they once knew, whose face they cannot remember, and for whom they have a photograph that looks nothing like the real person.

To this extent, sin means we desperately need changing, but part of its nature means we cannot change ourselves. Sin and its consequences as de-creation mean redemption must indeed be a new creation. This was seen with startling clarity by the great fourth-century bishop of Alexandria, Athanasius, who comments on the situation post-Genesis 3 that 'the work of God was being undone'.[46] Thus he insisted that because redemption was a new creation, none but the Creator himself could redeem. He puts it this way, speaking of the Son:

> What – or rather Who was it that was needed for such grace and such recall as we required? Who save the Word of God Himself, Who also in the beginning had made all things out of nothing . . . For being Word of the Father, and above all, He alone of natural fitness was both able to recreate everything, and worthy to suffer on behalf of all and to be ambassador for all with the Father.[47]

In more Reformational language, it must be God the Holy Trinity who saves us, for we cannot.

For God

For God on the other hand, sin emerges as something that opposes and frustrates his creation purposes, and is to that extent to the detriment of his glory. As such it is no surprise to find that God reacts to deal with sin and to remove it. There is a constraint here, however. God cannot simply overlook sin and refuse to attach penal consequences to it on the ground that he could by those means preserve his creation purposes. If he were to do that, he would be 'undoing' the word of Genesis 2:17. Again, this is something Athanasius saw very clearly: '[It] was unthinkable that God, the Father of Truth,

---

[46] *On the Incarnation*, trans. and ed. a Religious of CSMV (New York: SVS, 1953), 6.
[47] Ibid. 7.5.

should go back on his word regarding death in order to ensure our continued existence. He could not falsify himself.'[48]

Here Athanasius reminds us that if the word of Genesis 2:17 is not fulfilled, then God's word is not effective and he is shown not to speak the truth. It is worth noting just where Athanasius's stress lies: it is on the character of God himself. God is never a liar. Consistently in this part of his argument in *On the Incarnation* 6–7 Athanasius uses truth/falsehood language, and his thrust is that God is certainly truthful (Gk. *alēthēs*). The stipulation of Genesis 2:17 is part of God's created order and for God not to fulfil it would itself be an act of de-creation of the same order as that achieved by Adam. Ironically, it would show the serpent to have been truthful about God.

Now, is Athanasius really saying that some law or necessity outside God binds God? If he were, that would amount to saying that there was something more authoritative than God, for God himself must abide by it. However, this objection does not apply here, because the point is that God binds himself by his own word; he is not bound by some necessity outside himself. The reason why he is bound is because of his own character, not because of a moral code imposed by some third party. We know from Scripture that God does regard himself as bound by his word.[49] Furthermore, to insist that God be 'released' from his word of Genesis 2:17 undermines the reliability of his promises *tout court*. If released from this one, why is his promise to forgive sins (1 Jn. 1:9) any more reliable? On this basis the objection that Athanasius is allowing God to be bound by an external constraint proves ill-founded.

This discussion of God's truthfulness with respect to enforcing Genesis 2:17 recalls an incisive comment of Aulén: '[It] is in some conception of the nature of God that every doctrine of the Atonement has its ultimate ground.'[50] The strength of Athanasius's formulation is that he is attempting to respect a characteristic we know from other aspects of salvation history to be central. In

---

[48] Ibid. 7 see also 6.

[49] Cf. Heb. 6:13–18, esp. v. 18, which states that it is impossible that God should prove false. Note too Titus 1:2, where Paul rests our hope on the character of the God who makes the promises.

[50] Aulén, *Christus Victor*, p. 29.

stressing the truthfulness of God, and the importance of an atonement that conforms to his character, Athanasius has been followed by many. It is not satisfactory to reduce this to a concern to safeguard 'justice' or to prevent 'moral laxity', for those renderings substitute impersonal ethical abstractions for the concrete personal nature of God.

The problem generated by sin as de-creation

At this stage of the discussion the question has become: 'How can a de-creating creation be re-created?' This cannot be done by a creature, not merely because of the problems arising from the limitations of being a creature rather than an uncreated Creator , but more specifically because human creatures are caught in the network of de-creation, so captivated by it that fulfilling their original creation purposes lies beyond them. Hence Packer is right both to include in his description of penal substitution the idea of a judgement for which we are 'inescapably destined' – that is the way the cosmos has been created – and also to stress that salvation lies not through us, but through the action of Jesus. All this takes us to the next section and the matter of recreating creation.

Creation and 'Recapitulation'

As a point of departure, I adopt the idea that God's glory requires that his creation purposes be fulfilled. Thus redemption at least includes the idea of renewed creation. This was one of the great themes of Irenaeus of Lyons in the late second century. He observed that God must act with respect to creation to recapitulate his handiwork 'in order that [He] might not be conquered nor His wisdom lessened'.[51] The term Irenaeus used is 'recapitulation' (Gk. *anakephalaiōsis*), the idea that God must go over again, so to speak, the imperfect features of creation to bring them to fulfilment.[52]

---

[51] Irenaeus, *Against Heresies* 3.23.1.

[52] Using this central insight of Irenaeus's theology does not entail a wholesale adoption of all his typological readings of the Bible (e.g. Eve as a type of Mary).

Now the imperfection in an important sense focuses on humanity. Genesis 3 indicates that the dislocation of creation originates in humanity, while Romans 8:19 indicates that what is lacking in creation revolves around humanity ('the creation waits with eager longing for the revealing of the children of God'). Irenaeus rightly observed that this means that for creation to be recapitulated, humanity must be recapitulated.

A true Adam

Thus what is required is a new Adam, another Adam who is what Adam should have been. This second Adam must succeed where the first Adam did not. Jesus does just that (see e.g. Heb. 4:15). The temptation in the wilderness makes this very clear (Mt. 4:1–11; Mk. 1:13; Lk. 4:1–13), especially as Satan attempts to disrupt the relationship between Jesus and God by tempting him to worship something other than God (Mt. 4:9–10; Lk. 4:7–8). Irenaeus concludes that Jesus' obedience recapitulates our disobedience.[53]

Our Adam

Now if this were all, then God would have achieved a second creation in which the ideal humanity described in Psalm 8 is found in its proper place, albeit in one case only, that of Jesus. But this would not be a redemption of the first creation. For part of the creation provision of Genesis 1–2 is for a human race, not just one solitary human individual. Genesis 1:28 envisages a human community exercising dominion, and Genesis 2:18 is explicit that it is not good for Adam to be alone. Furthermore, it was not just one individual that fell in Genesis 3, but the race, exemplified in both Adam and Eve. But that purpose of a human race or human community under God and over his creation is not fulfilled by Jesus' existence as an individual, perfect though it was. The communal aspect of Jesus' work emerges in Romans 8:29 where God's predestining will is exercised that Christ 'might be the firstborn *within a large family*'. Without that communal aspect the first creation would still have been, at that level, a failure, and the stain on God's glory to which Irenaeus points would remain.

---

[53] Irenaeus, *Against Heresies* 5.19.1.

It is worth briefly dwelling on the notion of new creation. Vernon White is correct to observe that a complete and total restoration of the *status quo ante* is not possible,[54] for one cannot undo the history of a relationship. If one party damages that relationship, this action remains as a historical fact, even though the relationship may be healed. But equally the healed relationship is not an entirely new relationship. The idea of reconciliation[55] presupposes an existing relationship which is to be repaired. Equally, by 'new' creation, the Bible does not mean a creation unrelated to, and completely independent of, the old. It cannot. There are obvious continuities with the old, notably in the fact that individual persons originating in the old are found in the new. This is precisely the promise of redemption, that humans created in the old cosmos are placed within the new.

This underlines the fact that to renew the old creation, the recapitulation effected by Adam must in some way be applied to us. The new and true Adam must become our Adam. For we need an alien righteousness, a righteousness that comes from outside ourselves. Let it be noted at this stage that the 'no transfer of merit' argument, long waiting in the wings, is about to make its entrance, since it clearly bears on this. For restoration to take place, creation must have its ravaged relationships reconfigured. Put shortly, the cosmos, and humans in particular, must be or become righteous, in right relationship with God. But, as the foregoing discussion reminds us, this right relationship cannot be self-generating on our part because of sin. We cannot provide what we need. Turretin sums it up like this:

> However, since no mortal after sin has such a righteousness in himself (nay, by sin he has been made a child of wrath and become exposed to death), it must be sought out of us in another, by the intervention of which man (sinful and wicked) may be justified without personal righteousness.[56]

That is, we need an alien righteousness.

However, how can we have an alien righteousness in view of the 'no transfer of merit' argument, which asserts that there can be no

---

[54] White, *Atonement and Incarnation*, pp. 96–7.
[55] Which is a conceptual point of departure for White, ibid., p. 87.
[56] *Institutes of Elenctic Theology*, Topic 16 Q. 3 III.

shifting of positive merit or demerit between individuals? It was noted earlier that, for some, this arises from a fundamental principle of ethical theory – that humans are given personal responsibility and must abide by their own actions. Put like this, the argument is open to the methodological objection that it assumes humans can by themselves correctly formulate fundamental principles of ethical theory, something that sin renders at least problematic.

Nevertheless, the 'no transfer of merit' argument need not be put that way. A critical text here is Ezekiel 18:20 (see also Gen. 18:23; Deut. 24:16; 2 Kgs. 14:6; Ezek. 18:4), which obviously has been read as ruling out shifting positive merit or demerit between persons. It is vital to note that when resting on texts like Ezekiel 18:20, the 'no transfer of merit' argument does rule out positive merit as well as demerit. Naturally, when the argument is used in the context of the debate about penal substitution – where in Packer's terms *Jesus* 'endured and exhausted the divine judgement for which *we* were otherwise inescapably destined' – what is in view is the idea that the demerit of person A (that she or he deserves punishment) cannot be transferred to person B (who does not have that demerit from her or his own actions). But the objection applies to more than penal substitution alone. It also means that the positive merit of person A (that she or he deserves reward) cannot be transferred to person B who does not have that positive merit from her or his own actions. For transferring positive merit on those terms equally undercuts the principle of individual responsibility.

Several things need to be said in the light of this discussion of the full impact of the 'no transfer of merit argument'. Obviously, some might feel more comfortable transferring positive merit than demerit. After all, transferring positive merit is doing people good and can be defended on the basis that person A may consent to giving away, and person B consent to being given, an alien positive merit. In that way, they might feel there is an asymmetry between the transfer of positive merit and the transfer of demerit. One can do the former, but not the latter.

Yet reflection shows this is unsatisfactory. First, the textual basis of Ezekiel 18:20 is in precisely symmetrical terms. This nuancing of the 'no transfer of merit' argument thus starts to depart from its exegetical base. Secondly, this asymmetrical application of the 'no transfer' argument depends on nuancing the principle of personal responsibility by reference to other principles. Put bluntly, it arranges principles in an order of importance, in this case allowing conceptions of benefit and consent to nuance the principle of personal responsibility. This is highly problematic. The ravages of sin leave us without the competence to arrange ethical principles with certainty and it is not at all clear on what biblical basis this nuancing of Ezekiel 18:20 is to be done. Moreover, if one appeals to benefit and consent as higher principles, this ought to apply equally to the transfer of demerit from A to B. If both A and B agree to this, why does consent not nuance personal responsibility here too? Hence, the form of the 'no transfer' argument that needs to be faced is that embodied in Ezekiel 18:20, for it is biblical, and it covers the transfer both of merit and demerit, symmetrically.

It is just here that the New Testament's language of participation, being 'in Christ', becomes so important. This language is surprisingly prevalent in the New Testament, ranging from John's concepts of dwelling in Christ (Jn. 15:1ff.) and he in us (14:20; 17:23), through to Paul's ideas of 'in Christ' (e.g. Eph. 1–2). Indeed, R.B. Gaffin comments of Paul, 'There is no element in the whole of Paul's soteriology more basic than this existential union with Christ.'[57]

In the present context, Romans 5:19 talks of the many who were sinners being made righteous (*dikaioi katastathēsontai*). This by no means fits easily at first glance into a strict 'no transfer of merit' framework, which would insist that sinners reap the consequences of their actions. But 2 Corinthians 5:21 starts to show how this may be possible. We are made righteous in Christ. Christ is our righteousness. Here we echo the point made in chapter two by David Peterson. It is through faith-union, being 'in Christ', that we have Christ's righteousness – the righteousness, of course, of the new and true Adam. Martin Luther uses the analogy of marriage to explain this. In marriage there is a union between a man and a woman whereby the goods and wealth of the one may be enjoyed by the other, although originally the other was not entitled to them. So with Christ and the believer. The goods of Christ are available to the one united with Christ. This theme of faith-union having these

[57] R.B. Gaffin, *Resurrection and Redemption: A Study in Paul's Soteriology* (Phillipsburg: P. & R., 1987²), p. 51.

consequences has been a heart-cry of Reformation theology and much subsequent Protestant theology. As well as Luther, Calvin highlights the centrality of faith-union when he talks of the application of redemption to the individual at the start of Book 3 of the *Institutes*. In this he is followed by Reformed theologians from Turretin to John Murray and Robert Reymond.[58]

Some further observations are in order. First, faith-union is conceived of as a reality. It is not a fiction. It may be spiritual, constituted between us and Christ through the Holy Spirit, but that does not make it unreal any more than the Holy Spirit himself is unreal. Now, if there is a real union so that Christ is mine and I am his, then his goods are transferred to me, just as Luther's marriage analogy indicates. Viewed this way, it is missing the point to dismiss the imputation of righteousness to me from Christ as a mere 'legal fiction'. Real union suggests real imputation.

The second observation is this. God's imputation of righteousness on these terms is not covertly unjust. The principle of Ezekiel 18:20 is indeed observed, and the word of God is not abolished. Turretin writes:

> Although God justifies us on account of the righteousness of Christ, his judgement does not cease to be according to truth, therefore he does not pronounce us righteous in ourselves subjectively (which would be false), but in another imputatively and relatively (which is perfectly true). Thus God truly estimates the thing and judges it as it is, not in itself and in its own nature, but in Christ.[59]

As such the 'no transfer of merit' argument does not rule out imputed righteousness, because imputed righteousness rests on a union of persons. For the 'no transfer' argument to bite here it would have to be extended so that union of persons itself is seen to be contrary to the principles of personal responsibility. Yet here again it is not clear why passages such as Ezekiel 18:20 should be taken in this way. In fact, Israelite thinking did permit one person to

---

[58] See J. Murray, *Redemption: Accomplished and Applied* (Edinburgh: Banner of Truth, 1955); R. Reymond, *A New Systematic Theology of the Christian Faith* (Nashville: Nelson, 1998).

[59] *Institutes of Elenctic Theology*, Topic 16 Q. 3 XXVI.

impose obligations and accrue benefits for another on the basis of a relationship between the two. This is present in the relationship of *shaliach* or agency, under which the *shaliach* could bind and benefit his principal.[60] Now it may be objected that the *shaliach* is not a specifically biblical institution. Even so, the point remains that the institution was not perceived to be at odds with the issues of personal and individual responsibility arising out of Ezekiel 18:20 and similar passages. On this basis, it is not clear why the 'no transfer' argument should be seen as barring the personal union involved in faith-union. With this in mind we now move to consider the 'exclusive re-creation' argument.

The 'exclusive re-creation' argument evaluated

Advocates of 'exclusive re-creation' do use faith-union as a means by which the righteousness and resurrection-life of Christ are shared by others. The range of those who are in union with Christ may differ with the various proponents, as may the degree of awareness required for this union, but the point remains that some version of personal union is present.[61] In other words, the 'exclusive restoration' argument in the forms examined here uses faith-union in some form to counter the thrust of the 'no transfer of merit' argument. For the reasons given above, in principle, use of the concept of faith-union in this way is justified, although one might disagree over the precise way in which that doctrine is applied.

So far, however, discussion under this heading of recapitulation has been about imputed righteousness and not transferred guilt. It may fairly be said that asserting recapitulation through the obedience of Jesus and the imputing of alien righteousness through faith-union does not vindicate penal substitution. For penal substitution deals not with transferred righteousness but transferred guilt.

---

[60] For a useful summary of the *shaliach* institution see P. Borgen, 'God's Agent in the Fourth Gospel', in J. Neusner (ed.), *Religions in Antiquity* (Leiden: Brill, 1970), pp. 137–48.

[61] White, *Atonement and Incarnation*, pp. 66–7; Smail, 'Can One Man Die', in Goldingay, *Atonement Today*, pp. 73–92 (90–1); Atkinson, 'What Difference', in Goldingay, *Atonement Today*, pp. 253–71 (259–60). The particular definition of faith-union will determine whether every human being is in union with Christ or some only.

The question here is: does the transfer of righteousness to us in and of itself achieve the full renewal of creation? If it does, then the 'exclusive restoration' argument is made out and penal substitution shown to be a redundant feature.

Up to here the discussion under this heading has been to the effect that Jesus as true Adam recapitulates the original creation purpose for humanity by living in a righteous, obedient relationship with God. Yet that still leaves part of the original creation order, stipulated in Genesis 2:17, outstanding. It was earlier explored why it is that this ordinance cannot simply be ignored, without forfeiting the very creation purposes that recapitulation wants to safeguard and denying those characteristics of God that Genesis 3 saw challenged. In fact, a restoration or recapitulation theory of redemption has to give an answer to two things, not one. It has to answer not merely how we can become righteous, but also how our unrighteousness can be dealt with without breaching the creation order. If it fails in *either*, then it does not meet the purpose of God acting with respect to the cosmos, 'in order that [He] might not be conquered nor His wisdom lessened', to quote Irenaeus again.[62]

In fact, faith-union meets the first of these requirements, how we can become righteous, because by it Christ's righteousness becomes ours. Yet faith-union also helps answer the second. Our guilt and the penal consequences of our sin are transferred to Christ. It is well known that this is just how Martin Luther develops his marriage analogy for faith-union. In marriage, the couple share the goods one partner brings. They can also share the burdens and debts of the one. Thus one partner may carry all of a particular obligation, even though he or she may not be the one who incurred it. The union is symmetrical in that through it both benefits and burdens flow. Indeed, modern psychological insights show just how true this can be. In marriage one faces not simply the financial obligations one's partner has incurred, but also their life history with its experiences and emotional legacies – an inability to trust, perhaps, or a heightened tendency to selfishness because of previous relationships. Yet while there is a symmetry in that both benefits and burdens can be transferred under this kind of union, the burdens borne and the benefits enjoyed may not fall symmetrically between the parties. One party may end up bearing more than the other.

---

[62] *Against Heresies* 3.23.1.

Luther, of course, was not simply being speculative in his symmetrical statement of the benefits and burdens of faith-union. Reference has already been made to 2 Corinthians 5:21b and the clause 'so that in him we might become the righteousness of God'. But this is related to, indeed to some extent depends on, the first half of the verse, which deals with the other half of the equation, what becomes of our unrighteousness: 'God made him who had no sin to be sin for us.' In this way there is an interchange: we are clothed in his righteousness and he in our guilt. Clothed in our guilt he bears our penalty completely. Packer thus rightly insists that Jesus 'exhausted the destructive divine judgement'.

In the light of this twofold application of faith-union, the 'exclusive restoration' argument therefore faces a difficulty. For it to exclude penal substitution, the transfer of demerit, it must deny that faith-union permits the transfer of guilt and punishment. Yet to accept that objection is cutting off one's nose to spite one's face. If one denies the transfer of demerit, on what basis does one allow the transfer of positive merit? For the biblical basis of Ezekiel 18:20 deals with both positive merit and demerit. It is thus highly problematic that Smail, for example, can simultaneously rely on faith-union to establish our participation in Christ's positive merit[63] while utilizing the 'no transfer of merit' argument to deny penal substitution. Moreover, he[64] does this after citing a version of the 'no transfer of merit' argument which deals explicitly with transfers not only of positive merit but also demerit as equally obnoxious to the principle of moral responsibility.[65]

Any version of the restoration argument needs some kind of alien righteousness if it is to remain biblical in its conception of sin. The Bible points us to faith-union as the way that this alien righteousness is properly transferred without breaching the rule of Ezekiel 18:20. If Ezekiel 18:20 is not breached by the transfer of righteousness on the basis of faith-union, then on what grounds can we assert it is breached by a transfer of unrighteousness on the basis of faith-union? This difficulty is all the more acute when the party who donates his righteousness and receives the unrighteousness

---

[63] 'Can One Man Die', p. 91.
[64] Ibid., pp. 89–90.
[65] Ibid., pp. 77–8.

consents to the process, as Jesus does, and is even one of those wronged by the unrighteousness. The 'exclusive restoration' argument cannot consistently rely on the 'no transfer of merit' argument to block out penal substitution, because restoration theologies in any case do not accept the 'no transfer' argument when faith-union is involved. The exclusivity would prove fatal not just to penal substitution, but to restoration.

The upshot, then, is this. If one accepts redemption as being in some sense re-creation (which is biblical), and stresses the imputation of Christ's righteousness (which is biblical), one also has to accept penal substitution, for this is equally part of faith-union, and equally a necessary part of re-creation. Furthermore, the consequences of denying faith-union go beyond demolishing imputed righteousness and penal substitution. It also affects adoption, sanctification and glorification. For, as Turretin remarks, 'from union with Christ depends the communion of all his benefits'.[66]

Conclusion

Drawing all this together, the conclusion is that the doctrine of penal substitution can and must be reasserted. It is not a severable part of the theology of the cross. It was earlier observed that part of the debate over penal substitution relates to

- restoration of creation
- 'in Christ' language
- the 'no transfer of merit' argument

What emerges is that both the 'no transfer' and 'exclusive re-creation' objections to penal substitution fail. The 'no transfer' fails at the point of faith-union. The 'exclusive restoration' argument likewise fails. It presents a false antithesis between penal substitution on the one hand and restoration of creation on the other. In reality, the very cosmos that is being restored and vindicated is one which upholds a penalty for sin. So a soteriology stressing the restoration of this cosmos has to face the question of what happens to the penalty

---

[66] *Institutes of Elenctic Theology*, Topic 16 Q. 6 VIII.

for sin. A restoration soteriology that does not deal with the aspect of penalty has either failed to achieve a full restoration or, as Guillebaud observed, leaves the penalty still in operation (scarcely an encouraging thought). It is thus clear at this point that restoration of this cosmos, the one God actually created, demands a penal substitution. Restoration may well involve more than penal substitution, but it cannot be less and still be restoration. A restoration exclusive of penal substitution is thus not a full restoration, for it involves a God whose word has been and remains broken. To preach creation restored necessarily involves penal substitution.[67]

Secondly, this restoration soteriology utilizes faith-union with Christ. That union explains how Christ's righteousness may be ours, and our sin Christ's, and much else besides. In pursuing this, much use has been made here of the theologies of Athanasius (that only the Creator can redeem) and Irenaeus (that creation must be recapitulated by a true Adam). Neither are perceived as being unthinking endorsers of the 'exclusive re-creation' position. Irenaeus in particular appears as an influential figure in the 'exclusive re-creation' arguments, but a problem arises when central insights of both are not appropriated and the internal logic of their positions not properly developed. It is unsatisfactory that Irenaeus's penal views of sin, and Athanasius's stress on the truthful character of God with respect to Genesis 2:17, find such slender representation in the 'exclusive restoration' argument. However, this development of Athanasius and Irenaeus serves to remind us that although penal substitution is much emphasized by evangelicals and rightly so, it is not their exclusive possession. Rather, it lies in the positions of the common Fathers of many traditions. This kind of theology was articulated rather than invented by the Reformation.[68]

Thirdly, it can be said with justice that the church is the collection of those in faith-union with Christ. Ephesians 3:10 states that this church vindicates the manifold wisdom of God. It is easy to see

---

[67] This does have implications about what the Church must proclaim, but proper discussion lies outside the scope of this paper.

[68] For further comments on the thoughts of the Fathers on penal substitution see G. Williams, 'A Critical Exposition of Hugo Grotius's Doctrine of the Atonement in *De Satisfactione Christi*', unpublished DPhil thesis (Oxford, 1999), pp. 78–95.

why: the church shows the fulfilment of God's creation purposes. Its existence vindicates God's wisdom as Creator, for he has upheld the creation order as he established it, including Genesis 2:17, and, as has often been said, has shown in the cross both his mercy and his justice. This, too, is a note of Packer's description of penal substitution, that Christ died 'moved by a love that was determined to do everything necessary to save us'.[69]

Questions for Further Study

1. How far should Christians expect to see the restoration of creation in their social and individual lives before the return of Jesus?

2. What do you think we lose in our Christian lives if we do not think of redemption in terms of the restoration of creation?

3. What would God be like if he did not punish wrong-doing?

4. Do you think Christians have a proper understanding of faith-union with Christ? How can we deepen our appreciation of it?

5. How can humans trapped in 'false faith' come to have true faith in Jesus Christ? See John 6:35–51; Ephesians 2:1–10; and 2 Corinthians 4:1–6.

---

[69] Thanks are due to Lee Gatiss, James Robson and Garry Williams for helpful critiques of earlier versions of this chapter.

Select Bibliography

For the link between being Creator and Redeemer

Athanasius, *On the Incarnation* , trans. and ed. a Religious of CSMV (New York: SVS, 1953)

For the significance of faith-union

J. Calvin, *Institutes of the Christian Religion* 3.1
J. Murray, *Redemption: Accomplished and Applied* (Edinburgh: Banner of Truth, 1955)
R.B. Gaffin, *Resurrection and Redemption: A Study in Paul's Soteriology* (Phillipsburg: P. & R., 1987[2])

For idolatry

R. Keyes, 'The Idol Factory', pp. 29–48, in O. Guinness and J. Seel (eds.), *No God but God: Breaking with the Idols of Our Age* (Chicago: Moody, 1992)

For a helpful review of metaphors for sin

P. McCormick, *Sin as Addiction* (New York: Paulist, 1989)

5

Proclaiming Christ Crucified Today: Some Reflections on John's Gospel
Paul Weston

John 19:16–30 (NRSV)

Then he handed him over to them to be crucified.

So they took Jesus; and carrying the cross by himself, he went out to what is called The Place of the Skull, which in Hebrew is called Golgotha. There they crucified him, and with him two others, one on either side, with Jesus between them. Pilate also had an inscription written and put on the cross. It read, 'Jesus of Nazareth, the King of the Jews.' Many of the Jews read this inscription, be-cause the place where Jesus was crucified was near the city; and it was written in Hebrew, in Latin, and in Greek. Then the chief priests of the Jews said to Pilate, 'Do not write, "The King of the Jews," but, "This man said, I am King of the Jews."' Pilate answered, 'What I have written I have written.' When the soldiers had crucified Jesus, they took his clothes and divided them into four parts, one for each soldier. They also took his tunic; now the tunic was seamless, woven in one piece from the top. So they said to one another, 'Let us not tear it, but cast lots for it to see who will get it.' This was to fulfil what the scripture says,

> *'They divided my clothes among themselves,*
> *and for my clothing they cast lots.'*

And that is what the soldiers did.

Meanwhile, standing near the cross of Jesus were his mother, and his mother's sister, Mary the wife of Clopas, and Mary Magdalene. When Jesus saw his mother and the disciple whom he loved standing beside her, he said to his mother, 'Woman, here is your son.' Then he said to the disciple, 'Here is your mother.' And from that hour the disciple took her into his own home.

After this, when Jesus knew that all was now finished, he said (in order to fulfil the scripture), 'I am thirsty.' A jar full of sour wine was standing there. So they put a sponge full of the wine on a branch of hyssop and held it to his mouth. When Jesus had received the wine, he said, 'It is finished.' Then he bowed his head and gave up his spirit.

Introduction

C.H. Dodd in his classic treatment of John's Gospel says of this chapter:

> It appears . . . that the passion narrative is given in the main as a straight-forward story, with only a minimum of intruded interpretative elements . . . It is as though the evangelist, having sufficiently set forth the meaning of the death and resurrection of Christ, turned to the reader and said, 'Now I will tell you what actually happened, and you will see that the facts themselves bear out my interpretation.'[1]

Dodd's words introduce us to one of the most intriguing aspects of this remarkable chapter. At one level, it *is* a straightforward retelling of the factual circumstances surrounding Jesus' last hours. It tells of Jesus' suffering and death. It speaks of his final words. It describes the reactions of those looking on. Yet at another level, his words indicate that the chapter cannot be read in isolation from the narratives that have preceded it. Indeed, what Dodd calls the 'interpretative elements' function at a number of levels, leading the reader into a wider context into which the events of Calvary need to be placed if they are to be understood properly. They invite the reader into a deeper understanding of who Jesus is, and of what is going on here at the crucifixion scene. In this sense Dodd's words need to be nuanced. It is not that chapter 19 is somehow 'pure' history, following on from the more obviously 'theological' or 'explanatory' chapters that precede it. It is rather that within the text of the chapter itself, we are given the clues that will lead us to make the right connections and establish the truth about what is going on at Calvary.

---

[1] C.H. Dodd, *The Interpretation of the Fourth Gospel* (Cambridge: CUP, 1953), pp. 431–2.

My purpose in this chapter therefore is to explore some key aspects of John 19, focussing upon some of the connections that John makes, and then to discuss some of the insights that these offer to those who are engaged in the work of preaching and teaching. I suggest that there are three major themes emphasized by John, but that all of them are stated in the form of apparent 'paradox'. Each draws us into a central aspect of the meaning of the death of Jesus and each illuminates this meaning from a different perspective.

'Paradox' as a tool of discovery

The very presence of 'paradox' is itself a potent tool of discovery. On a recent university mission, I was struck by the reader response of outsiders to the narrative of John's Gospel as I tried to open it up and explain it night by night. We had distributed copies of the Gospel to every undergraduate, and additional copies were made available each evening so that I could refer explicitly to the text. On the second evening, a science student came to talk after the meeting clutching a copy of the Gospel. As we began our conversation, it was clear that he was in earnest, and I was intrigued to see that he had annotated nearly every page with pencil markings, comments and questions.

It soon became evident that this man was not a believer, but had become engrossed by John's Gospel. Like so many today he was completely ignorant of the Bible, and had never come across it at school. 'It's a bit like a detective story,' he said. 'I'm fascinated by it.' The nature of the 45-minute discussion that followed was a series of questions about how the various characters and incidents in the Gospel 'fitted' with each other. On two subsequent evenings we sat down again and worked through his fresh margin jottings – following up clues and hints, resolving questions and finding new ones. It was clear that here was something that was genuinely intriguing: something that he felt himself to be 'inside', even though he knew that he was not yet a 'part' of it. The biblical narrative had 'involved' him in its thought-world, and he was energetically anticipating its outcomes whilst being drawn into further discovery.

John is a master of irony and paradox. Why this is so is never explicitly stated, but both literary tools are potent as triggers of exploration and discovery within a developing plot-line. And this particular student was hooked by it. What he was discovering was that what is *really* happening in John's narrative cannot be ascertained simply by means of a surface reading. This is especially true of the crucifixion narrative in chapter 19. I want to suggest that a powerful strategy in our contemporary culture is to preach and teach in a manner that imitates John's method. We need to open up the questions and paradoxes of the text in such a way that others are enabled to enter them and begin to discover answers. Three great paradoxes emerge from the following examination of John's account:

(a)   Despite appearances, the death of Jesus is the fulfilment of God's plan (vv. 24, 28, 36, 37).

(b)   Despite appearances, the death of Jesus is entirely voluntary (vv. 17, 25–7, 28, 30).

(c)   Despite appearances, the death of Jesus is a revelation of divine glory (vv. 19–22).

John's Crucifixion Narrative

What then does the newcomer to John's crucifixion narrative find on first reading? One of the clearest features is John's tendency to keep informing the reader that some text or prediction of the Old Testament is being fulfilled in what he describes as happening. This has the effect of tending to 'break' the narrative flow of the story, while at the same time anchoring the drama in a wider context, and giving it a greater and deeper significance.[2]

It occurs first in 19:24 with the reference to the soldiers dividing the garments. Their initial division of Jesus' clothes into four parts has been followed by the dilemma over what to do with the tunic. For John tells us that it was 'seamless, woven in one piece from the top'. So they said to each other, 'Let us not tear it, but cast lots for it

---

[2] Some of the descriptive statements I have used in this chapter are based upon observations made by people who have never read John's Gospel before.

to see who will get it.' Then comes John's interpretative comment (quoting Ps. 28:18):

> This was to fulfil what the scripture says,
>
>> 'They divided my clothes among themselves,
>> and for my clothing they cast lots.'

This technique is repeated in verse 28, where Jesus' thirst is quenched by some sour wine and this is set in the context of Psalm 69:21 ('They gave me vinegar for my thirst').

The reference in verse 36 to the fact that none of Jesus' bones were broken is particularly rich in interpretative significance. It recalls the comment about the soldiers' intention to speed up the process of death by smashing the criminals' hip joints so that they could no longer lift themselves on the footpiece of the cross (the *patibulum*) in order to breathe (v. 31).[3] This action was taken in response to the Jewish request to Pilate that he might prevent shame being brought to the Jews as a result of having bodies hanging from crosses on the coming Sabbath (v. 31). But, when the soldiers came and broke the legs of the first and of the other who had been crucified with him, they came to Jesus and saw that he was already dead.

> [T]hey did not break his legs. Instead, one of the soldiers pierced his side with a spear, and at once blood and water came out. (He who saw this has testified so that you also may believe. His testimony is true, and he knows that he tells the truth.) These things occurred so that the scripture might be fulfilled, 'None of his bones shall be broken.' (vv. 33–6)

The 'scripture' referred to here is most likely either Exodus 12:46 or Numbers 9:12, both referring to the Passover regulation that the Jews were not to break the bones of the lamb used in the ritual. Immediately, therefore, the reader of the Gospel is taken into a wider interpretative context that draws connections between what is going on at the cross and what Jews did each year to celebrate their liberation from Egypt at the Passover.

---

[3] For the historical background to the 'methods' of crucifixion in the ancient world and their significance, see M. Hengel, *Crucifixion in the Ancient World and the Folly of the Message of the Cross* (Philadelphia: Fortress, 1977).

John makes these connections more suggestive and compelling by consciously placing the whole account of the crucifixion at the time of the Passover (cf. 13:1; 18:28, 39; 19:14, 31, 42), and by appearing to place the death of Jesus on the day of the preparation of the Passover when the sacrificial lambs would have been slaughtered at the temple.[4] It is in this context that the extraordinary statement on the lips of John the Baptist that Jesus is 'the Lamb of God who takes away the sin of the world' (1:29, 36) must be interpreted.[5]

In addition to these indicators is the cursory reference to the 'sponge full of wine' being placed on a 'hyssop branch' (19:29) in order to reach Jesus on the cross. It was a hyssop branch that was used to smear the blood from the Passover lamb around the lintel of the door at the time of the Passover (Ex. 12:22). Some have argued that the word for hyssop John uses here (*hyssōpō*) has been mistakenly substituted for *hyssō* ('a javelin'), but this suggestion lacks manuscript support. It is much more likely that John intends us to set this detail in the context of a thematic presentation of the crucifixion that assumes a fundamental parallel between what happened to Jesus and what happened to the Lamb at the Passover. It is difficult to escape the conclusion that John intends us to understand this man hanging on the cross as 'the true Paschal lamb, slaughtered for

---

[4] For a concise discussion of the timing of the Last Supper in John and its relation to the Passover meal, see the discussion in C. Blomberg, *The Historical Reliability of the Gospels* (Leicester: IVP, 1987), pp. 175–8.

[5] There is continuing scholarly debate about the precise identification of 'the Lamb' referred to here – whether the Passover Lamb of Exod. 12, or the Lamb referred to in Isa. 53. Either way, John's appended affirmation that it is the Lamb 'who takes away the sin of the world' puts the identification firmly within a sacrificial/atoning context, and it may be that he is drawing here (as elsewhere) a *general* reference to the redemptive role of the Lamb in the Old Testament as a whole in such a way as to show that all these references are seen to point forward to, and find their fulfilment in, Jesus (especially at the cross). Though the Passover reference may be part of a wider fulfilment scheme, it is nonetheless prominent. See the brief discussion in P. Head, 'Christ as Sacrifice in Gospels and Acts', in R. Beckwith and M. Selman (eds.), *Sacrifice in the Bible* (Grand Rapids: Baker; Carlisle: Paternoster, 1995), pp. 111–29.

the deliverance of his people'.[6] In the context of such a sacrificial framework, Rudolf Bultmann's estimation is surely mistaken:

> The thought of Jesus' death as an atonement for sin has no place in John, and if it should turn out that he took it over from the tradition of the church it would still be a foreign element in his work.[7]

The evidence of chapter 19 suggests that John clearly intends his readers to draw sacrificial conclusions about the significance of the cross. The Passover parallel signifies that Jesus is God's sacrificial lamb, whose death draws the divine judgement. Just as under the Old Covenant, the Jews remembered that their forgiveness and freedom rested upon the fact that God's judgement had fallen upon the lamb, and not upon *them*, so now – in a complete way – Jesus' death means that God's judgement falls upon the Son, and not upon the sinner. All this may be *implied* rather than spelt out by John in chapter 19, but the clues are firmly in place, enough to draw the intended conclusion implied by the comparison.

In addition, we might add that there is a theological 'framework of substitution' that John employs elsewhere in the Gospel, which serves to set up the theological context in which the reader is invited to interpret the cross. First, there is the thematic (and dramatic) use of 'either/or' categories in relation to 'faith' and 'unbelief', and 'life' and 'death'. These categories highlight the fact that for the believer a transfer and substitution has taken place in the work of the Son on the cross. In chapter 3, for example, in the context of Jesus' death (v. 15), the sending of the Son is the means whereby the believer *avoids* death ('in order that those who believe in him shall *not* perish', v. 16). The 'perishing' of the Son is substituted for the 'perishing' of the sinner. Similarly, later in the chapter, belief in the Son is said to bring 'life', but disbelief results in the 'the wrath of God remaining' on the sinner (3:36). By a similar process the believer is spared the 'wrath' of God by the action of the Son. Who then 'endures' God's wrath? The implication is that it is transferred from the sinner to the Son (cf. the similar way in which the notion

---

[6] C.K. Barrett, *The Gospel According to St. John* (London: SPCK, 1978[2]), p. 553.

[7] *Theology of the New Testament* (London: SCM, 1955), vol. 2, p. 54.

of condemnation functions in v. 18). Secondly, John repeatedly uses *hyper* ('for, on behalf of') sayings as a substitutionary framework within which he interprets Jesus' death (6:51; 10:11, 15; 11:50–2; 15:13; 18:14). Take, for example, the statement by Caiaphas (11:50, repeated in 18:14) that 'it is better for you to have one man die for the people than to have the whole people perish'. John here combines a statement of the deepest theological significance with the most profound irony. For, on the lips of an opponent, the death of Jesus is interpreted as a substitutionary action, effected in place of others.[8] This is the framework (informed by sacrificial overtones) within which John understands and proclaims the cross. It is an initiative on behalf of others that is sacrificial in form and life-giving in effect.

This leads us to a statement of the first great paradox in John's crucifixion narrative.

Despite appearances, the death of Jesus is the fulfilment of God's plan

What is the implication of all these allusions and quotations? At one level, they anchor the events of the crucifixion in a pattern that is apparent in the Old Testament and is shown to be in line with them. But, at the same time, they do something more fundamental still. They show that what is happening to Jesus is in line with God's plans and purposes. What God has said in the Old Testament is now being shown to refer to his chosen one Jesus. What God predicted through the Old Testament is now coming true. And this divine corroboration is shown to apply to the last seemingly insignificant detail – even at the point where Jesus' helplessness and humiliation appear to be greatest. Moreover, as these fulfilment quotations tail off at the point of crucifixion in John's Gospel, the careful reader is left with the clear impression that it is actually *at the crucifixion itself* that John wants us to understand God's redemptive plan and purpose finding its truest and noblest expression. Jesus' last words from the cross ('It is finished', 19:30) occur immediately after the last fulfilment of scripture (v. 28) and serve not only to indicate (with a

---

[8] Note the logical parallel between the substitution of 11:50 and that of 3:16 (with the repeated use of *apolētai*, 'to perish').

note of triumph) that his God–given sacrificial task is now accomplished, but perhaps also that all the prophecies of scripture in relation to his death have now been fulfilled.

In drawing lessons from this first theme, we recognize therefore that there is a *theological direction* about the crucifixion. It begins in the mind and purposes of God, and moves in the direction of fallen humanity. 'For God so loved the world that he gave . . .' (3:16). Or, as the great congregationalist theologian P.T. Forsyth put it:

> When Christ did what He did, it was not human nature doing it, it was God doing it. That is the great, absolutely unique and glorious thing. It is God in Christ reconciling. It was not human nature offering its very best to God. It was God offering His very best to man.[9]

Any understanding of the atonement that fails at this point fails to grasp its most fundamental reality. This is *God's* doing.

Immediately, this view of the cross excludes any understanding derived exclusively from an understanding of some aspect of Jesus' own human motivation. This is of course a common understanding today: what Jesus undergoes on the cross has – in the light of human reason – to be explained exclusively by some motivation arising from his own psychology or mission. Indeed, some such human explanation is naturally the *only* one available, once any divine involvement is excluded. The Jewish writer Hyam Maccoby writes, for example, that

> Jesus' life and death are best understood as simply the life and death of another of the chain of brave would-be messiahs, who at that time and later tried to liberate the Jewish people and restore their political and religious independence.[10]

Equally, a *purely* 'exemplarist' view of the cross (in which Jesus shows his love in voluntary self-sacrifice as a means of drawing a responsive love and devotion from his disciples) is also inadequate as a Christian interpretation. John, as we shall see, does not dismiss this

---

[9] P.T. Forsyth, *The Work of Christ*, orig. 1910 (London: Independent, 1983), p. 24.

[10] 'The Politics of Jesus', *New Society* (6 January 1983).

aspect of the cross, but on its own it fails to explain the depth of the divine initiative that he sets out to emphasize.

A divine initiative

One of our challenges today is to communicate to a world that has no conception of God and the truth that it was God's plan and purpose that Jesus should die. Perhaps because we find Jesus' own motivation easier to communicate (and easier for people to understand) we may tend to blur this perspective. But the New Testament never does so.[11] And it is precisely this divine dimension that makes the message of the cross completely *sui generis*. For, to emphasize – in Paul's succinct words – that on the cross '*God was in Christ* reconciling the world to himself' (2 Cor. 5:19), is to bring the divine being himself into the messy business of crucifixion, without which it is empty of meaning. God *himself* is the author and executor of the cross.

This – as Martin Hengel has convincingly demonstrated – was the real offence that the preaching of the cross engendered right from the start. For it was not the sacrificial aspect, even in its 'propitiatory' dimensions, that caused problems among early hearers, both Jewish and Greek. Hengel shows that these were current in the ways of thinking that would have made them comprehensible to Greeks, no less than to Jews. As he puts it:

> The message of the death of Jesus of Nazareth, the Son of God, on the cross for all men, was not incomprehensible even to the educated audience of the gentile world. That is to say, its linguistic and religious categories were largely familiar to this audience.

But what sets the Christian message of the cross apart in the ancient Greek world was that it was

> an event which more than the death of a pure martyr and religious sufferer, stemmed from God himself and therefore at the same time recognised the crucified one as the pre-existent Son of God and mediator

---

[11] Note, e.g., Luke's emphasis on the divine origin and plan of the cross and resurrection in his recording of the evangelistic sermons in Acts (e.g. 2:23–4, 32, 36; 13:27–30, 32–3).

of creation, whom the father had sent into the world to redeem his creation . . . In the last resort, in the man Jesus of Nazareth, God took death upon himself . . . This did not in any way diminish the 'scandal of the cross'; indeed it *accentuated it, to an unprecedented degree for the ancient world.*[12]

The reputation of this 'scandal' was well-known to Paul as he preached around Asia Minor. He repeatedly found that his preaching of the cross was a 'stumbling block' (Gk. *skandalon*) to Jews, and 'foolishness' (Gk. *mōrian*) to Gentiles (cf. 1 Cor. 1:23 in the context of the whole section 1:18ff.).

Uniqueness

Reflection on the implications of this central emphasis of John is much needed in our own day. A number of perspectives emerge. Most importantly, the involvement of God with and in Jesus on the cross makes the death of Jesus – by its very nature – totally unique. There has never been anything to approach it in conception, either in terms of comparison or of analogy. As a result, the biblical gospel of the cross – whether preached to ancient Greeks, or postmodern men and women – will *always* transcend our frames of rational understanding, simply because nothing like it has ever taken place before or since.

We should be cautious therefore about some calls to revise our 'models' of the atonement in order to make them more comprehensible today. Perhaps some who make this call are assuming that during some 'golden era' in the past, the message of the cross was somehow more 'acceptable' or 'comprehensible' than it is today. What is needed – it is argued – are more contemporary idioms and metaphors ('models' if you like) that will help to translate atonement into contemporary categories of understanding that will help our hearers today to understand what it means.

This process (that missiologists have come to describe as 'contextualization') is of course the cross-cultural missionary's daily task and struggle. We do indeed need to strive to make the gospel accessible to our contemporary hearers. But two notes of caution

---

[12] M.Hengel, *The Atonement: The Origins in the New Testament*, tr. J. Bowden (London: SCM, 1981), p. 74 (emphasis original).

need to be sounded. First, we need to remember that it has been precisely a desire to contextualize what appears to be incomprehensible that has sometimes led thinkers on the atonement into problems. In the desire to explain the doctrine logically and cogently from a human point of view, the danger is that our culturally accessible frameworks pull the biblical doctrines themselves out of shape, or distort important aspects of them. As a salutary example, one could develop the case, as Packer has suggested, that the debate in the late sixteenth century between the Unitarian scholar Faustus Socinus and the Reformed scholastics was carried out along lines more influenced by an understanding of moral government in the sixteenth century than by the Bible. As Packer comments:

> in trying to beat Socinian rationalism at its own game, Reformed theologians were conceding the Socinian assumption that every aspect of God's work of reconciliation will be exhaustively explicable in terms of a natural theology of divine government, drawn from the world of contemporary legal and political thought. Thus in their zeal to show themselves rational, they became rationalistic.[13]

The truth is that God's involvement at the heart of the atonement has always been beyond the rational grasp of the human mind. And history often shows that where attempts are made to make the atonement *more* rationally acceptable, the core of the message begins to disappear.

'Illustrations' of the cross

We need to remember that we too are 'contextualizers' of biblical truth. We too face the same desire to take the scriptures and allow them to live in the minds of our hearers in such a way that their message has an impact. But sometimes we also are tempted to blunt the divine uniqueness of the cross by expressing it in rather-too-human categories. Take our use of illustrations as an example. So many of them are – strictly speaking – *ad hominem*. They arise out of a circumstance (or set of circumstances) deemed to be 'analogous' to

---

[13] J.I.Packer, 'What did the Cross achieve? The Logic of penal substitution', (orig. 1974) in A.E. McGrath (ed.), *The J.I. Packer Collection* (Leicester: IVP, 1999), p. 100.

what in scripture we are trying to elucidate. Very often, however, the analogy ultimately breaks down, because such illustrations are nearly always *anthropomorphic*, and therefore do not actually get us very far in explaining concepts that derive from the nature and character of the divine.

Our attempts therefore to explain God's activity by relying upon particular illustrations or analogies may end up obscuring rather than illuminating the message of the cross. An example of this was the repeated use by evangelists of the horrifying story from the book *Miracle on the River Kwai*. An innocent soldier steps forward to be punished in place of his fellow prisoners on account of some missing tools. Though innocent, he takes responsibility for the tools, and is immediately butchered at the end of an array of rifle-butts, while his fellow internees are allowed to go back to their huts, spared and profoundly moved by their colleague's act of self-sacrifice. But, as events turn out, the missing tools are later re-counted and none is found to be missing.

This story may be profoundly moving as an example of supreme self-sacrifice, but as an illustration of the cross it fails to get near the unique nature of God's self-giving in Christ. In fact, it is in danger of driving the Trinity apart in a way that totally subverts the scriptural truth of John 19. In John's Gospel, Jesus the Son is a willing participant and co-worker with the Father in a divinely planned and executed mission to redeem humanity from its chosen path of rebellion and destruction. By contrast, the River Kwai illustration suggests some rather different analogies and connections. In this case, God the Father is pictured as a sadistic camp guard screaming for vengeance on charges that turn out to be entirely false; Jesus the Son is represented as an innocent bystander unwittingly caught up in the drama but motivated on impulse to sacrifice himself at the hands of the enemy (God the Father by implication); and the resulting bloodbath is portrayed not only as a senseless waste of human life, but also as a complete travesty of justice. I caricature to make the point, but the point still stands.

Preachers use illustrations all the time of course, sometimes well, and sometimes not so well. If they are good, such illustrations are inherently powerful, involving the listener, suggesting connections by means of imagination and analogy. But if they are bad, suggested connections will divert attention and distort the truth. If our illustrations lead *away* from biblical truth, then we have lost the plot at the point where we should be striving for the utmost clarity.

It is worth reflecting also upon the *way* that illustrations about the cross are used. I've noticed that often they are used at the *conclusion* of material on Jesus' death – as a way of 'clinching the argument' (so to speak) in the mind of the listener. But if what we have been saying about the unique nature of the cross is sound, then analogies will simply not exist (and are not needed) to do this kind of job. Leaving our listeners at this point with inadequate illustrations may undo much of the work already done.

I wonder whether this tendency towards the use of what we might describe as 'clinching' illustrations owes its origin to the *style* of evangelistic preaching many of us were brought up on. Ex-hibiting – as it often did – a 'modernist' tendency to explain the gos-pel by synthesizing from scripture the three or four doctrinal principles by which we felt the good news was most clearly pre-sented, we ended up communicating these (almost inevitably) in a rather abstract manner, using various 'structures' and frameworks. This immediately put pressure on the communicator to 'earth' these propositions in real life by employing more personal illustra-tions and analogies so as to connect the concepts with the people being spoken to. As a result – particularly in evangelistic contexts – the 'telling illustration' on the cross characteristically came to bear a weight it could never sustain. Perhaps then, our illustrations might help listeners to get nearer to the truth about the cross when we dis-tance ourselves from them and emphasize their inadequacies in the light of scripture.

Scriptural logic

These reflections lead us back to a crucial principle. We have seen from John's material that chapter 19 demands to be set within a wider theological context, and that it is only within that context that the divine 'logic' of the cross begins to make sense. This logic is scriptural, both in the sense that it is scripture that defines it (by the God-given connections and fulfilments that tie the two Testaments together), but also in the sense that the means whereby this logic is best communicated is by *allowing scripture to speak for itself*. This, after all, is John's hermeneutical purpose in detailing the fulfilment quo-tations that we have just been exploring. It is a technique that invites the listener to explore the text further. It signals that something big-ger needs to be grasped if the true significance of the cross is to be understood. And, of course, if we have a confidence in the scrip-tures, we believe that to explain them in the power of the Spirit is the God-given means whereby their divine author still speaks today.

My experience as an evangelist seeking to communicate the real-ity of the atonement today is that the temptation is to look for the *contemporary* connections too quickly, whether these be new illus-trations for sermons or new apologetic 'paradigms' with which to explain the atonement. What John reminds us is that the *biblical* connections are fundamentally more important. Trust them by preaching them. The goal for the author is that the reader reinter-prets the person of Jesus in the light God's redemptive purpose ex-pressed in the scriptures. Only in this context does the cross gain its true perspective. We have to take time, therefore, to make these connections in our preaching and apologetics. John never allows us to abstract the 'moment' of the cross from its scriptural moorings, but keeps drawing attention to them in order that the meaning of the cross might become clearer.[14]

Despite appearances, the death of Jesus is entirely voluntary

The emphasis upon the *divine* origin of the cross finds a dynamic balance in John 19 with an equal emphasis upon Jesus' personal willingness to carry through his God-given task. Indeed, one might argue that this element takes us close to the heart of the chapter. Again, it is couched by John in terms of an apparent paradox – the paradox of who it is who is taking Jesus' life from him. On the sur-face, the chapter is all about others crucifying Jesus: the religious leaders, Pilate, the soldiers. But John subtly refocuses our attention

---

[14] See the similarities between John's method and those of the other Gos-pel writers. Luke, e.g., emphasizes that a true interpretation of Jesus' suf-fering and death must be grounded in the light of revelation as a whole (Lk. 24:26–7, 32, 44–7). In the context of our discussion of divine pur-pose, note also his emphasis on the divine origin and plan of the cross and resurrection in his recording of the evangelistic sermons in Acts (e.g. 2:23–4, 32, 36; 13:27–30, 32–3).

by allowing another perspective to emerge. It is not actually the soldiers, or Pilate, or the religious leaders who take Jesus' life from
him. Rather it is Jesus himself who holds on to his life until the moment when all is accomplished. Then – at the moment of death –
rather than having his life taken *from* him, it is *he* who willingly
yields it up.

This second remarkable paradox is introduced in verse 16. John
records here that 'Pilate handed him over to them [i.e. the soldiers]
to be crucified' and then records that 'the soldiers took charge of
Jesus'. Yet in the next verse the grammar suddenly changes. Jesus is
no longer the object of the verbs, but becomes instead a dominant
subject: '*carrying the cross by himself*, Jesus *went out* to what is called
"The Place of the Skull", which in Hebrew is called "Golgotha" '
(v. 17; my emphasis). With this subtle shift in subject and emphasis,
John brings into focus a picture of Jesus as one who, though undergoing crucifixion, is supremely in control of all that is happening.

This new perspective is drawn out further as the narrative proceeds. First, Jesus takes the initiative from the excruciating pain of
the cross in order to meet the needs of others, uniting his mother
and the beloved disciple in a new bond of care:

> When Jesus saw his mother and the disciple whom he loved standing
> beside her, he said to his mother, 'Woman, here is your son.' Then he
> said to the disciple, 'Here is your mother.' And from that hour the dis-
> ciple took her into his own home. (vv. 26–7)

His movement at this point is away from the cross. He does not focus on his own suffering but demonstrates care for others. Then,
even at the very end, still maintaining control of events, he retains a
consciousness of his place in the divine plan, and is purposeful to
carry out his task and mission. 'After this, when Jesus knew that all
was now finished, he said (in order to fulfil the scripture), "I am
thirsty" ' (v. 28). Finally, 'When Jesus had received the wine, *he*
said, "It is finished." Then *he* bowed his head and [*he*] gave up his
spirit' (v. 30; my emphases).

This is a subtle but striking paradox. In a narrative which is
ostensibly all about others taking Jesus' life, John shows us that in
reality they have no power to do this at all. Instead it is Jesus who
lays down his own life. Back in chapter 10:11, 18 he had said:

I am the good shepherd. The good shepherd lays down his life for the sheep . . . No one takes it from me, but I lay it down of my own accord. I have power to lay it down, and I have power to take it up again. I have received this command from my Father.

We have here in the supreme and awesome willingness of Jesus to go to the cross, the mirror image to the first truth that it was the Father's will and purpose that he should die. For you cannot speak of God's sending of Jesus without Jesus' own supreme willingness to be 'sent'. You cannot speak of God's love in sending Jesus without Jesus' own love in going. Perhaps nowhere is this willing self-giving of Jesus more powerfully expressed than in the foot-washing of chapter 13, where John introduces the narrative with the words

> Now before the festival of the Passover, Jesus knew that his hour had come to depart from this world and go to the Father. Having loved his own who were in the world, he loved them to the end[15] (v. 1).

Jesus' actions here are often interpreted in a purely 'exemplary' manner. Indeed, Jesus himself accepts this interpretation. 'So if I, your Lord and Teacher, have washed your feet, you also ought to wash one another's feet. For I have set you an example, that you also should do as I have done to you' (vv. 14–15). But equally powerful are Jesus' words to Peter in verse 7, which interpret his actions as a 'visual aid' (ahead of time) of the cross, 'You do not know now what I am doing, but later you will understand.' And so the divesting of his robes in order to do the menial task of washing his disciples' feet is a visual aid of a far greater theological truth. It is a picture of the total 'washing' that Peter cannot accomplish for himself but without which he could have no fellowship with Jesus (v. 8). In this context, Jesus' actions mirror the words of Paul when he describes the Son as the one who:

> though he was in the form of God,
> did not regard equality with God
> as something to be exploited,

---

[15] The NIV renders this last phrase idiomatically as 'he now showed the full extent of his love' (*eis telos ēgapēsen autous*).

but emptied himself,
taking the form of a slave,
being born in human likeness.
And being found in human form,
he humbled himself
and became obedient to the point of death –
even death on a cross. (Phil. 2:6–8)

Divine partnership

These two ideas (the command of the Father and the willing self-giving of the Son) are never separated in the Bible. They are held together and expressed one alongside the other without a hint of tension or disagreement. Indeed, reading John as a whole, one gets the awesome impression of divine agency and purpose jointly shared by Father and Son together.

Again, we have much to learn here. We have noted already the tendency sometimes to stress Jesus' *self*-motivation in going to his death in a way that separates it from the notion of God the Father's purposive involvement: that what Jesus did was somehow motivated by his own love and desire irrespective of the Father's will. The other side of this tendency is to stress the Father's 'sending' of the Son in a way that excludes the Son's own active and willing involvement and co-operation in all that this 'sending' would involve. This can happen in different ways. Some of our well-worn gospel 'frameworks' or 'tracts' utilize and expound their material in terms of the great biblical categories of 'creation', 'fall', 'redemption' and so on. Often, when such frameworks are used, God the Father is the subject of all the actions: creating humanity, being unable to endure human rebellion, sending his Son to redeem it in its fallen state, and so on. The 'redeeming' part of such presentations is very often couched in variations on the theme of 'God sent Jesus to die'. This element of the redemptive plan carries profound truth of course, as we have seen. But sometimes such language begins to *dominate* our way of explaining the cross, and our hearers can pick up the false idea that Jesus was some kind of 'pawn', caught up unwittingly and unwillingly in his Father's plans.

Reflection on the Johannine material should warn us against the exclusive use of such ideas if they imply a non-participation or passivity on the part of the Son. The ideas of 'substitution' and 'transfer' by the Father are clearly present, as we have seen: whether in the sacrificial language of 1:29 or the matrix of Passover allusions that we have already noted in chapter 19. Thank God for them. For they enshrine the glorious and life-giving truth that Jesus' death on the cross was a death that should have been mine. He died in my place, bearing my sin, accepting my punishment. Or, as Calvin put it, 'he bore in his soul the dreadful torments of a condemned and forsaken man'.[16] But the mysterious glory of the cross is that he did all this in perfect unity of purpose and participation with the Father. In this context, John Stott's words are worth reflecting upon:

> We must not . . . speak of God punishing Jesus or of Jesus persuading God, for to do so is to set them over against each other as if they acted independently of each other or were even in conflict with each other. We must never make Christ the object of God's punishment or God the object of Christ's persuasion, for both God and Christ were subjects not objects, taking the initiative together to save sinners. Whatever happened on the cross in terms of 'God-forsakenness' was voluntarily accepted by both in the same holy love which made atonement necessary.[17]

We need therefore to work at communicating the profound truth that presents both Father and Son as equal participants in the glorious accomplishment of the cross. When we talk about God 'sending' Jesus to die, we need to speak also about Jesus 'willingly taking upon himself' the full consequences of all that this meant, in willing self-sacrifice. When we speak of God's 'wrath' being laid upon Jesus, we should also speak of the full divinity of Jesus in willingly enduring the judgement of that divine wrath that our own sins alone deserved.[18] When this divine partnership is held together in unity, the initiative of the cross is seen to shine at its most majestic.

---

[16] *Institutes* 2.16.10.

[17] J.R.W. Stott, *The Cross of Christ* (Leicester: IVP, 1986), p. 151.

[18] John Stott strikingly names the central chapter of his book on the cross 'The Self-Substitution of God', which effectively unites Father and Son in the redemptive mission that finds its culmination at the cross (pp. 133–63).

As teachers and preachers, we need constantly to stop and reflect upon the willingness of the Son to carry through his divine commission. It will test our motives and fuel our ambitions. As an evangelist, I need to ask myself, 'Does this gospel still move and compel me?' One of the greatest needs in our generation is for Christians to recover the *wonder* of this gospel. Many is the preacher who can communicate well, can argue persuasively, can tell the finest stories, but who has lost a passion for the gospel. I am reminded of the words of the great eighteenth-century evangelist George Whitefield who said, 'I am persuaded that the generality of preachers talk of an unknown and unfelt Christ.' He went on, referring no doubt to unconverted clergy ministering in numerous parishes of his day, 'The reason why congregations have been so dead is because they had dead men preaching to them.'[19] But there is a reminder here to preachers and teachers to pursue that energy of heart and spirit that informed the ministry of the apostle Paul when he wrote, 'For the love of Christ *compels* us, for we are convinced that one has died for all, therefore all have died' (2 Cor. 5:14).

Despite appearances, the death of Jesus is a revelation of divine glory

The third paradox of John 19 is perhaps the greatest of all. Its nature was summed up over one hundred years ago in the words of Brooke Foss Westcott, who wrote that the crucifixion in John 'is from beginning to end a revelation of majesty'.[20] Having used the title 'King' of Jesus sixteen times in his narrative, leading the reader to expect a revelation of regal power, John now faces us with the extraordinary paradox that it is *on the cross* that Jesus is crowned, and *on the cross* that this regal power is revealed. This – the greatest paradox of all – is unsurprisingly completely 'veiled' to the naked human eye. The naked eye sees in Jesus' pierced and bleeding body nothing but humiliation and degradation. It sees defeat and surrender. But the eye of faith is led to see something quite different by John, who delights to introduce us to what is *really* going on from the lips of Jesus' most powerful human opponent, Pontius Pilate.

---

[19] Quoted in J.C. Pollock, *George Whitefield and the Great Awakening* (Tring: Lion, 1982), p. 162.
[20] *The Victory of the Cross* (London: Macmillan, 1888), p. 95.

Majesty

John has used this heavily ironic strategy before. Back in chapter 11
we saw that it was Caiaphas who makes what turns out to be a prophetic comment about Jesus when he says that it is better that 'one
man die for the people than to have the whole nation destroyed'
(11:50). Just as this comment illuminates (unintentionally from
Caiaphas's point of view) the true meaning of Jesus' death, so here
in chapter 19 it is Pilate who is unwittingly responsible for telling
the reader what is *really* happening on the cross. All four Gospel
writers record that a 'plaque' was nailed to the cross above Jesus'
head (Mt. 27:37; Mk. 15:26; Lk. 23:38; Jn. 19:19), but only John
records the reaction to it (vv. 20–2). The title – 'King of the Jews' –
was written in Hebrew, in Latin and in Greek (every significant language of the ancient world). But, as John alone records, 'Then the
chief priests of the Jews said to Pilate, "Do not write, 'The King of
the Jews,' but, 'This man said, I am King of the Jews.' " Pilate answered, "What I have written I have written." ' As with Caiaphas,
there is the deepest irony here. Pilate challenges the onlooker (and
by implication, the reader), 'You think this man is a "king"? Just
look at him.' But at a far deeper level, his words are recorded by
John because they properly encapsulate the truth. What Pilate says
is *precisely* true. What you see on the cross is a king, and this is the
moment of his coronation.[21]

'Victory'

The cosmic consequence of the cross being Jesus' 'throne' is that his
revelation of majesty is also a revelation of victory. If Jesus is
crowned as King on the cross, then every other rival claimant

---

[21] John has already advertised this truth by his repeated use of the phrase
'lifted up' (Gk. *hypsoō*), with both its literal sense of being crucified, but
also its metaphorical sense of being glorified and exalted in relation to the
cross (e.g. 3:14; 8:28; 12:32, 34). This bringing together of the ideas of being 'lifted up' and 'glorified' also inform Isaiah's vision of the Servant of
the Lord in Isa. 52–3. Cf. esp. the Septuagint version of Isa. 52:13 ('See,
my servant shall prosper; he shall be exalted and lifted up, and shall be very
high'), where both *hypsoō* and *doxazō* are used in close connection (as in
Jn. 12:28, 32). Note also John's periodic reminder throughout the Gospel
that Jesus' 'hour' had not yet come, culminating in the arrival of this 'hour'
at the cross (12:23 and 13:1; cf. also 7:30; 8:20).

is thereby *de*-throned. While this is implicit in chapter 19 itself, the narrative acts as a fulfilment to Jesus' own explicit prediction about this victory back in chapter 12: 'Now is the judgement of this world [referring to his coming death]; now the ruler of this world will be driven out. And I, when I am lifted up from the earth, will draw all people to myself' (12:31–2).

Yet once more therefore, what 'appears' to be happening to Jesus at his crucifixion is not the complete story. If you had stood at the foot of the cross and a fellow bystander had said to you that here was a cosmic battle raging between the ultimate force of good and the ultimate force of evil; that one side was winning and one side was losing; and that the crucified man above you represented one of the sides; on which side would you have placed Jesus Christ? But what looks for all the world like defeat turns out to be the most emphatic victory. It is gained by the Son's complete obedience to the Father – even to death. Satan cannot gain a foothold on Jesus in order to manipulate him, or gain power over him. Nothing can separate him from the Father.[22]

Christus Victor

Gustaf Aulén brought this emphasis powerfully to the fore in the 1930s in his book *Christus Victor*.[23] He emphasized the victorious perspective of Jesus' defeat of Satan and the forces of evil as the 'classic' view of the cross, in distinction from what he described as the 'objective' view (that God the Father is reconciled by Jesus' action on the cross) and the 'subjective' view (that sinners are transformed and inspired by his sacrificial love shown there). Aulén is rather dismissive of these two latter perspectives, and argues that they are subservient to the 'classic' victory theory. His work is committed and powerful and highlights a theme much neglected at the time his book was published. The 'victory' theme is clearly powerfully present in John's narrative. But his dismissal of what he considers to be 'rival' views is misplaced. Instead, what we find in John's Gospel is that each perspective is stressed in its proper place. John does indeed highlight Jesus' victory over evil, but he also presents

---

[22] For the theme of obedience and freedom, see 8:28ff.
[23] G. Aulén, *Christus Victor: An Historical Study of the Three Main Types of the Idea of the Atonement*, tr. A.G. Hebert (London: SPCK, 1931).

those perspectives that Aulén wants to downplay. What he describes as the 'objective' perspective is emphasized in John's
handling of the sacrificial material we have discussed already, and
one could argue that the 'footwashing' episode in chapter 13 is 'subjective' in the sense that Jesus' actions, specifically related to his
death (13:7), are intended to evoke a pattern of life in his followers
in imitating the ultimate expression of love that is shown there
(13:14–15).

Variety in unity
Aulén's approach is interesting therefore not least for his tendency
to want to isolate *one* perspective on the cross.[24] The simple but profound lesson from these observations from John, however, is that
we should give each perspective on the cross its appropriate place in
our preaching and teaching. Much of our preaching of the cross
tends to be one-dimensional – particularly in our evangelism. As a
result, we slip into patterns of explanation that are often in danger of
missing the variety of the New Testament material. This can
happen for a number of reasons. If our preaching is not specifically
tied to systematic exposition, then the danger becomes greater, because we will not be exposing ourselves to the different strands of
New Testament teaching, and so be compelled to expound the
perspectives that we find.

   This is not of course to suggest that such differences in emphasis
are non-complementary. There is an inescapable element of 'substitution' at the centre of each. Even in the 'subjective' dimension of

---

[24] The danger of trying to find a unifying 'theory' of the cross could be il-
lustrated from the work of P.T. Forsyth. In many ways his treatment of
the cross is admirable. His vigorous defence of its centrality and indispen-
sability to Christian faith was a much needed corrective in the early years
of this century. He stresses too the unity of action of the Father and the
Son which resulted in the crucifixion (laying aside a crude third-party understanding, whereby Christ somehow 'stands in' between a holy God
and sinful human beings). Yet his material on the means of atonement
suffers from an attempt to unify in one theory the New Testament strands
of 'substitution' and 'representation' rather than seeing them as complementary perspectives. As a result the 'substitutionary' nature of the
atonement is downplayed in favour of its 'representative' quality. See
p. 182; also the discussion in pp. 113–14.

the foot-washing in chapter 13 lies the fundamental insistence by
Jesus that Peter can have no fellowship with him unless he allows
Jesus to 'wash' him: he needs to have something done 'for' him
before he can serve Jesus by loving others (v. 8). But they are nonetheless different in emphasis, and will communicate in different
ways to different people.

Concluding Observations

Confidence in biblical 'narratives'

I believe that we are increasingly moving into an era in which we
need to rediscover ways of using biblical narrative in our evangelism
among those with little or no biblical knowledge. As Barbara Hardy
has written about our contemporary culture, 'we dream in narrative, day-dream in narrative, remember, anticipate, hope, despair,
believe, doubt, plan, revise, criticise, construct, gossip, learn, hate
and love by narrative'.[25] Postmoderns especially love stories, but
there is nothing new about the particular ability of stories to engage
and hold attention. Significantly, nearly 50 per cent of the revelation given us in scripture is in the form of 'narrative'. We need to rediscover these forms, recognizing the evangelists' supreme literary
skills, and find fresh ways of redeploying the Gospels for the evangelistic purposes for which, after all, they were originally written.

One of my most vivid student memories is of sitting and listening
to a series of expositions by Tom Wright on the last chapters of
Luke's Gospel. They opened my mind I think for the first time to
the potential and power of 'gospel' exposition: that is, of explaining
and preaching Luke – *as Luke* – and allowing it to teach and evan-
gelize in equal measure. My student experience hitherto had been
rather straightjacketed. 'Teaching' was the exposition of the text of
scripture; whereas evangelistic preaching was nearly always 'thematic' in its drawing together of different texts from scripture in order to provide a framework of logically and theologically related
themes which made up 'the gospel'.

---

[25] Quoted in A. MacIntyre, *After Virtue: A Study in Moral Theory*
(London: Duckworth, 1985[2]), p. 211.

I have nothing against this tendency towards thematic preaching in evangelism, for I have learnt a great deal from it. But in my own evangelistic ministry, I have been a firm believer in a strategy of preaching and evangelism that invites the listener to enter into the narrative of the Gospel material itself: to allow the words of scripture to interpret themselves.

Confidence in the text

Of course, I do not imagine that many evangelicals would disagree with such an approach, but it often strikes me that we do not rigorously pursue it. We tend to move from the text too quickly in our evangelism to a modern-day illustration or analogy (particularly as we have noted already, when it comes to explaining the cross). These departures often fail to allow scripture to have its sustained impact, imagining – as such departures imply – that a contemporary voice is more able to interpret scripture than scripture itself.

We need to rediscover the powerful dynamic behind the truth that there is one voice in scripture: the voice of God himself. If you want to know what somebody means when they use a particular word, you ask them. If therefore in evangelism I want to know what is meant by the scriptural word 'love', I should ask the author of the scriptures – God himself. The word 'love', after all, is redolent of any number of meanings today, almost none of which has anything to do with the Bible. They seldom if ever encompass the idea of 'holiness'. They cannot comprehend or communicate – as an aspect *of* love itself – the biblical idea of 'wrath'.[26] How, therefore, am I to explain this idea to my contemporary listener? As evangelicals we jump rather quickly at this point to an illustration. But a far better strategy is to linger with the text for longer, to allow God to explain what *he* means when he uses these words.

This may, as I say, be a very obvious point. But it needs to become more of a hallmark of our preaching and teaching and

---

[26] As an evangelist I prefer the older word 'wrath' to its modern equivalent 'anger'. This is partly because of the associations of the word 'anger' – which imply to most contemporaries some sort of irrational or emotional outburst on the part of the Father, rather than to what Leon Morris describes as 'the stern reaction of the divine nature towards evil' (Morris, L.,

evangelism. If it is true that God speaks in the scriptures, then we must allow him to explain ('in his own words') what he means by his speech.

Confidence in the gospel

I had a salutary experience on the first night of a recent mission, arriving at the church where the first meeting was to be held. It was the end of the evening service and people were pouring out. I was about to go in to prepare for the mission meeting that was to take place later in the evening. As I walked in, a man passed me coming out. He stopped for some time, before asking me who I was. He had recognized me from a similar meeting some years previously when he had come to personal faith. 'How are you feeling about the week to come?' he asked. 'I'm terrified,' I replied. 'You should not be terrified.' he said. 'All you did when you spoke to me that night was to tell me what God said about himself. For that I am eternally grateful.'

It was a short, but exhilarating conversation. But, most importantly, it was a humbling reminder that what we are about as teachers and evangelists is the task of unfolding the scriptures: allowing God to 'speak for himself'. Perhaps the greatest need in our generation, when cultural change is so rapid that Christians seem always to be playing 'catch-up', is to recover a baseline confidence in the fact that God continues to speak for himself through the scriptures. An evangelical commitment to the scriptures is a commitment to the belief that to communicate the words of scripture is to communicate the voice of the living God. The cross is not something I can fully explain: I cannot dot the i's and cross the t's; I cannot bring it together in a rationally coherent way, or explain it logically in a way

---

[26] (*continued*) *The Apostolic Preaching of the Cross* [Leicester: IVP, 1965³], p. 209). I also prefer it because to use the word 'wrath' begs some further explanation which will help me to explain what the Bible means when it uses the idea. I agree with Morris's further comment (ibid., p. 209): 'It may be that wrath is not a perfect word to describe such an attitude, but no better has been suggested, and we must refuse to accept alternatives which do not give expression to the truth in question.' For a helpful discussion of the relationship between God's love and his wrath, see D.A. Carson, *The Difficult Doctrine of the Love of God* (Leicester: IVP, 2000), pp. 75–96.

that is plainly incontrovertible. But I do know that as I seek to explain the cross as scripture explains it, God delights to speak for himself through 'the foolishness of what we preach' (1 Cor. 1:21) and to bring people into fellowship with himself.

Questions for Further Study

1. Try to sum up in one sentence John's message about the cross in Chapter 19.
2. In what ways are we in danger of 'abstracting' the moment of the cross from its theological moorings, and how might we redress this tendency in our preaching and teaching?
3. How might the different perspectives on the cross in John be used to speak to different kinds of people?
4. In what ways does John's presentation of the cross challenge your own ways of sharing the gospel?
5. In what ways does John's presentation of Jews challenge you personally?

Select Bibliography

Commentaries on John

Barrett, C.K., *The Gospel According to St. John* (London: SPCK, 1978²)

Carson, D.A., *Gospel According to John* (IVP, 1991)

A survey of the notion of 'sacrifice' in the Gospels

Head, P., 'Christ as Sacrifice in Gospels and Acts', in R. Beckwith and M. Selman (eds.), *Sacrifice in the Bible* (Grand Rapids: Baker ; Paternoster, 1995), pp. 111–29

The doctrine of the cross

Packer, J.I., 'What Did the Cross Achieve? The Logic of Penal Substitution', in A.E. McGrath (ed.), *The J.I. Packer Collection* (Leicester: IVP, 1999), pp. 98–136

Stott, J.R.W., *The Cross of Christ* (Leicester: IVP, 1986)

Pastoral application

Carson, D.A., *The Difficult Doctrine of the Love of God* (Leicester: IVP, 2000)

Jenkins, G., *In My Place: The Spirituality of Substitution* (Cambridge: Grove, 1999)

Appendix

Justification by Faith:
The Reinstatement of the Doctrine Today
Alan M. Stibbs

The title of this appendix[1] virtually makes two assumptions, first that the doctrine of justification by faith ought to be reinstated because it is worthy, and second that it needs to be reinstated because it is neglected, and does not hold the place that it should either in our praise to God or in our preaching to men. A proper sense of its full glory and wonder is weak, if not lacking, among many Christians. What is worse, there is no consciousness that truth of inestimable value is lying unappreciated; we are not aware that we are losing much by our failure to dwell upon it. Indeed, to many who occasionally try to think about it, it seems rather unreal, theoretical and abstract; it has even been disparagingly described as a legal fiction, a method of reasoning by which it is pretended that something is true which is not true. So thinkers and preachers pursue it no further; and it is certainly not preached from our pulpits as it ought to be.

Not only so, many Christians who personally rejoice before God in the blessings of justification by faith cannot worthily declare to others what they themselves enjoy. So the truth is not preached and taught as it ought to be even by them, because its theology is inadequately understood; and this unsatisfactory situation is made worse because able thinkers, with no evangelical experience of its truth, often misunderstand it themselves and then misrepresent it to others in their teaching.

---

[1] Originally given as the Latimer Day Lecture of the Fellowship of Evangelical Churchmen, 1958.

Also, the ancient historic Creeds, which in our day many tend to regard as an adequate theological basis for Christian reunion, make no explicit mention of justification by faith, while the great Reformation Confessions, which do recognize the importance, and expound the truth of this doctrine, tend to be obscured and forgotten.

Is it not time, therefore, to ask whether Luther was wrong when he asserted that justification by faith is the article by which the Church stands or falls? Or was the discernment of the late Dr H.R. Mackintosh at fault when he wrote, 'The doctrine of justification by faith . . . has a way of turning up again with new majesty and power in every period of revival'?[2] Or was Paul a fool when he chose to suffer the loss of all things that he might gain Christ and be found in Him, not having a righteousness of his own, which is of the law, but that which is through faith in Christ, the righteousness which is of God upon faith (see Phil. 3:7–9)? Or ought we to wake up to our own error, our own lack of discernment, our own folly in choosing? Ought we to choose afresh and to set ourselves to reinstate the truth which is after all the indispensable secret of personal salvation, of spiritual revival, and of the very existence of the true Church of God?

If we are thus to move towards worthy reinstatement we need first of all to realize that the very phrase 'justification by faith' tends to limit or misdirect us by its incompleteness. It would be theologically wiser, and in practice more profitable, always to state explicitly by whom and in relation to whom the believer is justified, in whom his faith rests, and who is thus justified when he does believe. In other words, we ought to speak not merely of 'justification by faith', but rather of 'the justification of the sinner by God and in God's sight by faith in Christ, crucified and exalted'. This would then make plain that 'justification by faith' is no mere legal fiction or subjective fancy, no mere formal dogma or illusory experience, but an action of God wrought in the sphere of our personal and individual relation to Him.

In *F.D. Maurice and the Conflicts of Modern Theology*, Archbishop A.M. Ramsey summarizes Maurice's exposure of the weakness of the Protestant by saying, 'The Protestant, because he treats his principle of justification by faith as a shibboleth, slips from faith in Christ

---

[2] *The Christian Experience of Forgiveness* (Nisbet, 1938), p. 5.

the justifier into belief in an experience of being justified, and great is the fall.'[3] However unfair this may be as a generalization, let us acknowledge its measure of truth, let us heed its implied warning, and let us fix our faith, and urge others to place theirs, not in a dogma nor in an experience of justification, but in the living God who justifies us freely by His grace through the redemption that is in Christ Jesus.

Similarly, in the second place, if the doctrine of justification by faith is to be properly appreciated and thus worthily reinstated, it ought not to be considered in isolation, but rather viewed from varied standpoints in explicit relation to every essential feature of the gospel. For instance, the apostle Paul has indicated that the meaning of 'to be justified' needs to be interpreted in the divine and eternal context of being foreknown, foreordained and called by God on the one hand, and being glorified by Him on the other (see Rom. 8:28–30). Let us then survey more in detail and one by one these complementary considerations which are indispensable to the full and worthy understanding of justification by faith.

The Sovereignty of God in Holiness and Grace

We need with fresh acknowledgement and full awareness to be recalled to the recognition that God is sovereign in the universe, the First and Final Cause of all things; and particularly we need to be recalled to the conscious confession that the only righteousness which ultimately matters is to be accepted as right in God's sight and to be acting in harmony with His will. In contrast to the godless or secular thought so widely and so subtly prevalent, we need deliberately to return to theocentric thinking, in which from first to last God is the supreme pole or rather Person of universal reference. Sin can, for instance, only be seen in its true character and full horror, if it is seen not just as transgression of some impersonal law but rather as rebellion against God and His appointed ways.

What matters supremely is not just that right is right and wrong is wrong, but that God is God, and that He loves righteousness and

---

[3] *F.D. Maurice and the Conflicts of Modern Theology* (CUP, 1951), p. 29.

hates iniquity. Things sinful are the inevitable objects of His wrath. In relation to the sinner the God of holiness is a consuming fire. Yet in His sovereign freedom to do His own pleasure this same God delights to show mercy to the unworthy and the undeserving, and to devise means by which the estranged should be reconciled and the banished reinstated. Nor are these two complementary activities of holiness and grace satisfactorily held together in outworked harmony anywhere else except in the propitiation of Christ's sacrifice, and in the consequent gospel which offers to the sinful God's own way of being Himself just, and yet at the same time the justifier of him who has faith in Jesus (see Rom. 3:21–8).

The Primary and Final Authority of the Word of God

Nothing has perhaps undermined more our hold on and appreciation of the truth of justification by faith than modern criticism of the Bible; for it has subtly deprived most of us of any adequate awareness of the supreme sanction belonging to the God-given word. We need to realize afresh and with compelling force that what settles things in the universe is God's will as it is declared by His word. Once God speaks, then either it is, or it shall be, as He says. Of this there can be no final gainsaying, for every word will be vindicated by corresponding fulfilment. Therefore, than this there can be nothing more certain and secure. So our Lord Himself said, 'Heaven and earth shall pass away, but my words shall not pass away' (Mk. 13:31).

Nothing, therefore, can be more important and more decisive for the individual man, and most of all for the convicted sinner, than to be declared righteous by God Himself. For if God says that in His sight I am righteous, then I am righteous. I may boldly ask, as Paul did, 'Who shall lay anything to the charge of God's elect? It is God that justifieth; who is he that shall condemn?' (Rom. 8:33, 34). I now have no possible accuser or gainsayer to fear in earth, heaven or hell. Nor is this word of God an empty declaration or legal fiction, pretending that something is which is not. For His word is the decisive and creative word. What He declares is thereby constituted essential truth and infallible or incontrovertible fact.

For instance, if it is proper in this British Realm to regard a verdict of the High Court or an Act of Parliament to which the Royal Assent has been given as decisive, as indeed a word that can henceforth be acted on or proved operative, how much more is the solemnly declared word of the living God decisive in heaven itself. If the former borough of Cambridge, recently declared a city by Royal Charter, is now rightly able publicly to call itself a city, how much more may I who still know myself to be a sinner say with Luther – a sinner, yes – but '*simul iustus et peccator*'. For by the double sanction of God's word and covenant I have incontestable right to confess that as a believer in Christ and His redeeming work I am justified with God. Is not this something to wonder at and to glory in – the gracious pleasure and the royal writ of the Divine King, who has given me the standing of being righteous in His sight? For if God calls me 'righteous', who can call me otherwise? Is not this a boldness and a glorying which we need to see reinstated in our worship and our witness?

To this one may add that in the day in which we now live the fact that justification by faith is a revealed and scriptural doctrine, is in some quarters not only an original but also an up-to-date advantage. For, in the book previously quoted, Archbishop A.M. Ramsey has written of our times:

> The climate of thought has so changed that theologians commonly see it as their function not to demonstrate the validity of the Christian faith by the methods of contemporary secular thought so much as to study the Biblical revelation in its own categories and to draw from it some light to guide our steps in a dark world where diabolical forces are seeking whom they may devour.[4]

Man's Guilty, Helpless and Hopeless State as a Sinner

In comparatively recent times just as many have, on the one hand, lost faith in the supreme authority of God's Word, so they have, on the other hand, become blind to the extreme gravity of their own sinfulness. There has been, as we all know, a period of humanistic

---

[4] Ibid., p. 11.

optimism, a belief in natural evolution and inevitable progress. No wonder the relevance and the glory of the evangelical doctrine of the justification by God of the ungodly and the sinner ceased to be fully appreciated. In the last forty years, however, such hopes of human progress have been not only violently shaken but almost completely shattered. There is in consequence a new readiness to recognize the essential truth of the Christian insight concerning the inherent sinfulness and frustrating impotence of human nature. This new sense of depravity and proneness to despair provide just the field for the reinstatement of this doctrine of the salvation by God of the sinful and unworthy, this doctrine of a complete change in life's fundamental relations not only to things and people but above all to God Himself; a change offered, not as a reward of merit or as a prize to be won by good works, but as a free initial gift of divine grace to all who, confessing their need and unworthiness, cast themselves on the justifying mercy of God and the propitiating work of the God-given Saviour.

In contrast to the Englishman's inveterate Pelagianism, his persistent belief that God helps those who help themselves, there are fresh need and opportunity to make men aware, and to proclaim, that God helps those who cannot help themselves, and who do not deserve to be helped either; and that our Lord Himself taught that it was the publican who acknowledged with shame his sinfulness and counted on God's provision of propitiation, who went home justified with God rather than the Pharisee, who could honestly enough protest, by comparison, how much he had done of righteousness or had not done of sin. This message of the free justification of the sinful is the distinctive glory of the Christian gospel. Also, as our Lord made equally plain, there are in the end only these two alternatives – either condemnation or justification, either to exalt ourselves and be divinely humbled or to humble ourselves and be divinely exalted (see Lk. 18:9–14). Such is the message which ought afresh to be clearly sounded forth.

The Substitutionary and Penal Death of Christ

It is no mere chance coincidence that at the time of the Reformation a penal and substitutionary doctrine of the atoning work of

Christ and the full wonder and significance of the doctrine of justification by faith were appreciated and emphasized together. For the two doctrines are interdependent and complementary. The second rests upon the first as an indispensable and divinely ordained foundation. It was the Christ, who was first delivered up for our offences, who was then raised again for our justification (see Rom. 4:25). He had first to be lifted up on the tree to bear the sinner's condemnation as one cursed of God, before He was lifted up to the throne in vindication to secure the sinner's acceptance in God's presence; and both happened to Him as our substitute or proxy or federal head. Again to quote significant New Testament words, 'Him who knew no sin God made to be sin on our behalf; that we might become the righteousness of God in Him' (2 Cor. 5:21).

Justification, therefore, is no empty pretence, no mere legal fiction, because, although given to the sinner freely and apart from works, it does depend upon an objective work of propitiation wrought by Christ on the sinner's behalf and indeed in the sinner's stead. For Scripture does not teach that human sin can simply be pardoned. An objective work of redemption and remission is needed to set the sinner free from his burden and his guilt, and to give him a new standing of freedom and acceptance before God. This is exactly what is now ours because of what Christ has done for us. We cannot, therefore, reinstate the preaching of justification by faith without reinstating the preaching of a substitutionary and penal doctrine of Christ's atoning work. So it is of no small significance that, in spite of violent antagonism to the very idea on the part of many, there is a fresh readiness in more than one quarter to recognize that a substitutionary and penal doctrine of the atonement may, after all, be what Scripture teaches.

The True Significance of Christ's Resurrection and Exaltation to the Throne

The doctrine of justification by faith, the certain fact of the sinner's full acceptance as righteous in God's presence only through faith in Christ, is not realized and preached as it ought to be by many, because they know no corresponding certainty that Christ's atoning work is finished, and that He Himself as our High Priest is already fully accepted by God and enthroned at His right hand. They suppose rather that Christ is still making atonement by eternally presenting Himself to the Father as the Lamb that was slain. If, therefore, the Christ Himself in heaven is still only working towards our ultimate justification, justification can only be viewed and preached as a goal towards which believers are moving rather than as a God-given relation to God in which by grace they already and unalterably stand.

Such views, that the Christ in heaven and His Church on earth, by the continual offering to God of His sacrifice, are making propitiation for sin, and thus winning ultimate justification, sound devout and humble, and are obviously attractive to the religiously minded, but they are not scriptural. Indeed, they involve a fundamental and God-dishonouring denial of the eternal sufficiency of Christ's one sacrifice, finished once for all; and they completely deprive believers of the proper evangelical assurance of present and permanent peace with God. What we need to reinstate, therefore, is the preaching to believers of the glorious gospel truth that at the very throne of God Himself none can deny our access or condemn us as sinners. For there on the throne we have God Himself in Christ as our justifier. He who died for us and was raised from the dead is now at God's right hand for this very purpose to intervene on our behalf as our Advocate, to pronounce us righteous in God's sight, and thus to secure the acceptance and full salvation of all who come unto God by Him (see 1 Jn. 2:1, 2; Rom. 8:31–4; Heb. 7:25). So in Christ we have already and eternally an inviolable status as holy and without blemish in God's sight.

The Full Wealth of the Consequent Benefits; and the Full Weight of the Accompanying Obligations

Neglect of the full significance and consequent implications of the doctrine of justification by faith has caused very many true believers in Christ to be completely unaware of the wealth of their Christian inheritance and of the weight of their Christian obligations. As a result, instead of possessing the possessions which are already theirs in title, instead of seeking to cease from sin and to perfect holiness by regarding themselves dead to sin and alive unto God, many seek some 'second blessing', as though they still needed God to do something more for them before holy living and full salvation can be theirs. Whereas, actually, once we are 'in Christ' all things are ours; and so, not only our reconciliation to God but also our sanctification and our glorification are assured.

To quote the New Testament way of putting it: 'whom He justified, them He also glorified' (Rom. 8:30). 'Therefore, being justified by faith, we have peace with God through our Lord Jesus Christ: by whom also we have access by faith into this grace wherein we stand, and rejoice in hope of the glory of God' (Rom. 5:1, 2). In other words, once we are reconciled to God through the death of God's Son much more can we be sure that we shall be continually kept safe by the power of His resurrection life, and finally saved through Him from God's wrath against sinners, and conformed in resurrection glory to the image of God's Son (see Rom. 5:9, 10; 8:29).

The consequent obligation resting upon us is, therefore, so to live as those who are citizens of the heavenly Jerusalem and can no longer be earthly minded, as those who have the present available power of God's indwelling Spirit for holy living, and as those who have the future prospect of full redemption, when we shall at Christ's coming be clothed upon with a new spiritual body, fashioned after the likeness of our exalted Lord's own glorious body.

Such are the heritage and the high calling of the justified. The doctrines of justification, sanctification and glorification (or 'the redemption of the body' [see Rom. 8:23; 1 Cor. 1:30; Eph. 4:30]) belong thus together. And in this connection it is the worthy exposition of the relevant scriptural promises and exhortations to the justified, which particularly needs in our day widespread reinstatement in the ministry of the Word to Christian congregations.

The Proper Significance of the Two Sacraments of the Gospel

Christian baptism is the divinely appointed seal of our justification by faith. As an ordinance administered once for all it corresponds to the once-for-all character of the redeeming work of God in Christ. Just as the finished work of Christ is sufficient to procure the full salvation of all who are in Him, so baptism is administered once for all never to be repeated. Also it assures the recipient not only of initiation into Christ but also of every blessing of the justified life, including the final redemption of the body; as a sacrament it is thus eschatological as well as evangelical.

Adequate awareness of this comprehensive significance of the baptismal seal as pledging the sinner's full salvation from beginning to end is lacking in most Christian congregations. This is due, on the one hand, to the unworthy practice of infant baptism, to the failure frequently in the presence of the congregation both to baptize and to preach about baptism, and to the prevalence of mistaken views about baptismal regeneration. It is also due, on the other hand, to over-emphasis on the necessity of the candidate's personal confession of faith to the neglect of other and even more important truths about Christian baptism.

We all seem to have lost sight of the primary witness of baptism to God's justifying act, and still more to the full witness of baptism as pledging a complete salvation. For, on the one hand, Christian baptism is not just an initiation or beginning only; still less is it simply a provisional admission into the visible Church or local congregation. It is rather the visible seal of that incorporation into Christ which makes every blessing ours. All the promises of God which concern the sinner's full salvation, and not just the initial ones, are therein visibly signed and sealed. At the same time, on the other hand, while emphasis on the necessity of faith on the part of the candidate is important and indeed indispensable, such emphasis is overdone if a person's baptism is regarded more as the occasion of his public confession of faith than as the visible seal given to the candidate in God's Name of God's all-sufficient justifying act whose full benefit is thereby assured to the believer. We greatly need, therefore, first in our understanding and then in our exposition of the significance of Christian Baptism, to reinstate the doctrine of justification by faith.

Similarly, in contrast to the widespread and grossly misleading use of the Holy Communion service as a Godward plea or sacrifice of the altar, we need more fully to realize and rejoice in its divine sanction as a manward pledge or gift of the Lord from His table to His people. Far from any further pleading or spreading before God of our Lord's sacrifice being necessary, these symbols given under His hand to His disciples are visible seals of the conveyance to His believing people of the innumerable benefits of His passion as an already and once-for-all finished work. Further, their repeated administration assures believers that the one sacrifice that has secured their initial cleansing and peace with God is sufficient both to make theirs a fresh cleansing from sins of daily living, and to assure them of final preservation unto life everlasting of body as well as soul. In other words, the service challenges us to appreciate, and by faith either to appropriate or to anticipate, the full consequences and endless eternal blessings of being justified by faith. Also, many who devoutly use the service, desiring to find it a means of grace, need to be saved from the prevalent temptation to trust in the supposed virtue of partaking of the consecrated elements, and to be taught to fix their faith and hope on the justifying Lord, who by these visible tokens seals the conveyance to His people of the benefits of His finished work. If, therefore, the significance of the Lord's Supper is to be properly appreciated, and its administration properly enjoyed, we need fresh and frequent preaching in its fullness of the doctrine of justification by faith.

Justification by Faith Only

The distinctive character and the sole-sufficiency of the faith which justifies continually need afresh to be both recognized and expounded. This can only be adequately done when attention is directed not towards faith but towards the person and work of Christ. The faith of the individual must be seen as having no value in itself, but as discovering value wholly and solely through movement towards and committal to Christ. It must be seen as simply a means of finding all one's hope outside oneself in the person and work of another; and not as in any sense an originating cause or objective ground of justification. For true faith is active only in the man who is wholly occupied with Christ; its practice means that every blessing is received from another. For this reason faith is exclusive and intolerant of company; it is only truly present when any and every contribution towards his salvation on the part of the believer himself or on the part of the Church is absolutely and unequivocally shut out. Justification must be seen and received as a blessing dependent wholly and exclusively on Christ alone, on what He is and on what He has done – a blessing enjoyed simply through being joined directly to Him, without the interposition of any other mediator or mediating channel whatever. The one sufficient cause and the distinctive character of the salvation consequently enjoyed can only be properly expressed if it is made abundantly plain that it is justification by faith only. Religious man is so incessantly prone to introduce some contribution of his own works or of the Church's ceremonies and sacraments that this truth of justification by faith only unquestionably needs continual reiteration among those by whom it has all too often been lost.

True Evangelical Assurance

When hope is thus wholly and exclusively fixed outside oneself and outside one's fellow men on another, Jesus, the Son of God, the once crucified and now exalted Saviour, the believer finds a solid and unshakeable ground of full and abiding assurance. He knows that his sins are forgiven and forgotten by God. He knows that by His grace all is and all will be well. Possession of such assurance is an intended heritage, and should be a distinctive mark, of all who embrace the Christian Gospel.

Yet it is just this assurance which in our day so many lack, and not least those who profess and call themselves Christians. What is more, for lack of it many are disturbed and sometimes tormented by inner misgiving. They resort for relief either to the psychoanalyst and his psychotherapy or to confession to, and absolution by, the priest. The widespread prevalence of both these practices provides objective evidence that men are still hungry for, and in many cases far from enjoying, inner assurance. It is ours to declare that such full assurance of peace with God, of sufficient grace to face the uncertainties of this life, and of sure hope in the life beyond, is only to be possessed, and is meant fully to be enjoyed, by those who are justified by faith. For none can give the heart of sinful man true peace except the justifying Saviour. This is exclusively His prerogative; and this glory He will not give to another. Is it not time, therefore, that over against the well-meaning but ultimately insufficient ministries of the psychologist and the priest those who know the truth of the gospel of saving grace should set the renewed preaching of justification by faith?